An easy and simple explanation of āsana's and kṛiyās, established by Saint *Patanjali*. The eight *yogic* practices are meant for mental and physical cleansing, soul enlightment and have successfully cured diseases like diabetes, obesity, gastric trouble, constipation, chronic acidity and all other stomach related diseases, abdominal pain, cervical spondylitis, dislocation of disc, allergy, sinusitis, respiratory problems, migraine, depression, high blood pressure, stress, cholesterol and heart diseases etc.

Swami Ramdev

Publisher :  **DIVYA PRAKASHAN**
Divya Yog Mandir Trust
Kripalu Bagh Ashram, Kankhal
Hardwar – 249408 (Uttaranchal)

E mail : divyayoga@rediffmail.com

Website : www.divyayoga.com

Telephone : (01334) 244107, 240008, 246737

Fax : (01334) 244805

First Edition : 3,00,000 Copies

Latest Edition : 1,00,000 Copies (Improved and edited version)

Printer : **Sai Security Printers Limited**
152, DLF Industrial Area Faridabad -121003 (Haryana)
Phone: 0129-2257743, 2270309, 2272277, Fax: 0129-2256239

E mail : sspdel@saiprinters.com, saipressindia@yahoo.com

Distributor : **Diamond Pocket Books (Pvt.). Ltd.**
X-30, Okhla Industrial Area, Phase-II, New delhi-110020
Phone: 011-41611861, Fax: 011-41611866
Email: sales@diamondpublication.com
Website: www.diamondpublication.com

Price : **Rs. 125/-**
English : 0124
ISBN 81-89235-15-X

DEDICATION

Ṭwadīyaṃ Tuḅhyamev

The great freedom fighter, protector of the nation, religion and culture and one of the leaders of the freedom struggle - Revered Saint Swami Kripaludevji Maharaj had dedicated his entire life in the service of his motherland. He edited and published a periodical *'Viśhwagyān'* and gave a message of sacrifice to the youth and brave freedom fighters. He offered refuge to the main accused of the lord Harding bomb case – Rasbihari Bose in his difficult times. His entire life was spent in the worship of the almighty God, science of *Yog* and his motherland. He founded *Ḳripālubagh Āshṛam* in 1932 at Haridwar, the whole purpose of running '*Diṿya Yog Maṇdir*' at this ashram was to educate the masses about health, give knowledge of *Aḍhyaṭma* and *yogic* treatment and serve people for their benefit. I offer this humble creation of yogic science to the glorious memory of *Ḅrahmleen Mahaṛśhi* "*Pūjyāpad Rāśhṭriyasaṇt* Shradeya Swami Shri *Kripāludevji Mahārāj*" with regards and dedication.

With regards,
Swami Ramdev

EDITORIAL

It is a great pleasure to present the English edition of this popular book, '*Yog*-Its Philosophy and Practice', written by the revered *Swāmī Ramdevji Mahārāj*. The first Hindi edition of this book was published in the year 2002. In a span of just two years, this book has enabled hundred thousands of devotees to be a part of the *Yog* revolution. This edition is being brought out by using superior quality of paper and printing of international quality and standard. Attractive photographs have been added to give a new dimension to this book. Despite increase in cost of research and production, we have tried our best to keep the book at an affordable price, so that more and more people can buy the book and benefit from it.

Yog is complete in every aspect because it touches every sphere of human life. It is a complete science, a complete lifestyle, a complete medication system and above all, a complete spiritual insight.

The reason for the popularity of *Yog* lies in the fact that it is not bound by the narrow-mindness of gender, religion, caste, community, area and language. Anyone, be it a devotee, a philosopher, an amateur, an ascetic, a celibate or a householder, can be benefited from it. It has proven to be beneficial not only in the up-liftment and development of an individual but also in the overall development of family, society, nation and the world. *Yog* has the answer to the problems of our modern society, like stress, unrest, terrorism, neglect and ignorance. It is a divine science, which brings mankind on the path of positive thinking, which was discovered by the learned saints and seers of ancient India. Saint *Patanjali* compiled it and brought it out, in a disciplined manner, preserved and produced it in the form of the eight *Yogic* practices. Respected *Swāmīji* advices and practices these eight *Yogic* practices in his discourses and *Yog* training camps. He has arrived at a conclusion that a healthy individual and a happy society can be built only under the shelter of *Yog*.

Yog is not only meant for the ascetics, devotees and *Yogis* living in caves, but it is equally important and beneficial for the ordinary householders as well. It is surprising to note that we are ready to fall into the trap of the two hundred year old allopathic system of medication and willingly victimizing ourselves economically, physically and mentally, but are reluctant and ignorant towards the ancient knowledge of *Yog*, which is not only practical but is also a free medical treatment. Had this been just a mystic science, then why would Lord *Krishna* explain it to *Arjuna* in the battle field? *Yogiraj Swāmī Ramdevji* has done a great job by preserving this knowledge which was perishing in deep caves, by re-establishing it for the people of India. Therefore, he is not only worthy of the respect and regards that he gets from all the Indians and millions of people from all over the world.

We are confident and zealous that with your co-operation, respect, faith and devotion, this movement to bring back our divine culture will continue to progress and take the ascending journey of ancient spiritual knowledge including *Yog* and *Āyurveda* from zero to infinity.

-Acharya Balkrishna

PREFACE

I bow every moment to the God present within us and the supreme power of this universe which gives us happiness, with whose affection and compassion-the whole world is blessed with comfort, peace and prosperity. He has given shelter to an ordinary person like me and has filled my life with spirituality.

With the grace of the supreme soul and good *kaṛmas* of my past life, at the age of 14, I had studied almost all the literature, except *Dayanand Saraswati's* preachings on the *Vedas*. As a result, at a young age I got inspired to study the *Vedas* and was motivated to dedicate my life to serving the masses. As per God's will, I left home at the age of 15-16 years and began the journey to discover a *Gurū* who had good knowledge of *Vedas*, spirituality and philosophy. By the grace of Almighty, I got the proximity of a saintly, learned, worshipper of *Ḅraḥma*, *Āchāṛya Baldevaji Mahārāj*. He was kind enough to give me the knowledge of *Upanishads*, *Daṛṣhan* and *Vedas* including the Sanskrit grammar of *Pāṇinī*. He bestowed upon me the *deeksha* the insignia of a true *Ḅrāhmin* and made me a true devotee of *Ḅraḥma*.

I have understood that whatever good has come my way in my life is just because of the grace of God and blessings of my teachers. I bow my head in respect and gratitude to saint *Pataṇjali, Guru Gorakhnath* and other saints and sages with whose blessings I have mastered the traditional knowledge of *Yog*.

Revered *Gurūji* designated me as a religious instructor at the *Gurūkul* when I completed my education at *Gurukūl*. I was happy to be in *Gurūji's* proximity but God had other plans for me. Thus, I took the responsibility of a religious instructor at *Gurukūl Kisangarh, Ghaseḍa*. But the Supreme Being had a different role for me to play. I met *Āchāṛya Balkrishanji* in the caves of *Gaṇgoṭrī*. By grace of God, it was a meeting of like minded people on the path of celibacy. As we progressed on our mission with determination, we were joined by the highly learned, pious, respected *Āchāṛya Muktanandji* and *Āchāṛya Virendraji*, who also offered their dedicated services to the field of health, spirituality and education.

With the grace of revered and respected preceptor, *Swāmī Shankardevji* the *Diṿya Yog Maṇdir* Trust was established in the year 1995 and became the medium of providing services to the entire nation. It has all become possible as a result of the devotion, sacrifice and a lifetime of dedication of this learned teacher. I have written the present book as a result of inspiration and advice received from these teachers. My friends deserve an applause for their co-operation.

I bow to all the sages from all over India including *Harḍwār*, who have always blessed the social, spiritual, cultural and educational services offered by this institution.

I offer my sincere thanks to all those people who have contributed directly or indirectly in the writing or other works related to the book.

I pray to God to bestow honesty, strength, devotion, health, longevity, material and spiritualistic prosperity to all the devoted people who have offered their services to the tasks managed by the *āshṛam*, through which our social work has been strengthened.

I thank Sai Security Printers Ltd for bringing out this publication with coloured pictures, in a grand manner. I pray to God for their continued success.

There may be mistakes in the book, as it has been written in the short time taken out of my busy schedule of social services. The feedback received from our learned readers about our mistakes will help us to improve the book in the next edition.

-Swami Ramdev

Contents

Contents

Contents

Topic	Page	Topic	Page

Introduction to *Yog*

Form of *Yog*:

The word '*Yog*' has been used in *Vedas*, *Upanishads*, *Gītā* and mythological scriptures etc. since ancient times. It is a very important term in the Indian context, be it in devotion, self-realization or in the day-to-day work arena, *Yog* deals extensively with every aspect of our life according to these classics.

Mahaṛṣhi Patanjali defines '*Yog*' as '*Çhiṭṭavṛiṭṭi Niroḍh*' (eradication of negative moods) *Pramāṇ* (Fact), *Viparay* (Transposition), *Vikalp* (Alternate Option), *Niḍrā* (Sleep) and *Ṣmṛiti* (Memory) are the five moods. With the practice of *Yog* with dedication and devotion one eliminates these negative moods and the mind finds solace in merging with the soul – This is *Yog*.

Mahaṛṣhi Ṿyās describes *Yog* as *Samādhi*. The Sanskrit grammar shows that *Yog* is derived from the root '*Yuj*'. In short we can say that the controlled practices which result in the meeting of *Ātmā* and *Param-ātmā* (Soul and the supreme soul) is *Yog*.

The Sages believe that sole purpose of *Yog* is to merge with the Supreme Soul. When one eradicates all negative emotions by following *yog*, the detachment to momentary emotions and moods follows and control of one's life is achieved. The mind has five phases *Ḳṣhipṭa, Mudhā*, *Vikṣhipṭa*, *Ekāgra* and *Nirūḍha*. The first three phases are not capable of reaching the high state of *samādhi*. The fourth and fifth phase of mind enables one to reach a state, wherein one loses the bondage of *Kaṛma* and one can attain *Saṃpraḍnyāt Samādhi* and *Asaṃpradnyāt Samādhi*.

When *Samādhi* is obtained with the help of an object or idea (that is, by fixing one's thought on a point in space or on an idea), the stasis is called *saṃprajnāta samādhi* ('enstasis with support,' or 'differentiated enstasis'). When, on the other hand, *samādhi* is obtained apart from any 'relation' (whether external or mental) that is, when one obtains a 'conjunction' into which no otherness' enters, but which is simply a full comprehension of being one has realized *asaṃprajnāta-samādhi* ('undifferentiated stasis').

Indian literature has a unique place of honour for '*The Bhagvadgīta*'. Contemporary saints of India have spread the message of *Karmyog* from *Gītā* to the entire world.

Types of *Yog* :

The four types of Yog stated below have been described in the classic of '*Dattātrēya Yoga-sūtra*' and '*Yog-raj Upanishad*'. The characteristics of each type of *Yog* have been thus described in the elementary '*Yog Tattvopanishad*'.

1. ***Mantra Yog*** comprises of the chanting of the *Matrukadi Mantra* systematically over 12 years, which gives you *'Anima'*, it is Minuteness (This is the power which the *yogi* possesses to become as small as an atom, to identify himself with the smallest part of the universe, knowing the self in that atom to be one with himself. This is due to the fact that the *anima mundi,* or soul of the world, is universally spread throughout all aspects of divine life) and other spiritual powers.
2. ***Laya Yog*** is constantly remembering God all the time, while performing daily activities.
3. ***Hatha Yog*** comprises the practices of various *āsana's*, *mudrās*, *prānāyāma* and *Kriyās* for the purification of the body and concentration of the mind.
4. ***Raja Yog*** comprises the observance of *Yāma* (self-restraint, *Niyama* (scriptural prescriptions) etc which help to purify the mind, intellect and thereby enlighten t he soul (The meaning of the word '*raja' in Raja Yog*, is 'to illuminate' or 'to brighten' ('*rajru diptou*') and meaning of '*Yoga*' is *samādhi* or transdental meditation. The *Gitā* embodies the detailed analysis of *Dhyāna-Yog*, *Sānkhya Yog* and *karma Yog*. In the 5th chapter of '*The Bhagvadgītā*' *Karmyog*, is considered greater than *Sānkhya Yog*. *Maharṣhi Patanjali* has captured the essence of *Yog* by describing the *Ashtang Yog* in the *Yog-Sūtra*. When one looks into the classics of *Yog* to know the secrets, one arrives at the conclusion that methods and processes which are used for attaining spirituality and devotion may be categorized as *Yog*.

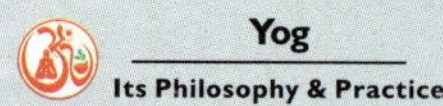

1. योगश्चित्तवृत्तिर्निरोधः *Yogścittavṛtti-nirodhaḥ yoga Darśana 1:2*
2. प्रमाणविपर्यय-विकल्प-निद्रा-स्मृतयः *Pramāṇa-viparyaya-vikalpa-nidrā-smṛtayaḥ--yoga Darśana 1:6*
3. अभ्यासवैराग्याभ्यां तन्निरोधः *Abhyāsa-vairāgyābhyāṃ tannirodhaḥ--yoga Darśana 1:12*
4. तदा द्रष्टुः स्वरूपेऽवस्थानम् *Tadā draṣṭuḥ svarūpe'vasthānam--yoga Darśana 1:3*
5. योगः समाधिः - व्यास भाष्य *Yogaḥ samādhiḥ--Vyāsa-bhāṣyam;* yog *Darśana 1:1*
6. ज्ञानस्यैव पराकाष्ठा वैराग्यम्। *Jñānasyaiva parākāṣṭhā vairāgyam-- Vyāsa-bhāṣyam; yoga Darśana 1:16*
7. क्षिप्तं मूढं विक्षिप्तमेकाग्रं निरुद्धमिति चित्तभूमयः। *Kṣiptaṃ mūḍhaṃ vikṣiptamekāgraṃ niruddhamiti citta-bhūmayaḥ--Vyāsa-bhāṣyam; yoga Darśana 1:1*
8. योगस्थ कुरु कर्माणि सङ्गं त्यक्त्वा धनंजय। *"Yogastha kuru karmāṇi saṅgaṃ tyaktvā DhanañjayaI* सिद्धयसिद्धः यो समोभूत्वा समत्वं योग उच्यते। *Siddhyasiddhayoḥ samo bhūtvā samatvaṃ Yoga ucyateII" --Gītā* 2.48
9. योगः कर्मसु कौशलम्। *Yogaḥ karmasu kauśalam--Gītā 1:50*
10. मोक्षेण योजनादेव योगो ह्यत्र निरुच्यते (यशोविजय कृत द्वात्रिंशिका १०/१) (मुक्खेण जोयणाओ जोगो हरिभद्र सूरिकृता योग विशंका १) *Mokṣeṇa yojanādeva* Yogo *hyatra nirucyate (Dvātriṃśikā 10:1 by Yaśovijaya)*
11. कायवाङ्मनः कर्मयोगः *Kāya-vāṅ-manaḥ karma-Yogaḥ--Tatvārtha-sūtra 6:1*
12. श्री अरविन्द *Shri Aravind- yoga Samanvaya;* page 605
13. मन्त्रयोगो लयश्चैव हठयोगस्तथैव च। राजयोगश्चतुर्थः स्याद् योगानामुत्तमस्तु स। *"Mantra-*Yogo *Layaścaiva Haṭha-Yogastathaiva ca I Rāja-*Yogś*caturthaḥ syād Yogānāmuttamastu saḥ II" Dattā.*Yoga*.18, 19*
14. योग तत्त्वोपनिषद् - श्लोक *Yoga-tattvopaniṣad*--verses--21-25 -- *Gītā 3:29*
15. ध्यानोनात्मनि पश्यन्ति केचिदात्मानमात्मना। अन्ये सांख्येन योगेन कर्मयोगेन चापरे। *"Dhyānenātmani paśyanti kecidātmānamātmanā I Anye sāṅkhyena Yogena karmaYogena cāpare II"* [*Gītā*]
16. संन्यासः कर्मयोगश्च निःश्रेयस्करावुभौ। *"Saṃnyāsaḥ Karma*Yoga*śca niḥśreyaskarāvubhau I* तयोस्तु कर्मसंन्यासात् कर्मयोगो विशिष्यते।। *Tayostu Karma-saṃnyāsāt Karma-Yogo viśiṣyate II"* [*Gītā 5:2*]

Effect of *Yog* on the Body

Yog gives an insight to know more about the self. The dormant inner powers blossom to give complete bliss and an introduction to the true self. It enables one to meet the supreme soul and attain complete bliss. Indian sages have prescribed many methods to achieve this goal. We will mainly follow the *āsana's* and *Prāṇāyāma's* given in *Ashtang yog (Yām, Niyam, Āsan, Prāṇāyām, Pratyāhār, Dhāraṇa, Dhyān and samādhi)* or the eight main aspects of *Yog*. We will also cover the six supporting actions or *shaṭkarma's* or *Haṭh yog*.

Practicing *Yog* revives our dormant energy. These exercises rejuvenate tissues and help new cell formation. Light *Yogic* exercises reactivate the nervous system, and regulate the blood circulation. They reinstate fresh energy in the body. According to the laws of physiology, when the body contracts and expands, energy is developed and diseases get cured. This can be achieved with the help of different *Yogic āsanas*. With the practice of *prāṇāyāmas* and *āsanas*, the glands and muscles of the body contract and expand, and diseases get cured naturally.

Yog also keeps the veins healthy. The pancreas becomes active and produces insulin in the right quantity, which helps in curing diabetes and related diseases. Health is directly linked with the digestive system. The improper functioning of the digestive system is the prime cause for most of the diseases. Even some serious problems like heart disease occur due to a faulty digestive system. *Yog* strengthens the entire digestion process, making every part of the body healthy, and active. Fresh air enters the lungs making them healthier which keeps diseases like asthma, respiratory problems, allergy etc away. Fresh air also strengthens the heart. *Yogic* exercises dissolve the fat deposits which make the body light, healthy and attractive. *Yog* is beneficial for thin and lean physique as well. Along with physical fitness, *Yog* also affects the subtle senses, the intellect and the mind. *Yog* controls the working of organs and helps the mind to detach itself. The follower of *Ashtang Yog* passes with great ease from the darkness of ignorance towards a joyous, peaceful and ever illuminated existence by connecting with the supreme soul. '*Tādā Drashtuh Swaroope, Vsthanam*'. Thus we can embark on the path of *Yog* and experience the inner happiness of connecting with the Supreme Being and attain physical, mental, intellectual and spiritual progress.

Daily routine of a healthy person

Good health is the key to happiness. Health is wealth. But who is healthy? Sage *Sushruta* writes in the Ayurveda text *'Sushrut Saṃhitā'*:

"Samdoshah Samagnishch Samdhatu Malkriyah
Prasnnatmendriymanah Swasth itymidhiyale"

(*su-15.41*)

This means, for a person who has all the three *doshas* – *Vāt, Piṭta* and *Kapha* in equilibrium, the *agni*(power of digestion) of the stomach is normal (neither very less nor very high). The seven substances or *dhātus* in body, *Rasa* (plasma), *raḳta* (blood), *Māsa* (tissues), *Med* (Fat), *Aṣthi* (bones), *Majja* (Bone marrow) and *Vīṛya* (Semen) are in the required quantity, urination and excretion is normal, the ten senses (ears, nose, eyes, skin, taste, rectum, genital organs, hands, legs and tongue), the mind and their ruler i.e. the soul remain happy. Such a person is said to be healthy. Sage *Sushrut* has given a broad and scientific definition to the word health. *Maharṣ̣hi* Charak has stated that the three pillars to attain this health are diet, sleep and celibacy.

"Trayopstambha Aharnidrabramhacharyamiti"

(*Ҫharaksanhita* - *Su 11.34*)

These are the three pillars on which the whole body rests.

Yogeṣ̣hwar shri *Krishna* says in *Gītā* :

"Yuktaharviharasya Yuktacheshtasya Karmasu
Yuktaswapnavhodhsya Yogo bhawati dukha"

(The *Bhagavaḍgīta 6:17*)

One whose diet, thoughts and behaviour are balanced and controlled and whose deeds have divinity, who has a pious mind and desires auspicious things, whose sleep and awakening is regular, he is the true *Yogi*. We will briefly discuss these three pillars of good health and how to acquire good health:

1. *Āhāra (Diet)*

"Yatha ch khadyate hyannam tatha sampdhyate Manah

Yatha ch peeyate vari tatha nirgdyate vachah"

A person's body develops with diet. Diet has its effect not only on the body but also on the mind.

"Aharshuddou Satvashudhih Satrashuddho dhruva smriti

Smriti labhde sarvgranthinam vipramokshah"

(*Ҫhhāṇdogyōpaniṣ̣had*)

Sage *Ҫharaka* has given an interesting anecdote with reference to diet. Once, *Ҫharaka* asked his disciples, 'who is not a patient? (in other words, who is healthy?') His best disciple *Vāgbhatt* replied, 'A person who does good deeds, eats as much as required and in accordance with the season, is healthy'. One should eat according to one's constitution i.e. *Vāta*, *Piṭta* and *Kapha*. If the constitution is *Vāta* then *Vāta* problems arise in the body. In this condition, starchy food like rice and sour food which aggravate *Vāta* should be avoided. Pepper, dry ginger powder and ginger should be consumed. If the constitution is *Piṭta* then hot, spicy and fried food items should not be consumed. Raw foods like gourd, cucumber etc is beneficial. People with *Kapha* constitution should not eat cold things like rice, curd, buttermilk etc in excess. Pepper and turmeric should be added to milk and then consumed. Food should be taken in the right quantity. Half of the stomach should be reserved for food, one-fourth for liquid items and remaining one fourth should be left for air. If the food items are consumed in accordance to the season then diseases do not attack the person. Meals should be eaten at fixed timings. Food consumed at irregular intervals causes indigestion and other diseases. Fruits and a light beverage should be taken in the morning between 8 and 9 am. It is better for health if you consume minimum food in early hours of the day. Persons who are above 50 years of age should not consume stale food. The afternoon meal should be eaten between 11 and 12 in the morning. Eating between 12 and 1 in the afternoon is considered to be less beneficial and after one O'clock it is considered to be bad for health. In the evening, the period between 7 to 8 PM is considered to be the ideal, between 8 and 9 PM is not so good for health. Eating after 9 O'clock is definitely bad for health. One should not talk while eating, as the food does get not chewed properly and as a result excess food is consumed. Therefore, one should be silent while eating and should chew the food properly. One morsel should be chewed 32 times or at least 20 times. Chewing as a habit reduces the violent tendency of an individual. We all are aware of the fact that an angry person grinds his teeth, which means grinding teeth expresses anger. If we want to eliminate these violent tendencies, we should pay special attention to chewing our food. You will know the result when you experience it first hand. One should begin eating food by chanting '*Oṃ*' or the '*Gāyāṭrī Manṭra*' and then sipping water at least three times. One should not drink water while eating food. If the food is dry then water can be taken in little quantity. One must not drink more than two to three sips of water after eating food. One could drink buttermilk if it is available. There is a shlok in Sanskrit which states that, " A person drinks water early in the morning, at night drinks milk after dinner and drinks buttermilk after his lunch at noon, such a person never needs to consult a doctor. He is a healthy person." Along with this one's diet should be balanced and comprehensive as per the needs of the body. The diet should include minerals and vitamin B in good measure. The diet should be rid of meat and eggs. Naturally, God has made human beings to be vegetarian. When one can survive on bread then where is the need to be violent? Where is the necessity to take life of other innocent creatures. Dying of hunger is preferable to eating meats. By eating non-vegetarian food the feelings of kindness, compassion, love, devotion, brotherhood and humanity are lost in individuals. Man becomes an animal. By eating non-vegetarian, the stomach becomes like a cemetry.

2. *Nidṛā (Sleep):* Sleep is a happy, soothing experience in itself. A person unable to sleep well can turn lunatic. It might seem like a trivial matter. But a person lacking sleep will realize its true importance. A healthy person needs atleast 6 hours of sleep. Children and elderly people require eight hours of sleep. As the saying goes – early to bed, early to rise makes a person healthy, wealthy and wise. The entire universe runs according to the rules made by God himself. All living beings except mankind retire to their resting place as the sunsets. All the birds with the exception of owls or bats wake up at the break of dawn, chirp away to praise the God and then get busy with their daily routine. The rooster wakes up to give the 'wake up' call to others as soon as the sun rises. Little sparrows sing praises of the God but the unfortunate human being keeps awake the whole night and sleeps away in the morning hours, inviting ill health. We should derive inspiration from the animal world. Retiring to bed at nighttime and waking up in the morning at the right time makes a man healthy and capable.

3. *Ḅraḥmachaṛya (Celibacy):* This means diverting our physical energy and mind away from material objects and focusing them on God and in serving others. Celibacy is not limited to control of the sexual organs. Celibacy or *Ḅraḥachaṛya* in the true sense is to convert the physical and mental energies in self realization to achieve proximity to '*Bramha*'

"Bhoga na bhukta vayamev bhuktastapo na taptam vayamev taptah
Kalo na yato vayamev yatah trishna nojirna vaymev jirnah"

(*Bhartuhari : Vairagyashatak – 12*)

We do not enjoy the pleasures but the pleasures enjoy us. Act of penance is not affected – we are. We cannot destroy time - time destroys us. We cannot finish greed - greed finishes us. Pleasures can never satisfy us. Desires have no end. *Mahaṛiṣhi Manu* says:

"Na jatu Kamah Kamanamupbhogen Shamyati
Hansha Krishnavartmev bhuya evabhivardhte"

(*Manusmriti : Adhyaya 2, Shloka 94*)

Sexual desires are insatiable. The act of satisfying sexual urges creates more urges, just like pouring oil into the fire. *Mahaṛiṣhi* Kapil expresses similar views in '*Sāṇkhyadaṛṣhan*'

"Na bhogat ragshantirmunivat"

(*Sankhya daṛṣhan : 4.27*)

The entire environment is indicating us to observe the discipline. Let us join hands with nature to enjoy this orderly world around us.

4. Vyāyām (Exercise): The human body requires regular exercise as well as a proper diet to remain in good physical condition. Lack of exercise makes the physique unwell and lackluster. Regular exercise can turn even a weak, ill or ordinary person into a strong, healthy and attractive person. Heart disease, diabetics, obesity, gastric problems, piles, blood pressure, mental stresses are the products of lack of physical exercise. If one practices Yog regularly then all these diseases will stay away from him. There are many ways of exercising but the best way to exercise is to practice *āsana's* and *prāṇāyāma*. Other types of exercises help to shape up the body but can never help in achieving the mental concentration or peace which *Yog* can do. Difficult exercises can only tone up the muscles but they cannot improve the nervous system. Gradually the muscles harden up and the flow of blood is reduced resulting in pain. The *āsanas* and *prāṇāyāmas* fulfil all the health requirements, do not have any kind of side effects and bring peace, concentration and tranquility to the person practicing them.

5. Snān (Bath) : One should wait till the body temperature returns to normal after exercises before bathing. Bathing refreshes the body. It cools off the body and it feels light and clean.

"Adabhirgatrani Shudhyanti manoh satyen shudhyati
Vidyatapobhyam bhutatma buddhir dnyanen shudhyati"

(*Manusmriti* : 5.109)

Water purifies the body. Truth purifies the mind. Learning and dexterity purifies the soul and knowledge purifies the intellect. If one is not ill then one should bath with cold water. Bathing with warm or hot water results in faulty digestive power and weak eyesight. Untimely graying of hair and hair-loss occurs. The body suffers from excess heat and essential ingredients of the body are washed away. One should rub the body with a rough textured cotton towel (*khādī*). The skin acquires a beautiful glow with this practice. If you suffer from constipation then rub your stomach with a dry towel. Bathing in a river or a pond is very beneficial for health.

6. Ḍhyān : Once completing the routine for personal hygiene like daily ablutions, bath etc, one must perform the *āsanas*. After that he can meditate at least for 15 minutes to 1 hour to gain peace, contentment and happiness. Chanting of *Pranav* or *Gāyāṭrī* or any such powerful mantras with faith can bring peace, joy and strength.

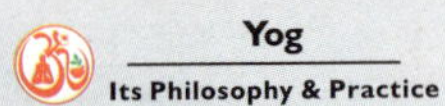

Ashtang Yog (Eight Yogic Practices)

Relevance of Ashtang Yog:

Every person in this world is craving for peace and happiness. Whatever we do, it is with the ultimate goal of achieving happiness. Not only individuals but every nation, the entire world is praying for world peace. Every year a person who has made a significant contribution towards world peace is honored with the Nobel Prize Award. But nobody knows the way to bring this peace to the world. There are many solutions to these problems but no agreement has been reached and universal peace still remains a distant dream. Some people are of the opinion that a single religion in the entire world is the key to this matter. Some people propagate Christianity or Islam, on the other hand some people swear by Buddhisam or Jainism. India is overflowing with such claims, teachers and *Gurūs* who make tall promises of world peace. But none of these religions or thought processes is broad enough to cover the entire world population with their philosophy. Each one has its own limitation. Efforts to spread one religion have always resulted in bloody wars. Violence is on the increase. In short, solutions for world peace are failing even though they are genuine because they lack in perfection and potential to address all aspects of the problems and a broad vision. All these religions or cults promise you plenty but fail to deliver 'peace' and one tends to fall prey to a lot of blind superstitions, myths and wrong practices in the process. A person gets entangled in the web of half-truths and moves away from reality. At times large population embracing Islam, Christianity or any one religion can also pose a threat to our national security. In this scenario can't we have a path which is free from any religious belief? Can't we have a philosophy of life that a person of any religion or nationality can follow? Can the entire world population join hands and walk on this path towards world peace? What is this magic solution that will protect each one's national pride, religious belief and is free from any selfish interest or greed? What is this magical word that promises individual's joy, peace and prosperity in their personal lives and shows them a path to world peace that they can adopt fearlessly? The word is *Yog*. The path of *Ashtang Yog* which has been propagated by *Maharṣhi Patanjali* is the answer we are all looking for. It is not a cult or theory but a complete way of life. This is the only solution to our quest for world peace. *Ashtang Yog* provides us with individual and social well-being, physical fitness, intellectual awakening, mental peace and contentment of the soul. Let us briefly consider all aspects of *Ashtang Yog*. *Maharṣhi Patanjali* thus explains with the help of *Yog-sūṭras*:

"Yam niyamasan pranayam pratyahardharnadyan samadhyoshta wangani"

(*Yog-darṣhan* : *2.29*)

Yām, Niyama, Āsana, Prāṇāyāma, Pratyāhāra, Dhārṇa, Dhyān and *Samādhi* are the eight principles of *Yog*.

A person cannot become a *Yogi* without following these principles. These principles are not only for a *Yogi* but for anybody who wishes to be completely happy, or see other living beings happy. These principles have proved themselves whenever they were tried by the yardsticks of religion, spiritualism, human behaviour or science. It is only *Ashtang Yog* that can stop the violence in today's world. *Ashtang Yog* includes common practices of daily life as well as higher stages of *Adhyatma* like *Dhyān* and *Samādhi*. Any person who is searching for his true identity or wants to find the true meaning of life must follow *Ashtang Yog*. *Yām* and *Niyam* are the basis of *Ashtang Yog*.

1. *Yām (Self-restraint):*

The first principle of *Ashtang Yoga* is resisting passions (*Yām*). The word '*Yām*' is derived from the root '*Yam uparame*' which means '*Yamyante upramyante nirvantantye himsadibhya indriyani yaste yamaha*'. It means following *yāma* diverts the senses and the mind from violence and other banal feelings and concentrates them on the soul. Saint *Patanjali* has described these *yamas* as follows:

"Ahimsa-Satyasteya-Brahmacharya parigraha Yamaha"

(Yog-darṣhan 2:30)

Non-violence, truth, not cheating, celibacy and not collecting unwanted things- are the five *yamas* defined below.

A. *Ahinsa (Non-violence):* Non-violence means to not trouble anybody by thoughts, words or deeds, to not wish ill for anybody, to not hurt anybody with words and to not kill any creature in any circumstance, at any place, any day. These are the features of Non-violence. Saint *Vyasa* has said:

"Tatrahimsa sarvatha sarvada sarva – bhutanam manbhidroha"

(Vyasa-bhāṣhya, Yog-darṣhan)

B. *Saṭya* (Truthfulness): Truth is to experience a positive feeling in your thinking process. The same attitude should be adopted in speech and actions should match our thoughts. One should not speak words which may deceive or confuse the other person. One should speak words which do not hurt others. The speech which harms others is sinful and causes grief. Saint Ṿyasa says :

"Satyam Yathartha Vangmanasi yathadrushtam. yathanumit yathashrutam tatha vangmanshcheti Paratra svabodh. sankrayank vagukta sa yadi na bodhita bhranta va. pratipattivandhya va bhavediti Eva. sarvabhutopakrartha pravrutta na bhutopaghatay"

(*Vyas bhashya, Yog-daṛṣ̣han*)

C. *Asteya* (Abstinence from stealing possessions of others): Taking over or using other people's possession without their permission and acquiring things by violating the codes of conduct given in the ancient texts is called stealing. A desire to acquire other's belonging is also stealing. Therefore a *Yogi* should never steal, rather he should feel satisfied with whatever God has given him and be happy.

D. *Ḅraḥmacharya* (Observance of Celibacy): Abstaining from the food which arouses sexual desires, avoiding situations of sexual temptations, sexually provocative audio and visuals, sexually provocative sights and dresses is called celibacy. Looking at the opposite sex with lust, touching, meeting alone, talking, discussing the subject, enacting the sexual acts, thoughts of a sexual nature and keeping company of people who distract or tempt, are eight types of intercourse. A celibate should protect himself from the above and use eyes, ears, nose, skin and taste for noble objectives. He should think of decent, good things and missions of one's life. A devotee should bear in mind that nature is inherently free of baser aspects. The natural qualities of water is coolness and free flow. Freezing, vaporizing and boiling are not the natural qualities and even after getting heated, evaporating, converting to snow and freezing to solid it returns back to its original form. Similarly celibacy is our natural form. One may meditate at a quiet place and introspect whether one is free from lust or not. Do you have Lust, Anger, Greed, Attachment, Ego and other shortcomings? These shortcomings enter our bodies like thieves, linger a while and within that time steal the strength of our body, mind and soul, deform, destroy and then vanish. Lust and Anger attach themselves to the body for a short time. In that period the whole body is shaken after which the body becomes charmless, weak and pale. One is exploited again and again but we accept it as an eventuality. Then my dear friend nobody can protect you. Wake up, rise and recognize your duty. Lord Shri Krishna says in Gita **"Svadharme nidhana Shreys para-dharmo bhayeva"**

Do not burn yourself in the kiln of lust, anger, greed, attachment and ego. You are the soul, your inherent qualities are friendship, sympathy, love, empathy, service, devotion, benevolence, happiness and peace. We are faultless, we invite the faults. When a person collects material wealth and riches attracting thieves and when the thieves robes of our worldly possessions, rob us of everything do we watch and say "Oh! What has happened! I called them and now they are robbing everything! Destroying everything!" we don't. A person never invites a thief to steal his wealth because he has earned it with hard work. But just think! In the body there are unlimited qualities like happiness, peace, contentment, strength, charm, brilliance, power, intelligence, courage, friendship, sympathy, compassion and others which God has provided us. Why do we destroy them? Control yourself and recognize the strength given by God. Establish a strong determination within yourself that you are faultless, celibacy is your prime duty, it is natural to remain celibate. Firmly believe that the unnatural outburst of these emotions will be short lived and you will return to your natural peaceful form in no time. Therefore do not throw yourself into such a situation. Be accomplished with the divine strengths given by the God and follow celibacy to obtain peace and immense happiness. Follow celibacy and become brilliant, clever, intelligent, strong and courageous. Have divine love towards others; serve the people, make yourself blissful by having a sympathetic and benevolent attitude to others. Walk on the path of *Yog*, only then you will connect with the happy form of God present within you. This is the ultimate truth. This is the objective of life.

E . *Aparigraha* (Abstinence from possessing unwanted things): Collection means attempt to hold on to material. To lead a life which is just the reverse, one should be satisfied with minimum wealth, garments and items of material comfort. What you collect to live on to achieve the main objective of devotion of God is not holding on for selfish purpose. Whatever wealth you have, according to God's grace, do not consider it to be your own. The devotees should not aspire for physical and external sources of happiness. Lead a life without selfish interest and make others happy with whatever things of joy and comforts are available. Saint *Vyasa* says :

"Vishayana margan rakshankshaysanghimsadoshdarshanathsweekaran maparigraha"

(*Vyasa-bhasya*, *Yog-darṣhan*)

Materialistic possessions induce desires. The desire to possess wealth is a sin, to hoard such wealth is a sin, to be attached to such wealth is a sin, and violence created by such desires - because it is not possible to possess such wealth unless you harm other living beings – is also a great sin. That is why a *Yogi* should be detached from possessions and observe 'aparigraha' ***"Nanupahatya bhutanupbhogaha Sambhavati"***

Therefore a *Yogi* should maintain distance from materialism and should not collect unwanted things. Self restraint, resistance of desires, following non-violence and truth through thought, words and deeds whole heartedly without inhibitions. Saint *Patañjali* says,

"Jati-desha-kala-samayanavacchinnah sarvabhauma mahavratam"

(*Yog-darṣhan* 2:31)

Complete and unbounded by the limits of nation, caste, time and period, whole-heartedly following non-violence in every situation is called the great ritual of non-violence. From an ordinary person's point of view, lot of difficulties arise in following these rituals. Therefore a person fixes limits and boundaries to non-violence, austerity and truth to himself with respect to caste, country, time, period etc. For example, let us consider a fisherman; he kills fish, sells and eats. This is violence on his part but he does not kill cow, sheep and goats, this is his non-violence. Similarly, non-violence can be limited to geographical limits. A person might say, I will not kill or harm anyone in '*Kāaṣhī*' or *Mathurā*. However, it will not be complete if it is only practiced at *Kāaṣhī, Mathurā* and *Harḍwār* and other holy places. That means he can indulge in violence in all other places except the holy places. A person with such thinking is non-violent only till the limits of a place. The same thing applies to time, for instance if one says 'I will not indulge in non-violence on certain auspicious days, full moon, new moon and Tuesdays etc. or on any festival'. This is non-violence bound in time frame. The same is related to time limits, I will not be violent in normal situations but special instances when I face some trouble I will indulge in violence. This is also not complete non-violence. Complete non-violence will take place when everybody rises above limits and follows it every time, everywhere and in all places, towards all creatures, in all situations and all circumstances without any exceptions. The same should be understood with respect to truth, *Asteya* (not stealing) and austerity. For example if one lies to protect a Brahmin or a cow, it is caste based non-violence. If one speaks truth only in a particular place – for example his own country or a holy place like *Gurūdwārā*, *maṭha*, *temple*, *Gurūkula*, mosque or church, but lies in a courtroom, business place or office – it will be place bound truth, and not a complete truth. If your vow to speak truth is limited by time factors, limited only to a certain day or festival etc – it will not be complete. We have to therefore break from all limitations and follow the rules of truth, *Asteya* and austerity.

2. *Niyama* (Scriptural rules):

The second basic factor in *Ashtang Yoga*'s principles is rules. *Saint Patañjali* says :

"Shaucha Santosh tapah swadhyayeshwar pranidhanani Niyamaha"

(*Yog-darṣhan* 2:32)

This means excretion, contentment, penance, regular study of *Vedas* and deep devotion towards God are the five rules.

A. *Shāucha* (Purity): Excretion is purification and cleansing. Excretion or purification is of two types – one is external and the second is internal. Saint *Manu* has aptly said,

'Adbhigatrani Shudhyanti Manalha Satyen Shudhyati
Vidyatapobhyam bhutatma budhirdnyanen shudhyati'

(*Manusmriti 5.109*)

It means the devotee should purify his body with water everyday, purify his mind with good behavior, purify his soul by learning and devotion and purify his intelligence with knowledge. The holy water of river *Gaṇgā* can purify the body. One has to follow the advices of the saints and sages for the purification of the mind, the brain and the soul.

B. *Saṇtosh* (Contentment): One should fulfill ones objectives with the available resources. To be fully satisfied with whatever results are obtained, to not desire unobtainable objects, to not disregard achievements acquired with the grace of God, and to not aspire for what is not available is contentment. Saint says –

"Santoshamrut truptanam Yatsukham shantchetsam
Kutastad dhanlubdha namitashchetashcha dhavatam"

Consuming the nectar in the form of satisfaction gives immense happiness to content people. It can never be achieved by people who are wandering aimlessly in the search of wealth and luxury. It has been said elsewhere that

"Santoshmulahi sukham dukhmulam viparyayaha".

Happiness is based mainly on satisfaction and cause for unhappiness is desire and aspirations. Sages have said in the *Upnishad*, ***"Na vittena tarpaniya manusha"*** which means a man never gets satisfaction with wealth. Therefore the devotee should perform his duty and whatever results God gives according to his justice and plans, one should feel fully content. One should never forget that God blesses us with more beauty, youth, wealth, prosperity and luxuries than what we are worthy of.

C. *Tapas* (Penance): Saint *Vyasa* says that tapas means tolerating challenges. He says, ***"Tapo dvandva-sahanam".*** This means whatever pains, troubles, adversities come in the path of accomplishment of our objectives, they should be accepted gracefully and we should march forward towards our goal continuously without deviating. In *Mahābhārata*, *Yakśha* asks *Yudhishtira*, ***'Tapasah kim lakshnam'?*** "What is the definition of Penance"? Kind *Yudhishtira* replies, ***''Tapaha sva-dharma-vartitvam"***, Oh, *Yakśh* whatever hardships, obstacles come in the path of duty, tolerating them and continuously dedicating yourself to fulfill your duties is penance. These hardships are hunger, thirst, cold, heat, happiness, unhappiness, gain, loss, fame, dishonor, worship, insult, honor, dishonor, victory, loss etc. To remain steadfast in all these adversities is penance. Penance is not just standing in fire or standing on one foot and giving pain to your body.

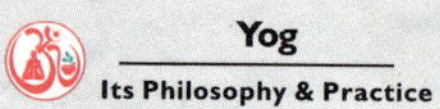

D. *Ṣwādhyāy* (Regular study of the *Vedas*): Saint *Vyasa* says, ***"Pranavadi Pavitranam japo mokshashastranam madhyayanam ya"*** which means that chanting *Oṃkāra* (*pranava*) mantra, true classics, the *Gītā* etc, with devotion is called regular study or swadhyay. If we look at the literal meaning of regular study of *Vedas*, we derive two meanings. ***'Su Adyayan ṣwādhyāy'***. One is the study of the classics written by the sages i.e. the *Vedas*. We get purity, good thoughts and deeds, divinity and determination makes our lives pious. The second meaning of study is knowing ourselves or realizing our internal self, thinking about our existence and introspecting on 'who am I? What should I do? What am I doing? What is the aim of my life? Who gave me birth? Why am I born?'

If a devotee thinks wisely, he will not be obsessed by luxuries of materialistic world and chanting *Pranava (Oṃkāra)* and reading scriptures written by sages will lead to proximity with God.

E. *Iṣhwar praṇidhān* (Deep devotion towards God): Saint *Vyasa* says, ***"Tasmin Paramagurau sarva – kriyanam arpanam"*** which means, devoting all our actions to the *Guru* of all *Gurus*, the supreme *Guru*, the Supreme Soul is deep devotion to God. Only pure, auspicious and divine things can be offered to God. Therefore, a devotee will give respect and make whole-hearted efforts in only such things, which he can offer to God and the sole aim of all his actions will be devotion to God. A true devotee always thinks that whatever he has achieved, body, mind, wisdom, strength, beauty, youthfulness, prosperity, luxury, status, honor and prosperity is all because of the blessings of God. Therefore, he uses all his might to please God. The ultimate objective of a devotee's life and efforts should be to dedicate each and everything that he has to God, including his existence. God bestows his blessings on devotees who are totally committed to him.

Obstacles in following *Yām*: Lot of obstacles come in the way when one follows *Yāma* which make us deviate from our path. Saint *Patanjali* says:

"Vitarka-badhane pratipaksha-bhavanam"

(*Yog – darṣhan* 2:33)

While following these principles, violence, falsehood, temptation to rob greed for material, impurity, dis-satisfaction, extra-vagance, irregularity in the study of *Vedas* and atheism is avoidable. One should plan to protect oneself from them. Having given up violence, falsehood, stealing and uncontrollable passions to protect himself from the lust for materialism, the devotee should be firm on his resolution. 'I have sacrificed it all and I will not embrace them again, because I did it after serious consideration. Now, I will not embrace what I have left. I will follow the great rituals whole heartedly and with full commitment, this is the object of my life. I am willing to die with the honor of having fulfilled my duties'. Such should be his thinking. Why are these obstacles created? What are the ways to avoid them?

Saint *Patanjali* says –

"Vitarka himsadayah krutkaritanumodita lobh krodh moh purvaka mrudumadhyadimatra dukha dnyanantphalaiti pratipakshbhavanam".

(*Yog – darṣhan : 2.34*)

The obstacles like violence, untruth and theft are of three types. *Krut* or self created, *karit* or committed by others with your instigation and third *Anumodit* or supported by you. Greed, anger and ignorance help you to create these obstacles. They are of mild, medium or strong nature and give limitless sorrow. If you think on these lines you can eradicate the obstacles. Let us take 'Violence' as example.

Types of violence against which devotees should avoid:

Violence is of three types. The **first is i.e.** violence which takes place through our thought, words and deeds. The **second kind** of violence is *Karit* i.e. one which we commit not by ourselves but we get it done through others and the **third type** is *anumodit* i.e. one when we relate to greed, anger and attachment. The three types of violence again have three differences. Indulging in violence by self, through others or by provoking others for skin, land, building and other things is greed generated violence. In the same way anger-generated violence comes with the aim of revenge. The violence generated through attachment (done by self), through others or through provocation with the selfish feeling will be generated for interests of wife, children and other well-wishers. The violence generated through greed, anger of attachment is further divided into three types – mild, medium and strong.

There are three stage of mild violence: 1. *Mṛidu mṛidu* (extremely mild): In this case the extent of violence is extremely low. 2. *Maḍhyā* (Medium): Slightly more violent. 3. *Tīvramṛidu*: Highest state of violence in the limits of mild violence. Likewise, medium and extreme violence have three stages each. Thus there are 81 types of violence. The 81 types of violence become manifold due to rules, alternatives and collective forms. Stealing and having other doubts are parts of the 81 different types of violence. Stealing, telling lies, leading an unchaste life and collecting unwanted things, either done by self, through others or provoking others to do so, are also obstacles for the devotee. Not speaking lies personally but making others speaks lies on your behalf and provoking others to speak lies is also evil. In the same way, stealing, making others steal things and provoking others to steal things is all included in stealing. Something wrong in meaning inspiring others to lead a life of a celibate and not following celibacy yourself cannot be called as being completely celibate. The same should be understood for not collecting materials, lies, stealing and other greed-anger-attachment generated different types of violence. The devotee should determine in ones mind that these doubts are form of unhappiness and give unending results in the form of ignorance. This way one should inculcate a reasoning against violence, protect one from lies and lead the way of *Yog* and rituals to meet with the individual soul.

Results of following '*Niyama*' :

A. Results of following of *Ahiṇsa* (Non – Violence):

"Ahimsa pratishthayam tatsannidhou vairtyagah"

(*Yog – daṛṣ̣han 2:35*)

When a devotee associates with *Yog* and respects non-violence, the feeling of violence and enmity is gone. If a *Yogi* follows the principle of non-violence through thoughts, words and deeds, and is simple, pure, selfless and affectionate towards all living beings, who can hate him? Proximity with a *Yogi* not only eliminates the feeling of hatred in human beings but also in snakes, tigers and other violent wild beings.

B. Results of *Satya* (Truthfulness):

"Satya – pratishthayam Kriya phalashrayatwam".

(*Yog – daṛṣ̣han 2:36*)

A person who believes in truth, in his speech and behaviour makes his predictions come true. That is why the words spoken by the great people and *Yogis* come true. It is equally important to note that *Yogis* never speak meaningless, unsuitable and harmful words. *Yogis* always speak the truth and avoid speaking ill words. A single word by a *Yogi* can change one's whole life and make life move towards a better world. Truthful personalities have great power.

C. Results of *Asteya* (Abstinence from stealing):

"Asteya-pratishthyam sarva-ratnopasthanam".

(*Yog – daṛṣ̣han 2:37*)

When a devotee leaves the habit of stealing other's belongings, he starts receiving valuable things in life. A *Yogi* does not desire anything because he does not have anything, leave alone stealing things. Whatever a *Yogi* requires, God provides him to it.

It is nature's rule that when a person has too much desire for wealth, the wealth runs away and when a person rejects wealth, it comes after him. Yogis are in the same position. They are greedless. Therefore the rich people from across the world provide them riches and *Yogis* donate it for the benefit of the mankind.

D. Results of *Ḅraḥmachaṛyā* (Observance of celibacy):

'Braḥmachaṛyā – pratishthayam Viryalabhah"

(*Yog daṛṣ̣han 2:38*)

A *Yogi* who leads a life of celibacy increases his vigour, sharpness, glow, chastity, strength and courage. A person cannot become *Yogi* when he does not lead a life of celibacy.

E. Results of *Aparigraha* (Abstinence from possessing unwated things):

'Aparigraha sthairye janma kathntarambodhah'

(*Yog daṛṣ̣han 2:39*)

The result of detachment of possessions is that a man remains uninterested in materialism and always emerges as the winner over his senses. Then he gets auspicious thoughts like 'who am I? Where have I come from? What should I do?' A *Yogi* is never attracted towards material wealth and thus he attains salvation by getting relieved from the bonds of life and death.

F. Results of *Shāucha* (Cleaning)

'Shauchatsavanjugutpsa Parairsansargah'

(*Yog daṛṣ̣han 2:40*)

When a devotee purifies his body with water again and again, he finds that the more he tries to purify it, the more dirty and stinky it gets. It develops hatred in the person for his own body parts and when he sees others, he finds their body dirty too and tries to avoid their touch. He hates hugging and other such acts. Saint *Ṿyasa* says that :-

'Sthand beejadupatmbhannirasya yandanni dhanadapi
Kaymadhey shouchtwat pandita Hyhuchi vidu bhoshya'

(*Yog daṛṣ̣han. Vyas bhashyam*)

It means that the physical body is not pure, because it comes from impure body parts. It is made up of blood, sperm and therefore it smells from the mouth, the excretory organs and the pores on the surface of the skin. Even after death the dead body stinks a lot. Therefore this body is a mass of filth. This body remains dirty in spite of purifying it with water etc. The devotee loses interest in his body with these thoughts. He does not have any attachment with the body. He does not love the body, but loves the soul. This is the result of external purification. *Saint Pataṇjali* speaks about internal purification:

'Satvashudhisaumansyekapraendriya jayatm darshan yogtvani cha'

(*Yog daṛṣ̣han 2:41*)

Truth, non-violence, study of *Vedas* result in internal purification, happiness of the mind, concentration, victory over senses and ability to recognize the soul.

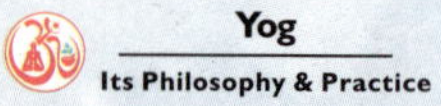

G. Results of *Saṇtosh* (Contentment):

Santopadnuttamah Sukhlabhah

(*Yog darṣḥan 2 :42*)

Happiness obtained through contentment is the best happiness. Happiness through contentment is called happiness of salvation. *Saint Vyasa* says :-

"Yacha kamsukham loke yaha divyam mahatsukham
Trishna kshay such marhatah shodashi kalam".

This means that pleasure of sex which is compared to the heavenly happiness, is not even equal to 1/16th part of happiness which is achieved by overcoming the desires. Therefore, there is no better form of delight than satisfaction; the desire troubles us at every step. *Ḅhartuhari* says –

'Trishna jirna vayamevajirna'

(*Vairagyashatak :7*)

This means a person who wants his desiresfulfilled, his desires never get over.

H. Results of *Tapas* (Penance) :

'Kayendriya sidhirashudhikshayat Tapasah'

(*Yog darṣḥan 2 : 43*)

When the impurities are destroyed with the ritual of devotion, the devotee's body and senses become strong and healthy. *Saint Dayanaṇd Mahārāj* comments with respect to devotion that "True feelings, belief in truth, speaking truth, not allowing the mind to be unreligious, performing right deeds through body; senses and mind, studying and teaching others the true knowledge of the *Vedas*, leading life according to the *Vedas*, performing religious deeds of high quality is called penance. Burning your bones and skin is not called penance.

I. Results of *ṣwādhyāy* (Regular study of the *Vedas*) :

'Swadhyaydisht devata samprahogh'.

(*Yog darṣḥan 2 : 44*)

A *Yogi* while regularly studying the *Vedas* meets scholarly, introspecting sages and accomplished personalities who further have devotion. A devotee who chants *oṃkār maṇṭra* and recites scriptures, never faces difficulties in devotion, accomplished holy sages guide him directly or indirectly. A devotee gets the guidance of God through holy preceptors.

J. Results of "*Īṣhwar praṇidhān*" (Deep devotion to God):

"Samadhi-siddhirswara – pranidhanat"

(*Yog darṣhan 2 : 45*)

With deep devotion to god or offering all actions to the supreme power and not being desirous of results of the deeds, a devotee attains the stage of *Samādhi*.

"Ishwar pranidhanam sarvkriyanam paramgurvrpanam"

(*Vyasbhashya 2 : 1, Yog darṣhan 2 : 1*).

After describing the results of *Yām*, we are now in a position to learn third principle of asana.

3. *Āsanas* (Postures):

"Sthira-sukham Asanam"

(*Yog darṣhan* 2 : 46)

Sitting in *parmāsana*, *bhadrāsana*, *sidhāsana* or *sukhāsana* or any other comfortable posture is called *Āsana*. Devotee should practice to sit attentively and comfortably for a long time while worshipping and meditating. According to *Maharṣhi Ṿyas* , Those who cannot sit in these postures and those who are sick, can do *sopashraya āsana* or take the support of chairs, walls and practice *prāṇāyām*, meditation etc.Posture is extremelyimportant for devotion meditation and worship.Practise of asanas is reqired to achieve *Japa* and meditation. Your spine should remain straight while practising any meditative *āsana*. Floor should be even. One can spread thick sheet, woollen blan cket or a grass mat as these are non- conductors of engery.A place which is quiet, peaceful ,gets fresh air and free from insects is ideal for practising *āsanas*. There are many people who claim to be a "*Yogi*" by doing a few *āsanas* and some people do believe in them. But it is just a myth. *Yogāsanas* are only part of *yoga*. A person has to follow the eight *yog* principals of resistance of passions, non- violence, truth, cheating, celibacy and other such principles, and practice meditation for long duration with complete devotion to become a *yogi*.

Haṭh Yoga describes 84 types of different asanas, these *āsanas* relate with physical and mental health as well meditative poses. As one practices these *āsanas*, the entire body gets activated, becomes flexible and healthy. Topics 5-10 contain complete details of *āsanas* which can help to cure different health problems the readers may refer to these pages.

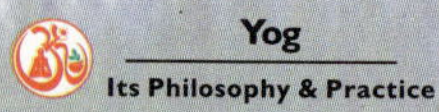

4. P̣rānāyām (*Yogic* Respiratory exercise, or balanced breathing)

"Tasmin Sati Shwasprashwasyogrtir Vichedah Pranayah"

(Yog darṣ̣han : 2.49)

After completing the physical poses or *Āsana*'s, with controlling inhalation and exhalation is called *P̣rānāyām*. *Yogdaṛṣhan* describes four categories of *Prānāyām.*

A. *Bahya Vritti Pranayama*
B. *Abhyantarvritti Pranayama*
C. *Stambhvritti Pranayama and*
D. *Bahyabhyantar-Vishaya kshepi*

"Bahbyabhyantar Stambhvrittirdesh Kalsankhyabhini Paridrushto Deerghsukshmaha"

(Yog darṣ̣han : 2.50)

"Bahyabhyantar Vishayakshepi Chaturthaha"

(Yog darṣ̣han : 2.51)

A. *Bahyavritti P̣rānāyām* (External Condition)

Method :

- Sit in *Sidhāsana* or *Paḍmāsana* and exhale breath as much as you can in one go.
- Hold on to your breath as long as you can and perform *Mōolbaṇdh*, *Udiyan* and *Jalandhara baṇdh.*
- To end the bandhas relax your muscles whenever you wish to breath again and inhale slowly.
- Inhale and repeat the entire exercise non-stop 3 to 21 times.

Benefits :

This *Prānāyām* does not cause any harm to the body. It improves calmness of mind and digestion capability. It is very beneficial in stomach disorders. It enhances and sharpens the intellect and purifies the body. It regulates energy from sexual organs upwards and helps to cure premature ejaculation, nightfall and other semen related problems. *Āḅhyāṇtaṛvṛiṭti Prānāyām* (Internal condition)

B. *Ābhyantara-vṛtti prāṇāyāma* (Internal condition)

Method :

- Sit in meditation pose, exhale and inhale as much as you can. Your upper chest should be bulging our and lower abdomen should be contracted when you inhale. Perform *Jalandhara baṇdh* and *Mōolbaṇdh* while you inhale.
- Hold the breath in as long as you can. Relax muscles to end the *baṇdh* and exhale slowly.

Benefits :

- It cures the respiratory (lung related) problems. It is extremely beneficial for Asthma patients. It increases vitality, vigor and enhances the complexion of the body.

C. *Stambhavritti Ṛrāṇāyām* (Arrested breathing)

To practice this *Prāṇāyām*, stop inhaling or exhaling as long as you can. Resume to normal breathe normally. You can perform all three bandhas while you arrest your breathing.

D. *Bahyabhyantara Vishayakshepi Ṛrāṇāyām* (Arrested breathing during inhaling and exhaling)

- **Method :** While exhaling hold the breath out for a short span and while inhaling hold the breath for a short span too. In other words, as you are breathing out *(Ṛrān Vāyu)* try to stop it by contracting air *(Apān Vāyu)*. When the fresh air enters the body it pushes the air inside and stops the fresh air. In this manner by doing opposite actions, the movement of both air passages stops and the breathing is in your control. By doing this *Prāṇāyām* the mind and the bodily senses are in your control. The vigour and vitality increases due to which the intellect sharpens, and masters difficult and minute aspects of a subject in a short span of time. The body becomes more virile; one becomes brave and his physical senses are under control. By practicing this *Prāṇāyām* the person absorbs and retains knowledge in short span of time. The mind is cleansed and it can concentrate in worship. Ladies can follow the same method of *Prāṇāyām.*

(*Sa. Pra* : Third Ch.)

"Prachardan vidharanyamam Va Pranasya" (Yog sūṭra 1.34) expresses similar views. Let us understand it in detail. Bring the *Ṛrāna* from above and *apāna* from below and let them fight in the nasal area. *Ṛrānvāyu* which is normally in the heart region and leaves body through exhalation, should be made to move towards *'Brahmānaṇda'* and settle between your eyebrows. *Apān Vāyu* which lives in lower abdomen and has the tendency to come in, it should be brought to the nostril area and should be reserved there. Now push both the *Ṿayus* and create a 'war' between twXo. In other words start friction between them. Do not allow the *Ṛrāna* to go out or *Apāna* to enter. This way both the *Ṛrāna's* will be in your control by performing this frictional action. While performing the *Prāṇāyām* concentrate your mind and all the organs between your eyebrows.

(Dhyānayoga Prakaśa : second chapter)

Bhagvaḍgītā explains about *Prāṇāyām* this way :

"Sparshan Krutwa bahirbahyamshchakshushcai wantare
Bhruwo, Pranapanau samo krutwa Nasabhyantarcharinau"

(Bhagwaḍgīta : 5.27)

Disconnect from all the worldly pleasures of beauty, taste or smells and concentrate your mind between your eyebrows (This point is called *Ṭrīkuti or Ḅhrukutī*). A true *yogi*, by doing thus normalizes the movement of both the *Ṗrānas* with the help of nostrils and is capable of controlling the mind, heart and senses. He aspires for salvation and he is free from anger, fear or desire.

"Yatendriya mano budhir munir moksha parayanoh
Vigatechabhaykrodho yah sada mukta eva sah"

(Bhagvadgita : 5.28)

The following *śhloka* describes the same topic :

"Apane Juvhati pranam pranepanam tatha pare
Pranapangati rudhwa pranayam parayanaha
Apare niyataharah pranan praneshu juvhati
Sarvepyete yadnyavido yadnyakshayit kalmashaha"

(Bhagadgita 4: 29-30)

These references about *Prānāyām* have been compiled and printed along with colored illustrations in an attractive book form. We request the readers to read '*Prānāyām* – its philosophy and practices' written by *Ṣwāmī ji* for in-depth knowledge of the subject.

-Publisher

Saint Pataṇjali prescribes these *Prānāyām* in *'Daṛṣhanśhaṣtra'*. In *haṭhyog* text the internal *kuṃbhaka* (*Āḅhyāṇtaṛ Kuṃbhak*), which is of eight types, has been prescribed for the benefit of physical and mental health.

"Suryabhedan mujjayi Sitkari sheetali tatha
Bhastrika bhramari murcha plavinityashta kumbhaka"

(Haṭhayoga-pradīpikā)

After the publication of intial edition of '*Yog* - Its Philosophy and Practice', the topic on *Prāṇāyāma* has been published separately with coloured illustrations. The readers are requested to read '*Prāṇāyāma* - Its Philosophy & Practice' written by *Swāmīji* for an in-depth knowledge of *prāṇāyāma*.

5. *Praṭyāhāra* (Withdrawal of senses from their subjects):

"Swavishaya samprayoge chittaswaroopa nukar evendriyanam Pratyaharaha"

(*Yog darṣḥan 2:54*)

When the senses do not have connection with their subjects, they change according to the condition of the mind (*chiṭta*). When one controls ones mind through detachment and wisdom, the senses get controlled on its own.

This victory over mind deviated from the subjects and diverting the senses and mind inwards is known as praṭyāhāra. The '*hru*' basic root is used with reference to attraction. *Saint Pataṇjali* explains the results of withdrawal of senses as follows:

"Tatah parama vashytendriyanam"

(*Yog darṣḥan 2:55*)

A learner has complete authority over the senses with the help of *Praṭyāhāra*. Interest and indulgence towards words, touch, beauty and smell divert's a person from the higher path of attainment of his soul. The person who has interest in sensual pleasures is inclined towards materialistic pleasures, not God. Therefore detachment and *yogic* practice provides true understanding and one accomplishes victory over the senses. Once this stage comes then one experiences immense happiness, contentment and the world seems nothing but the root cause of all the sorrows.

"Parinamtap sanskar dukhairgunvrutti virodhacch dukhmev sarv vivekinaha"

(*Yog darṣḥan, 2:15*)

The bodily pleasures which are created by speech, touch, vision of beauty or taste are nothing but enjoyment due to ignorance as far as a learned *Yogi* is concerned. Analyzing the worldly pleasure shows that these pleasures are based on sufferings of other human beings. These suffering leave minute impressions on our joyful experiences which a common person cannot sense but a *Yogi* can sense. Thus the worldly desires which satisfy others, do not make him happy. Therefore a *yogi* fulfills his duty to attain God and is free from all types of pain.

The description given from *yām* to *Praṭyāhāra* forms *Bahirang Yog*. Now we will give brief description about *Ḍhārṇa, Ḍhyān* and *Aṇtaraṇg Yog*.

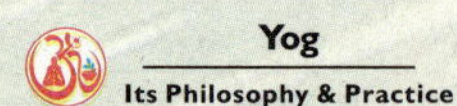

6. Ḍhārṇa (Concentration):

Deshbandshchittasya dharna

(Yog darṣhan: 3.1)

Nāḇhiçhaḳrā (Navel center), *Ḥriday puṇdarīk* (Heart), *Ḅhrūmaḍhya* (center of Eyebrows), *Murdha jyoti* (the light glowing on center of your forehead), *Bramharandhra* (top of your head), *Nāsikāgra* (Tip of your nose) or *jiṿhagra* (Tip of your tongue) are the physical points of your body. *Ḍhārṇa* is when you sit in one place and concentrate your mind (*Nigraha* or *Ekāgrata*) on any one of these points.

Thus the act of detaching your mind from the worldly objects and focusing it on the subtle subjects of Soul and Supreme Soul is called *Dhārṇa*. *Dhārṇa* is the foundation of *Ḍhyān*. As you perfect your practice of *Ḍhārṇa, Ḍhyān* will take place on its own.

7. *Ḍhyān* (Meditation)

Tatra Pratyayaiktanata dhyanam.

(Yog darṣhan : 3.2)

By performing *Dhārṇa* or concentrating on the physical points *(Nāḇhiçhaḳrā, Bhrumadhya* etc) one experiences tremendous rapport with the God. This concentrated flow of superior knowledge is called *Ḍhyān*. When a river enters the sea it submerges with the seawater. Similarly submerge your mind with the supreme divine presence and do not think of anything else. To lose yourself in this pure joy and divine peace of the God's presence is *Ḍhyān*.

Ḍhyān is associated with every moment of life. According to Indian culture *Ḍhyān* supports each action of your daily life. No wonder the elder members in the family always advice people to 'concentrate and do all the tasks with care'. We use the word 'concentrate' but never really concentrate on its true meaning. *Ḍhyān* or concentration is associated with every action of the world and is an inseparable part of our lives. Our lives are incomplete without *Ḍhyān*. We cannot achieve any spiritual or physical objective without *Ḍhyān*. We can lead a happy and blissful life only with *Ḍhyān*. Though *Ḍhyān* is in itself a very major yogic action, but we will give a short glimpse of the various methods of *Ḍhyān* to guide our readers.

Few directions or guidance for meditation :

- First, one should do *p̱rāṉāyām* before doing *ḏhyān* because *p̱rāṉāyām* makes the mind completely calm and concentrated. A calm and peaceful mind is a pre-requisite for proper *dhyān*.

- The mind becomes free and relaxed by practicing *Kapālḅhātī* and *Anulom-vilom p̣rāṇāyām* so the meditation takes place on its own. When you perform *Kapālḅhātī* for three minutes and *Anulom-vilom p̣rāṇāyām* for 5 to 10 minutes, *Ḅrahma*'s divine strength situated inside the muladhar chakras start moving upwards. With all the *Çhakṛās* and nerves get energized, the Supreme God starts positioning in the form of *Oṃkār* in the heart and divine light flame emerges. Even unstable mind can concentrate with the help of *p̣rāṇāyām.*

- At the time of *ḍhyāna* give the utmost importance to this process. Any other thought whether it is good or bad, is immaterial or secondary at that time. Even the good thoughts of donation, serving or helping others, studying *vedas* etc. should be kept off the mind at the time of *ḍhyāna*. At that time one's aim should be only the introspection, remembering and meeting the almighty and submerging yourself with him.

- While practicing *Ḍhyān*, guide your thoughts inwards. And everyday before such practice think over the following points. Tell yourself – I do not exist in material riches, glory, land, buildings. My existence is not in thoughts of my relations – my son, my grandson etc All this explicit or inexplicit thoughts are not my natural form. I am liberated from all living and non living matter. Even this body is not my actual form. I am not bonded by my body and senses like speech, touch, smell, or with mind and emotions of mind i.e. anger, passion, attachment and pride. I am liberated from jealousies, pride and other negative emotions. I am a pure soul with bliss and enlightened with peace. I am a child of immortal peace *(Aṃrit-Puṭra).* I rest in the super consciousness (*Ḅrahmi* consciousness) like, a drop that vaporizes and goes to the sky from the ocean and then comes back to earth as a rain drop and again merges back in the ocean. A drop of water cannot live without the Ocean. I too want to embrace almighty - the ocean of joy and make myself like a drop that merges with the ocean itself. The almighty provides us life, power, glory, peace, our parents, wealth and all the materialistic pleasures. He is showering blessings continuously from every direction. He never keeps us away from him for a single moment. I am always in God and God is always in me'. These thoughts of, being one with God, merging with God and becoming part of the supreme soul will give us ultimate happiness. The almighty will shower happiness on us. Inspite of this if you cannot experience God then who do you blame ?

- One should keep himself detached and discretionary. One should perform every action without any attachment and as a service to God Almighty. Look at life as an impartial viewer or a witness. Every action which is without any pride or the desire for its result is a form of *ḍhyānakriya.*

- All the means and thoughts of worldly comforts are ultimately sorrowful. Till the time one has a comfort-oriented mentality, he cannot be a true devotee. Without total devotion attaining *ḍhyāna* and *Samādhi* is impossible.

- ***"Tasya Vachakaha Pranavah*** **(*Yog darṣhan* 1:27)**

  Tajjpasta Aarthabhavanam **(*Yog darṣhan* 1:28)**

  Omityekaksharam bramha **(*Gīta8.13*)**

  Om kham Bramha" **(*Yajuṛveda*)**

Chanting of *Oṃkār* is the best way to begin *ḍhyāna*. Many of our organs created by god, for instance – eyebrows, eyes, nostrils, lips, ears, heart, chest and other parts of the body resemble the shape of *omkar*. A *Sādhak* should experience the omnipresent and omnipotent Almighty everywhere and experience his divine existence.

The entire universe is full of *Oṃkār*. A devotee chants the *Oṃkār maṇṭra* and he experiences the presence of *Ḅraḥmā* all over, loving its divine form. *Oṃkār* is not an individual word or a symbol. It is a divine power which rules the universe. As the soul is not visible in the body, similarly *Oṃkār* is not visible to the external eyes but regulates the universe with its divine energy. Along with *Oṃkār, Gāyaṭrī maṇṭra,* the powerful *maṇṭra from Vedas* can also be chanted after understanding it's meaning.

- The mind is concentrated on controlling the inhalation and exhalation. After concentrating the mind, *Oṃkār* should be chanted. All the senses are not flawless because the eyes can see good and bad things, ears can listen to decent and indecent words, nose can smell fragrance and bad odour, speech can express truth and lies, tongue eats both digestible and indigestible food and mind can develop both good and bad thoughts. Therefore, to meet the flawless *Ḅraḥmā*, the only pure part of our body is *'p̣rān'*. We should take it's help to chant *Oṃkār* (*udgeet*) and worship the purest of all - the God almighty and should experience the God. Whenever you get time, look within yourself and take long and deep breaths and with every exhalation chant *Oṃkār*. The speed of inhalation and exhalation should be so slow that one should not be able to hear it and a cotton thread kept in front of the nostrils should not move. Try to inhale and exhale only once in one minute. In this manner, try to feel the breath going inside your body. Initially the touch of breath will be felt on the tip of your nose and gradually you will learn to experience the deep touch of your breath. This way chant *Oṃkār* for sometime, while introspecting within yourself, and you will achieve meditation. This is *Sahaj Yog* (easy *Yog*). While meditating in this way the devotee sees God within himself (*sākṣāṭkār*) and thus experiences the divine joy of samadhi. The devotee should do the same at bedtime to enjoy the sleep, which is enhanced with *yoga* (*Yog Niḍrā).* With this practice the entire life of devotee becomes enhanced with *Yog*.

- Every person aspiring for salvation should meditate (i.e. *japa* (chant), *ḍhyān* & worship at least for an hour everyday. The worries of this world are thus destroyed and we experience the supreme soul of God. We should remember that the sole aim of life is merging the individual soul with supreme soul and reaching God, everything else is secondary. Therefore *Yog* and *ḍhyāna* are the necessities of our lives.

8. *Samādhi* (Transidental Meditation) :

"Tadevarthmatra nirbhasam Swaroop shunyamiv Samadhiti"

(*Yog darṣhan :3.3*)

When we achieve *ḍhyān*, our own bodily presence goes down to nil and the Godly presence illuminates our body. That state is called as *Samādhi*. While chanting *Oṃkār* a yogi gets engrossed, submerges and gets lost in glory of the peaceful presence of God. One forgets everything else and experiences the divine form of God. In meditation, the person meditating, the soul of a person meditating and the subject one is meditating on, all three are present. Whereas, in case of *Samādhi*, the mind, the divine peaceful form of God and the soul enlightened with knowledge are one, not having any difference in the three aspects. As a person takes a dip in the water and stays submerged for a while, in the same way the living soul submerges itself in the delight of God and experiences the divine joy of deep meditation. The sages narrate it in a different way. Like the iron when thrown in the fire takes the form of fire, similarly the soul should be enlightened in the divine knowledge of God. We should forget ourselves and our body completely and should be completely engrossed in the divine joyous form of God, thereby accomplishing *Samādhi*.

Sri Bhōj Mahārāj says with reference to *Samādhi*:

"Samyagadhiyat ekagnikriyate vikshepan paritritya mano yatra sa samadhih"

This means the stage when the mind is diverted from doubts, concentration is achieved and only the truth is grasped, is the state of *Samādhi*. The stage which includes doubts and queries described in the first *pāda* (chapter) of *Yog darṣhan* should be considered to be a stage of *ḍhyān* because it has words, meaning, knowledge and alternatives. The stage without doubts and queries should be considered as *samādhi*. This training of mind is the highest level of

Samādhi and at this stage the devotee obtains the knowledge in the form of blessings of God (*Prasād*). After the stage of *samādhi* another advanced stage is - *Nirbeeja Samādhi* in which desires and pleasures don't arise, even in the mind. Due to that all the moods (*vritis*) subside completely. The realization destroys the seed of all wanderings of the mind. Then the possibility of falling prey to worldly bonds is also destroyed, which is called the contemplation of the highest order. This is perfection of *Yog* or life, by achieving it a *Yog* in the words of Sant *Vyasa* is:

"Praptam prapniyam, kshinah kshetavyah kleshah, chinnha shlishtparvah Bhavasankramah
Yasyavichedajjanitva mriyate mrutva chyayat Iti
Dyanssaiva parakashtha Vairagyam
Etsaiv hi nantrakshiyakam Kaivalyamiti"

(*Yogsutras, Vyasbhashyam; 1.16*)

In other words the ultimate limit of knowledge is asceticism. Reaching this highest stage with *samādhi* leads to the salvation of the soul. One achieves fulfillment in life, the ignorance and other sufferings (pride, jealousy, hatred and attachment) are destroyed. The organs are joined and the entry of a soul in other body, or the circle of life and death (due to which a creature takes birth, dies and is reborn after death) is destroyed. Thus *Samādhi* is briefly described.

Eight *Yogic* Practices *(Ashtang Yog)*

(Light) Exercises

Following are some light exercises recommended for maintaining healthy joints and providing strength, agility and soundness to the nervous system:

Sitting positions in *Daṇḍāsan:*

Method:

All the *āsanas* that are done in sitting position are begun with *Daṇḍāsan*. Both feet should be stretched straight in the front, held together. Both hands should rest on the on either side of the waist with palms touching the ground and the fingers facing backwards. Keep the hands and the waist absolutely straight and practice as explained below.

1. For the fingers of the toes: Slowly but forcefully press the toes together in a forward movement while keeping the heels still. Do the same in a backward movement also. Repeat this exercise eight to ten times.

2. For the heels and the feet: With both feet joined together, press the entire feet slowly, forward and backwards. The heels will rub with the ground while doing this. This exercise is beneficial for sciatica pain and knees.

3. **For the toes:** Keep both the feet at a distance. First rotate the toes of the right foot in a circular motion trying to make a zero. Repeat this exercise five to seven times. Then do the same in the opposite direction. In the same way, exercise with the other foot and lastly with both the feet held together.

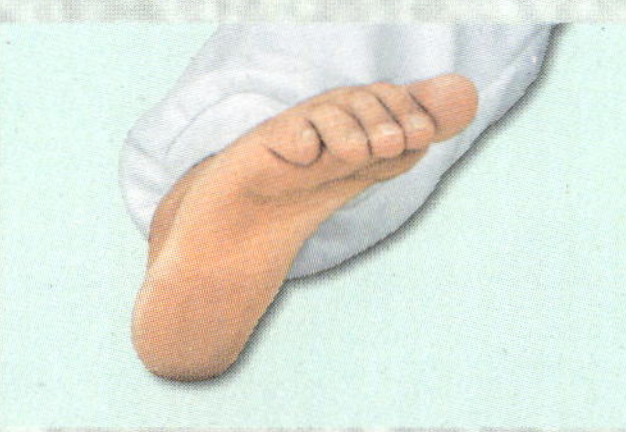

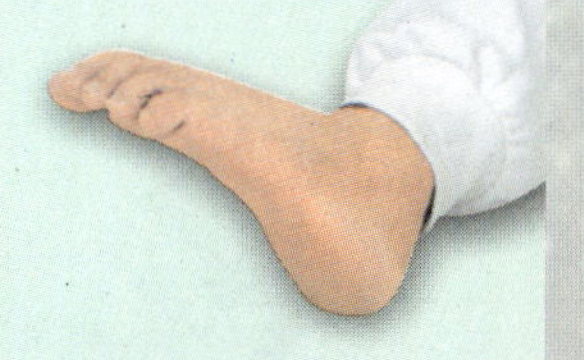

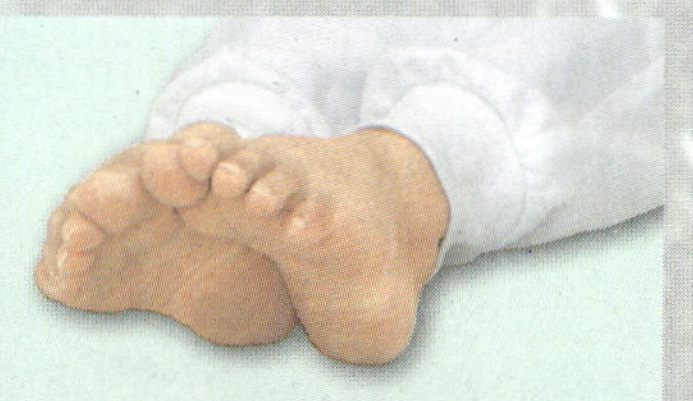

4. **For knees and hips : (a)** Fold the right leg inwards and place it on the left thigh. Hold the right toe with left hand and keep the right hand on the right knee. While supporting the right knee with the right hand from below, move the knee so that it touches the chest and then do the

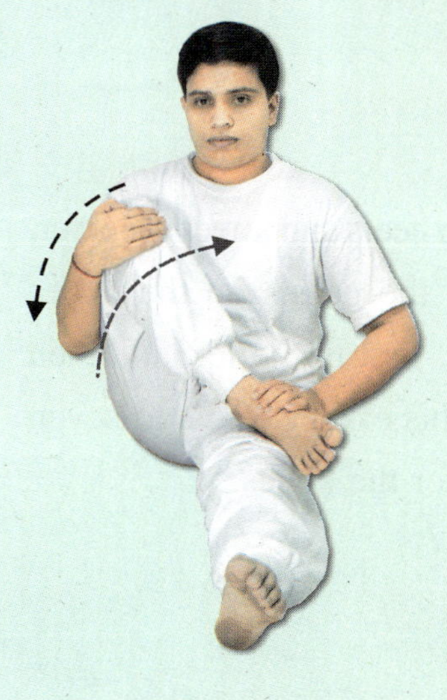

reverse so that the knee touches the ground. Similarly, repeat this exercise by folding the left leg, keeping it on the right thigh and then touching the chest with the left knee. At last, join both feet and hold the toes with both hands. Maintaining this position, touch both knees to the floor and then lift them up. Do this exercise a few times.

(b) ***Titli Āsan*** (Butterfly). After bending both the legs from knees hold the bases of the feet together, bring them to the joints of the thighs and move the knees up and down as the wings of a butterfly for two minutes, repeat this exercise. It helps in maintaining a healthy hip joint and also helps in reducing the excess fat around the hips and thighs. This will help in performing *Padmāsana* as well.

5. For the knees: (a) Keeping the legs straight, keep both the hands on the sides touching the floor. While pressing and releasing the kneecaps, perform the action of contraction and expansion. After this, interlock the fingers of both the hands underneath the right knee and hold the thigh. Then fold the leg inwards bringing it as close to the hip as possible and while performing the cycling action make a circle moving the foot forward. Repeat this exercise using the other foot in the same way.

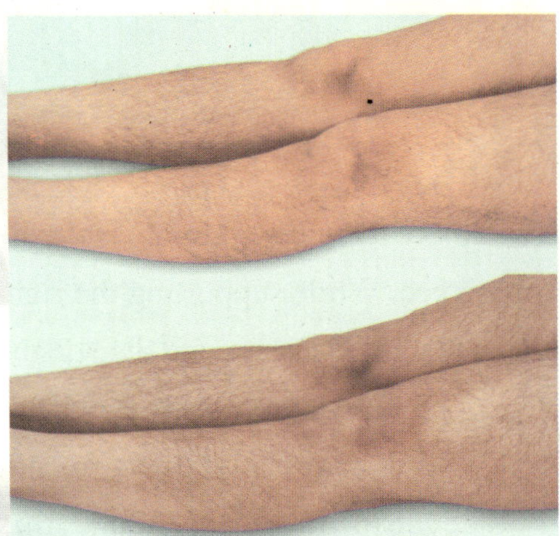

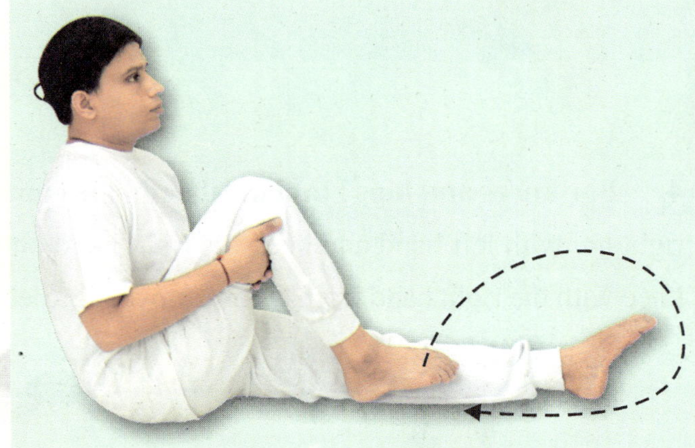

(b) Standing straight keep both heels and knees together, touching each other. Put both the palms on the knees and rotate in a circular motion, first in the left and then in the right direction. Repeat this exercise five to seven times. This exercise is useful for the knees.

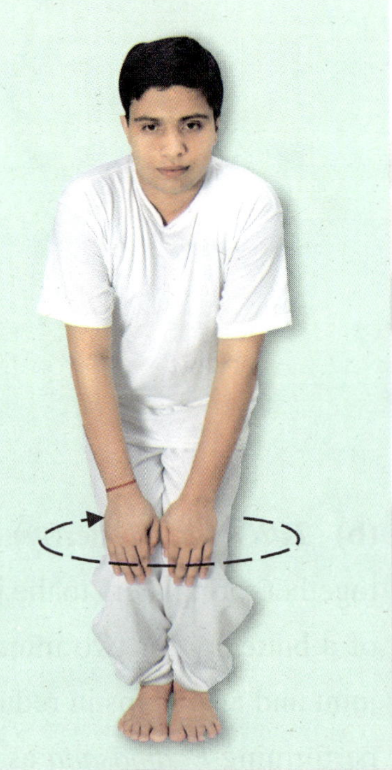

6. For the stomach and the waist (Grinding): (a) Hold the fingers of both the hands in an interlocked manner and stretch them in the front touching the feet. Turn the hands together from left to right in such a way that the waist bends forward, and the hands move in a circular path while touching the feet. When the hands reach the thighs, the waist should move backwards. Keep the legs stationary. Repeat this exercise in the same way, from right to left.

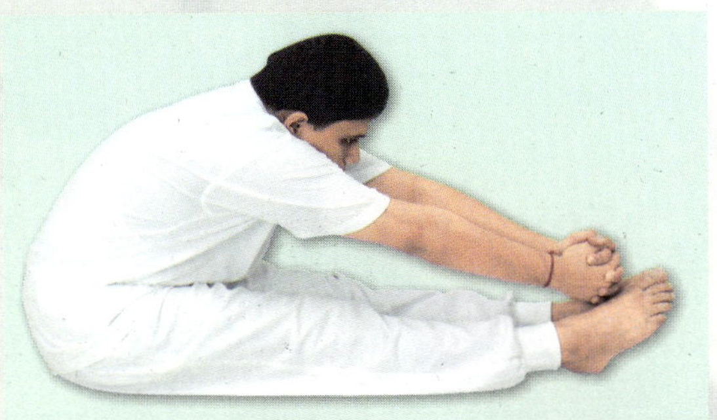

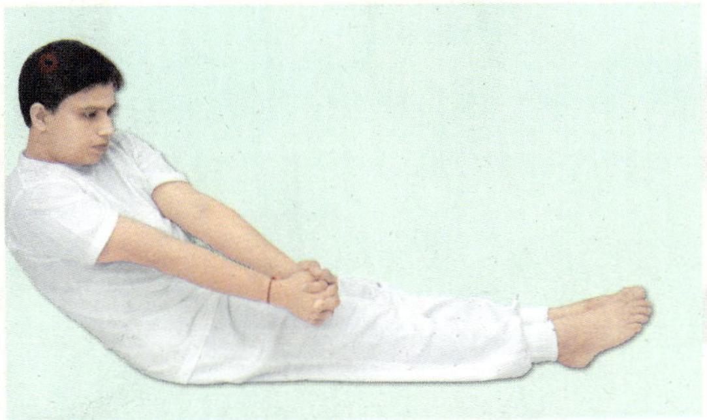

(b) Stretch both legs wide apart in the front. Raise the hands horizontally in line with the shoulders in each direction. Then catch the thumb of the left toe with the right hand and turning the left hand in an upward direction, keeping it straight, turn the neck so as to look at the left hand. In the same way repeat the exercise with the other hand. These exercises strengthen the stomach and relieve the backache, and also reduce accumulated fat on the waist. However, those suffering from severe backache should not perform these exercises.

7. **For the back:** Hold both the wrists with opposite hands, lift them and take them to the back of the head. While inhaling, pull the left hand with the right hand towards right side keeping the arm behind the head. Keep the head and neck still. While exhaling lift the hands upwards. Similarly perform this exercise from the other side.

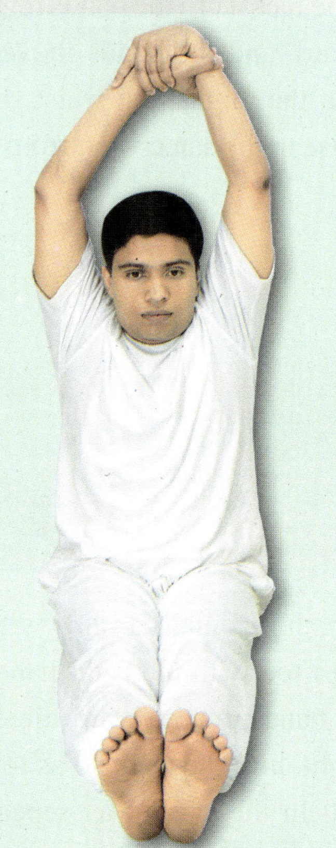

8. **For the fingers of the hands:** (a) Stretch both the hands in the front keeping them aligned with the shoulders and palms facing down. Fold the fingers slowly but forcefully and then release them.(b) Fold both the thumbs inside and press them with the fingers making a fist like shape, and then slowly open them. Repeat them 10 to 12 times.

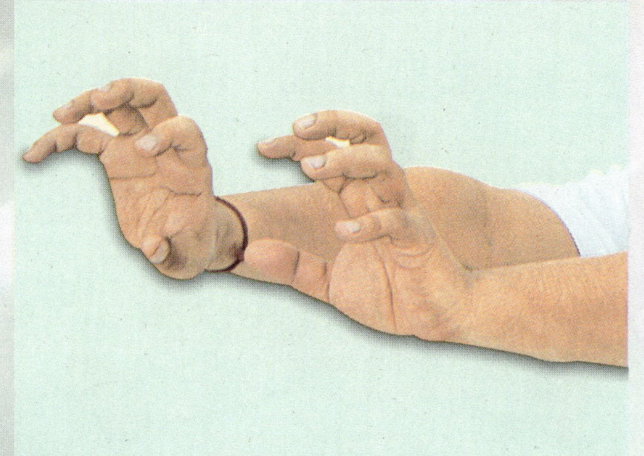

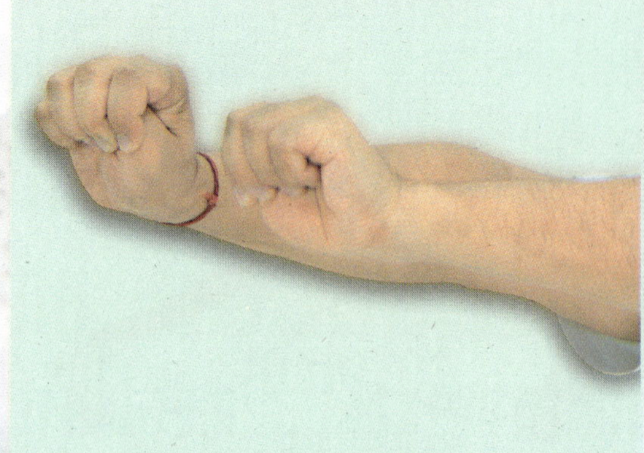

9. For the hands, cervical spondylitis and frozen shoulders:

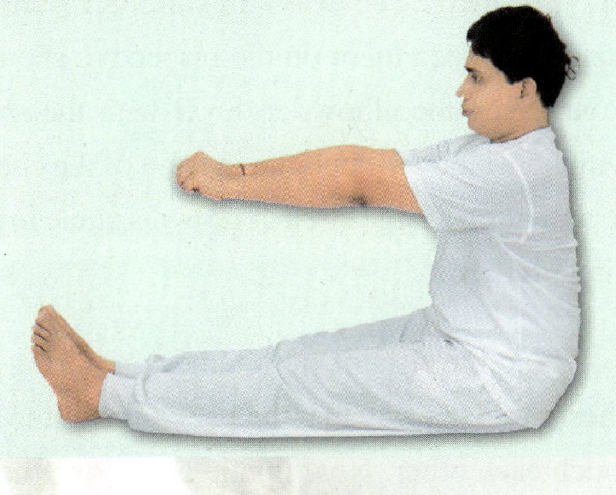

Fold the thumbs, press them with the fingers to form closed fists like shape and keep the hands aligned with the shoulders, stretched in front. Now rotate both fists together in both directions. The elbows should be kept straight throughout.

10. For the elbows: (a) Stretch both arms in front aligned with the shoulders and palms facing upwards. Now fold both elbows such that the fingers touch the respective shoulders. Then slowly straighten them. (b) Repeat the same exercise while stretching the hands sideways aligned with the shoulders.

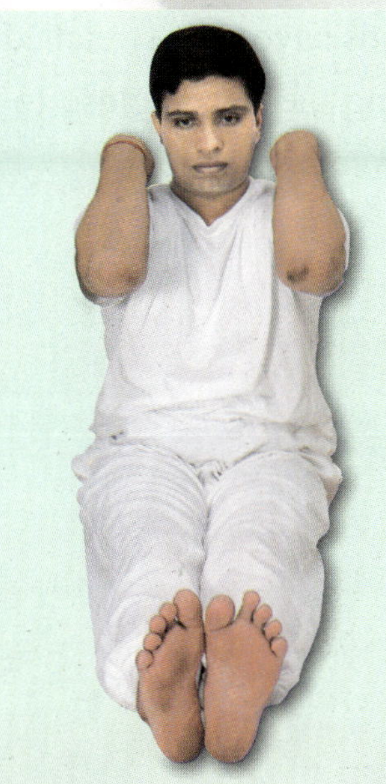

11. For heart, cervical and shoulder pain: (a) Fold both hands and keep them on the respective shoulders from the front. Keep the elbows in level with the shoulders. Then with both elbows touching, in front of the chest, rotate them so as to form a large circle. Form this circle from the opposite direction also.

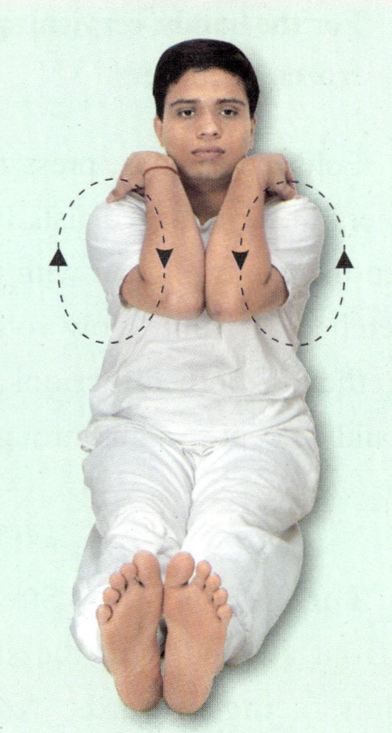

(b) Fold the fists of both hands and bring them near the chest in such a way that the back-side of the fingers should touch each other. Now inhale and move the hands slowly in the front, keeping the fingers together and touching. Once the hands have fully stretched in front, start exhaling while bringing the hands close to the chest. Repeat this several times.

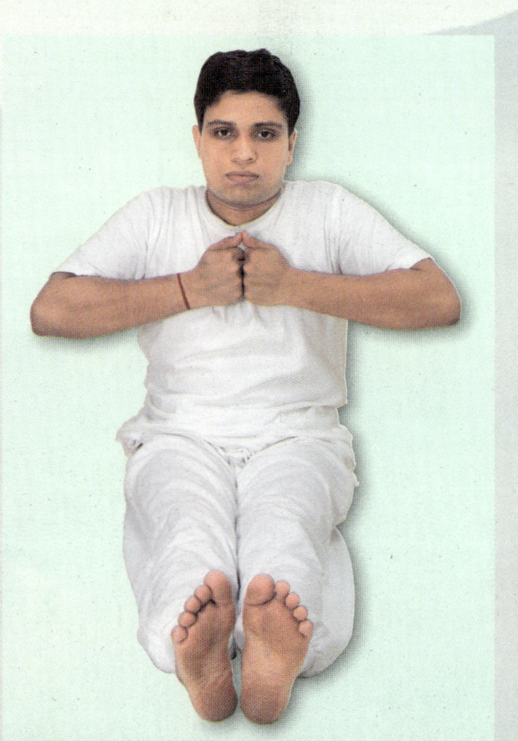

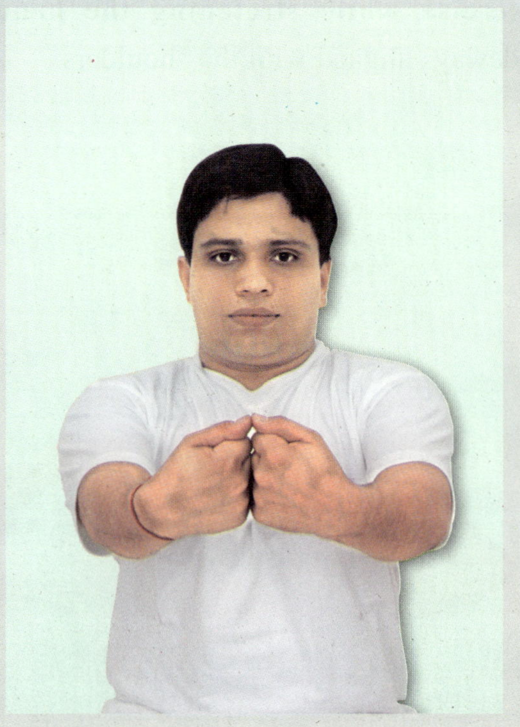

12. For the neck:

(a) Sit straight and rotate the neck towards the right to touch the right shoulder. In the same way, touch it with the left shoulder. After this, bend the neck in front such that the chin touches the chest and then slowly take it backwards bending as much as you can. In the end, rotate the neck in a circular motion in both the directions.

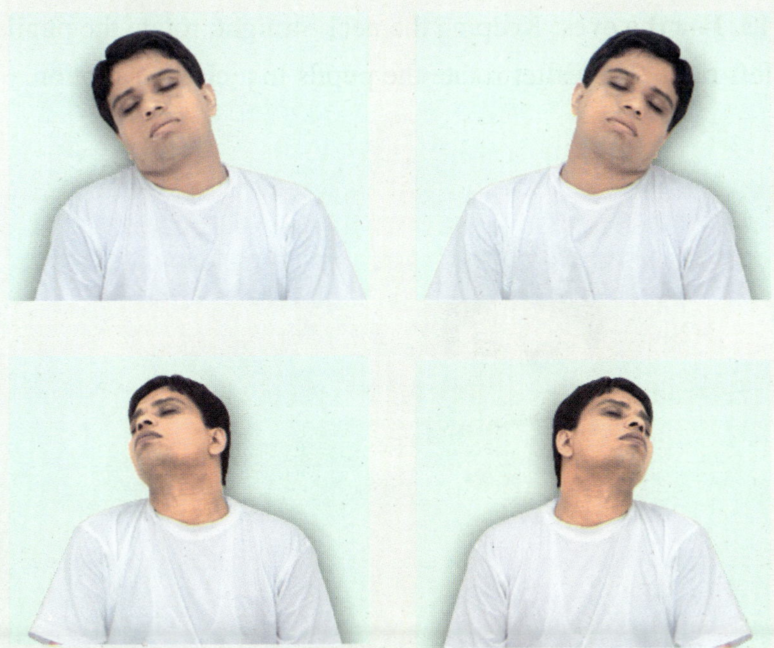

(b) Keep the right palm on the right side of the head above the ear and press the palm against the head such that both exert pressure against each other. This mutual pressure will create a vibration in the neck. Repeat this exercise 4-5 times. Now undertake the entire exercise with the left hand on the left side of the head.

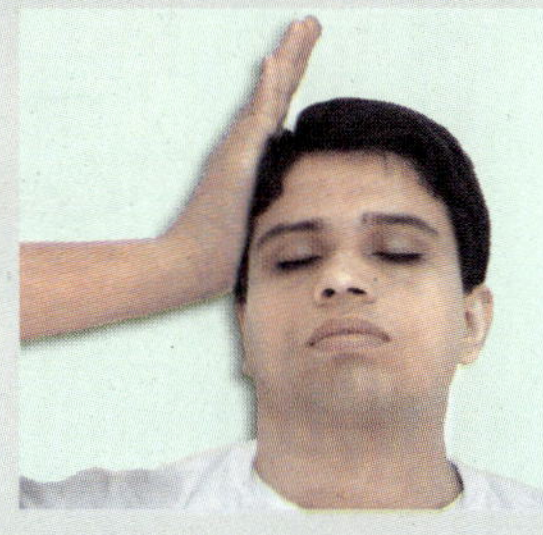

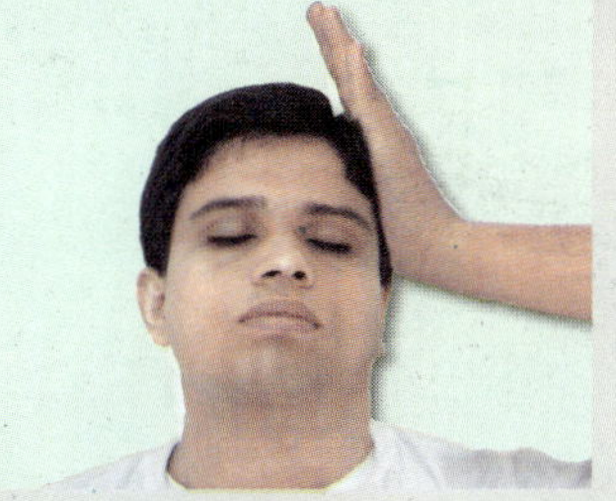

(c) Interlock the fingers of both the hands and press them together against the rear of the head, both exerting pressure on each other. While doing this, the neck and head should be kept straight. This mutual pressure will create a vibration in the neck, which would be beneficial for the neck and its proper blood circulation.

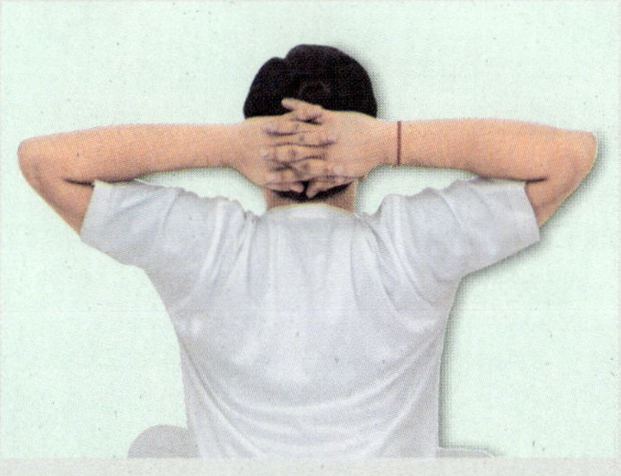

13. For the eyes: Keeping the neck straight, rotate the pupils of the eyes up-down and then left-right. Thereafter rotate the pupils in a circular motion.

Rules useful for the *Āsanas*

1. Time: *Āsanas* may be done both in the morning and evening. If one cannot do them at both the times, then morning time is better. The mind remains calm in the morning. *Āsanas* can be done in the morning after performing daily chores, on an empty stomach, or in the evening, 5-6 hours after lunch. If there is a problem of constipation then one should drink water kept in a copper or silver utensil, in the morning, and take a stroll. This helps in clearing the system. If it is a case of severe constipation, one should take *Triphalā* powder with warm water before going to bed.

2. Place: A clean, calm and secluded place is the best for performing *āsanas*. Places like greenery of trees, park, garden, pond or river side are the most suitable places. Adequate amount of oxygen is available in open spaces and near the trees, which is good for health. If *āsanas* and *prāṇāyāma* are being performed at home, a lamp *(dīyā)* or *guggulu* should be lit to fill the air with aroma.

3. Clothes: While doing *āsanas,* clothes should be minimum and comfortable. Males can wear half-pants/shorts and a vest. Ladies can wear *salwar*, blouse, etc.

4. Surface and duration: It is appropriate to spread a soft mat or blanket on the ground. Do not do *āsanas* directly on the floor/earth. Perform all the *āsanas* according to your stamina. Complete practice of the asanas takes about one hour, medium practice about 30 minutes and brief practice in about 15 minutes. Every person should preferably do these exercises for at least half an hour, daily.

5. Age: Practice should be according to ones own capacity, physical strength, age and with a happy and enthusiastic disposition and full concentration of the mind. Only then can the person achieve the benefits of Yog. Weak and old people should not practice too much of *āsanas and Prāṇāyām.* Children above the age of 10 can do all the exercises. Pregnant ladies should not attempt difficult exercises. They should only undertake deep breathing and *pranavnād* slowly, chanting *Gāyatrī-mantra* and other sacred mantras while meditating.

6. Stage and precautions: *Āsanas* and *prāṇāyāma* can be done in all situations. They enable healthy people become healthier. Such a person does not fall sick, whereas an unhealthy person will become alright. There are a few *āsanas* which a sick person should not perform or those who have discharge from ears, who have redness in eyes, who have a weak nervous system and heart, should not perform *Śīrṣāsana.* Weak hearted people should not perform heavy exercises like full *Śalabhāsana* and *Dhanurāsana*. Persons suffering from hernia should not do *āsanas* that put pressure on the lower part of the body, below the navel. Patients of high blood pressure should not do *Śīrṣāsana* and women should not perform exercises during the 4-5 days of menstrual period. Those who have pain in the neck and back should not do exercises, which require bending forward.

7. Food: Food should be taken at least half an hour after performing of *āsanas*. Food should be simple. Consumption of fried and spicy food leads to stomach disorder. Consumption of tea once destroys around 50 cells of liver and other delicate glands. You can yourself imagine the harmful effects of tea consumption. Tea is a bitter enemy of health, which deforms the whole body. Tea consumption has an addictive effect, which makes it habit forming. It affects the digestive system causing acidity, gas, constipation and several other problems. Tea and allopathic medicines are the two main factors causing deformation of the liver.

8. Inhale-exhale rules: While doing *āsanas,* it is a common rule to exhale while bending forward and inhale while moving backwards. Breathing should take place through nose only, not through mouth, as the air inhaled through nose gets filtered automatically.

9. Sight: *Āsanas* done with eyes closed, help increase concentration of the mind, and thus help in eliminating stress and instability of the mind. Normally *āsanas* and *prāṇāyāma* can also be performed with eyes kept open.

10. Sequence: Some *āsanas* are performed on one side only. If an *āsanas* is performed in one direction then it should be repeated in the opposite direction also. In addition, decide the order in which the *āsanas* should be done so that performing the succeeding *āsana* provides exercise of the muscles and joints in the opposite direction also. For example, one should do *Matsyāsana* after *Sarvāṅgāsana* and *Uṣṭrāsana after Maṇḍūkāsana.* The beginners will experience pain in the muscles and joints during the first 2-4 days, however they should continue to practice. The pain will subside by itself. Whenever you get up after doing the *āsanas* in the lying position, you should turn leftwards while getting up. At the end of practice, *Śavāsana* should be done for 8-10 minutes so that the body parts are relaxed.

11. Rest: Whenever one feels tired while doing *āsanas*, one should perform *Śavāsana or Makarāsana* to provide rest to the body. When tired, one may take rest in between also.

12. Gurū: *Gurupadishtmargen Yogmev sambhayset*

Yog is accomplished with the grace of the *Gurū* and by following the path shown by him. Therefore, Yog-*āsanas*, *prāṇāyāma* and meditation, etc. should be performed under the supervision of the *Gurū*.

13. *Yām-Niyam*: Yog practitioners must follow the principles of *Yām-Niyam* with full commitment. Without them nobody can become a *Yogi*.

14. Temperature of the body : If the person is ill or the environmental temperature is high, which rises further while doing the *Yog*-practice, then inhale through left nostril and exhale through the right nostril repeatedly, to bring the temperature back to normal.

15. Cleaning the stomach: If the bowels are not regular or there is a problem of constipation or indigestion, take *harad* or *TripHalā* etc., before going to bed, for a few days in the beginning. If the bowels are not clear, one may face problems relating to eyes, mouth, head or weakness in the nervous system. Therefore, it is essential to have clear bowels, no constipation and good digestion, sufficient sleep, appropriate food and proper living conditions.

16. Difficult *āsana*: Any person who has fractured his bone(s) any time previously, he/she should never undertake difficult *āsanas*, otherwise the concerned bone(s) may be damaged again at the same place.

17. Sweating: If one sweats while performing *āsanas*, the sweat should be wiped with a towel. This refreshes the body, makes the skin healthy and prevents germs from entering the body, through the skin. Yog*āsanas* should be undertaken preferably after a bath. One can take a bath after 15-20 minutes of exercises, when the body temperature becomes normal.

Main Āsanas for Stomach problems, Diabetes and Obesity

All the *āsanas* which have been described below, are specifically useful for the abdomen. Additional benefits of these *āsanas* have been mentioned at appropriate places. The health of our entire body depends on the healthiness of our abdomen. The word abdomen includes the entire digestive system, which has stomach, liver, spleen, intestines, gall bladder and pancreas. Fluid and blood are produced when the food is digested through this digestive system and blood so generated energizes the whole body. Therefore these *āsanas* will provide complete physical benefits to the person. Healthiness of the heart also depends on this digestive system. Majority of people suffering from heart diseases experience gas formation and indigestion, that effects the heart. Their ill-effects cause an increasing heart beat, therefore, these *āsanas* are useful for the heart patients as well.

Sarvāṅgāsana

Sarvāṅgāsana

Method:

- Lie down straight on your back. Keep the feet together, place the hands along the body with the palms touching the ground.
- Inhale and raise the legs slowly upwards to 30 degrees, then 60 degrees and finally 90 degrees. Take the help of your hands while lifting the legs. If the legs cannot be kept straight at 90 degrees take them ahead to 120 degrees with the hands supporting the back. The elbows should rest on the ground and the toes joined and straight. Keep the eyes closed or gaze fixed on the toes. Starting with about 2 minutes, the duration can be extended slowly up to half an hour.
- Bend the legs slightly backwards before returning to the normal position. Remove both the hands from the back and place them straight on the ground. Now regain the original position slowly in the reverse order, while keeping the palms pressed on the floor. Take rest in *Śavāsana* for approximately the same time as used for *Sarvāṅgāsana*. The reverse /complimentary of this *āsana* is *Matsyāsana*. Therefore, performing *Matsyāsana* before *Śavāsana* is more beneficial.

Benefits:

- It activates and rejuvenates the thyroid gland. Therefore, diseases like obesity, weakness, tiredness and insufficient increase in height, etc. are taken care of. It strengthens the adrenal glands, testicles and ovaries.
- Other benefits are similar to those of *Śirsasana*. But the specialty of this *āsana* is that those for whom *Śirsasana* is forbidden, even they can do this *āsana*. It is beneficial for 2-3 stages of asthma also because the shoulders become stable in this *āsana*. Respiration of the abdominal area also takes place. The abdominal muscles are exercised and the diaphragm gets toned due to participation in inhaling and exhaling process.
- Thyroid gland and pituitary gland are activated resulting in height increase.

Uttānapādāsana

Method:

- Lie down straight on your back, with palms touching the ground, legs straight and toes together.
- Inhale and raise the legs slowly upwards up to 30 degrees and hold for some time in the same position.
- While returning, place the feet slowly on the floor, avoiding any jerks. After resting for a while repeat the exercise 3 to 6 times.
- Those suffering from acute back-ache, should practice it using one leg at one time.

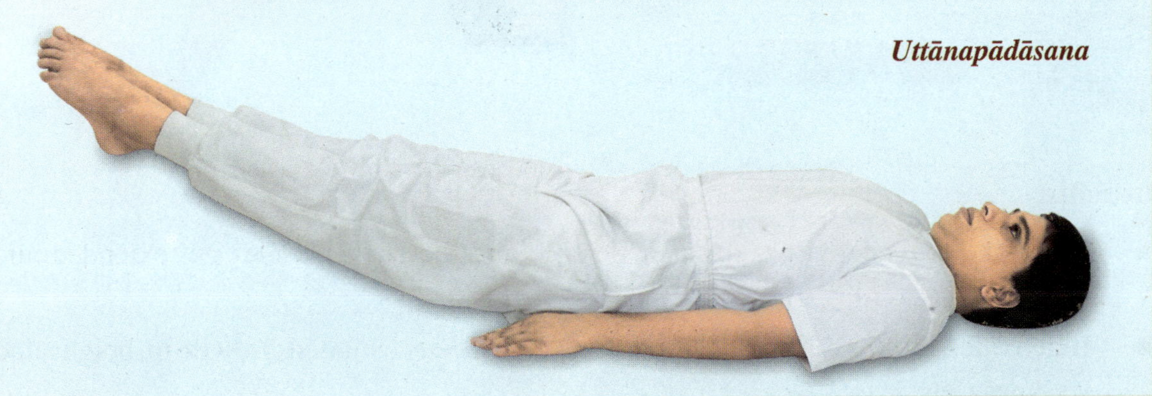

Uttānapādāsana

Benefits:

- This *āsana* strengthens the intestines and makes them free of diseases, and helps remove constipation, gas formation, obesity, etc. and improves the digestive system.
- It is useful in preventing displacement of the navel, heart disease, stomach pain, and respiratory problems.
- It is especially useful for back-ache, when performed using one leg at a time.

Halāsana

Method:

- Lie down straight on your back, inhale and slowly lift the legs. First 30 degrees up, then 60 degrees and finally 90 degrees up and then take the legs to the back of the head by lifting the back, while exhaling.
- Rest the toes on the floor behind the head and breath normally. In the beginning the hands can be used to support the back for comfort. At the completion stage keep the hands on the floor and stay in this position for 30 seconds.
- While returning, repeat the same process by keeping the hands pressed on the floor and keeping the knees straight, while the heels touch the floor.

Halāsana

Benefits:

- The spine is rendered healthy and flexible and the back muscles get extended and disease free.
- It activates the thyroid glands and removes obesity, stunted growth in height and weakness, etc.

- It is beneficial in dyspepsia, weak digestion, gas formation, constipation, spleen and liver enlargement and heart disease.
- It activates the pancreas and cures diabetes.
- It is beneficial in painful menstruation and gynecological problems.

Precautions:

- This *āsana is forbidden* for those suffering from excessive enlargement of liver and spleen.
- People suffering from high blood pressure, cervical and spinal problems also should not do this āsana.
- In case of slip disc and tuberculosis of spine also, this āsana should not be done.

Karṇa-pīḍāsana

Method:

- Like *Halāsana,* rest the legs at the back of the head and bend both the knees so as to be touching the ears. The remaining method is similar to *Halāsana*.

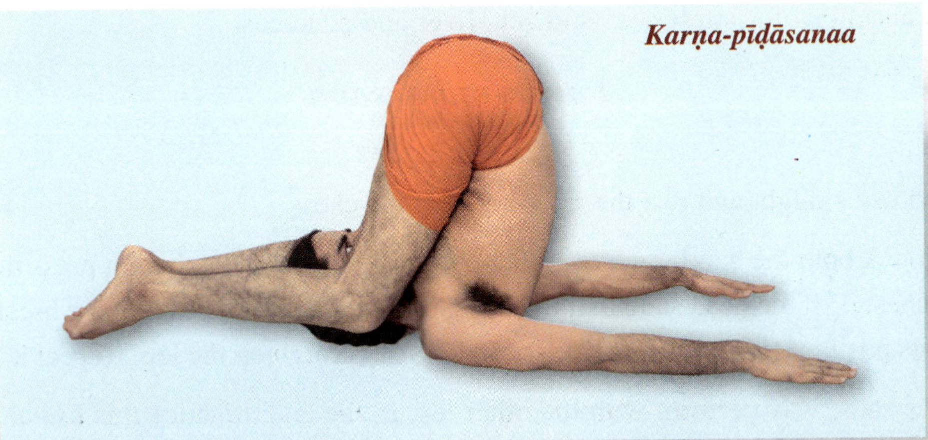

Karṇa-pīḍāsanaa

Benefits :

- All the benefits are similar to *Halāsana*. It is especially beneficial for ear problems, and hence the name *Karṇa-pīḍāsana.*

Naukāsana

Method:

- Keep both the hands on the thighs and lie down straight. While inhaling, first raise the head and shoulders upwards and then the legs. The legs, hands and head should be lifted to the same level, looking like a boat.

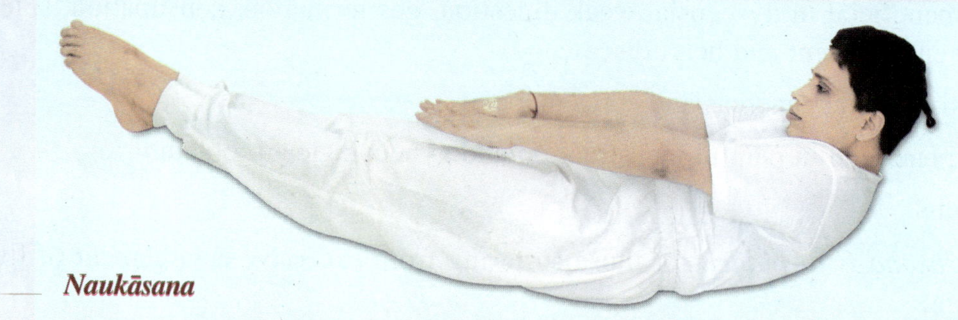

Naukāsana

- Stay for a while in this position and slowly bring down the hands, legs and head to the floor, while exhaling. Repeat it 3-6 times. The reverse *āsana* is called *Dhanurāsana*, i.e. *Dhanurāsana* should be done after *Naukāsana*.

Benefits:

- The benefits are same as of *Uttānapādāsana*.
- The lungs and heart become strong due to the inhalation of *prāṇa-vāyu*.
- It is beneficial for intestines, stomach, liver and pancreas.

Pavan-muktāsana

Method:

- Lie down straight and rest the right knee on the chest.
- Interlock both the hands and keep them on the knee. While exhaling press the knee on the chest. Lift the head such that the nose touches the knee. Holding the breath, remain in this position for about 10 to 30 seconds. Now straighten the leg. Repeat it 2-4 times.
- In the same way perform with the other leg. In the end, practice this *āsana* with both the legs together. This completes one cycle. Repeat this cycle 3-4 times.

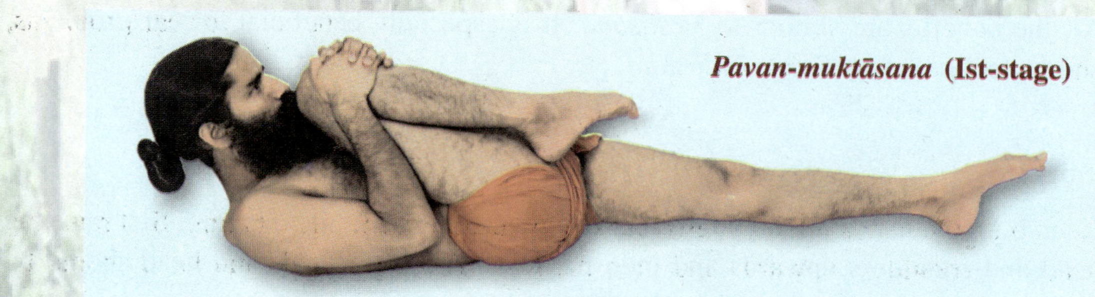

***Pavan-muktāsana* (Ist-stage)**

Pavan -muktāsana (IInd-stage)

- Hold both the legs and massage the back by rolling forward, backward and sideways.

Benefits:

- It is extremely beneficial for gas related problems of the stomach, thus justifying its name.
- It is useful in scanty/painful menstruation and uterus related diseases.
- It is beneficial in acidity, heart disease, gout and backache.
- It reduces excess fat on the stomach.
- If there is severe pain in the back, then do not lift the head at all. Press only the legs on the chest. In this way slip disc, sciatica and backache are sufficiently benefited.

Kaṇdhārāsana

Method:

- Lie down straight, fold the knees and keep the legs near the hips.

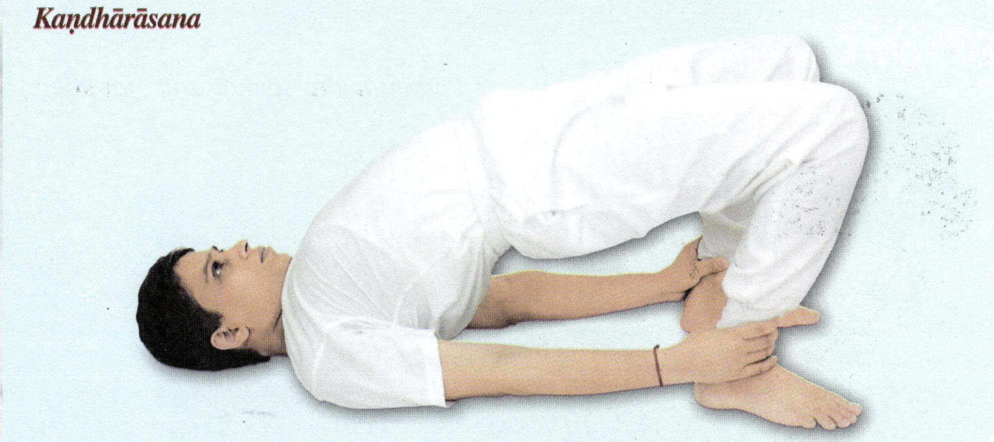

Kaṇdhārāsana

- Hold the upper portion of the ankle with the hands.
- Inhale and raise the back and hips. The shoulders and heels should rest on the ground. Stay in this position for 15-20 seconds.
- While coming down exhale and slowly rest the back on the floor. Repeat this 3 to 4 times.

Benefits:

- It is the best asana to keep the navel in its central position. It is useful for stomachache and backache.
- It is especially beneficial for uterus. It cures infertility, menstrual disorder, white discharge, bleeding and sex related problems in males.

Pādāṅguṣṭha-sparśāsana

Method:

- Lie down straight and bend the right leg and hold the toe with interlocked fingers of both hands, while exhaling, pull the toe and lift the head such that the nose touches the thumb of the foot.
- Repeat this with the right leg and then with both feet together.

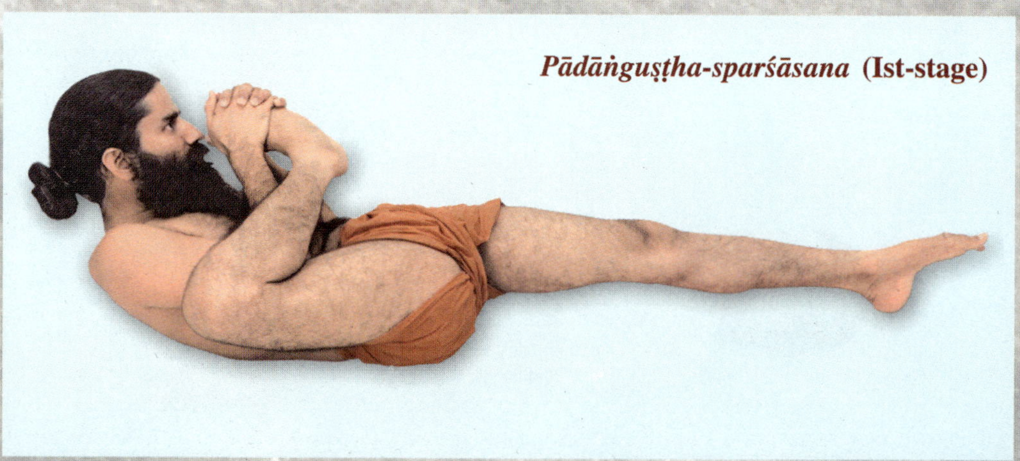

Pādāṅguṣṭha-sparśāsana **(Ist-stage)**

Benefits:

- This is an important exercise to set right the navel. This automatically takes care of gas formation, stomach pain, constipation, dysentery, weakness and laziness.
- It is beneficial for pancreas, stomach and intestines.

Pādāṅguṣṭha-sparśāsana (IInd-stage)

Dīrgha Naukāsana

Method:

- Lie down in *Śavāsana* and straighten both the hands while taking them to the back of the head together.
- Inhale, slowly raise the legs, head and hands at least one foot above the ground level keeping the hips and the lower portion of the back touching the ground. Keep looking at the chest. While coming down, exhale and slowly rest the hands, legs and head on the floor.

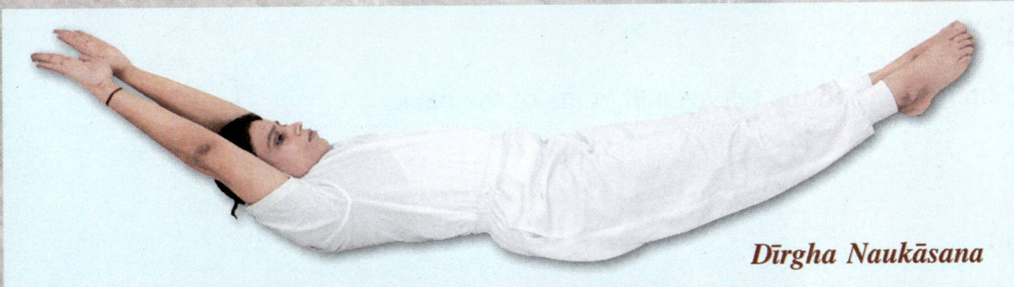

Dīrgha Naukāsana

Benefits:

- It is beneficial for the stomach and back just like *Naukāsana*.

- It is the best *āsana* to strengthen the heart. It is thus also called *Hṛdaya-stambhāsana*.
- Except for the period during pregnancy, females should do this exercise regularly. This gives good shape to the body and makes them active.

Pṛṣṭha-tānāsana

Method:

- Lie down on your stomach. Stretch the hands straight in the front of the head, keeping the palms one above the other, facing downwards. The legs should be straight and the toes stretched backwards. The forehead should rest between both the arms.
- Inhale and pull the hands forward while stretching the legs backwards. Perform this āsana while the body should remain stable. This will cause vibrations in the back. Exhale and relax the body. Repeat this 3-4 times.

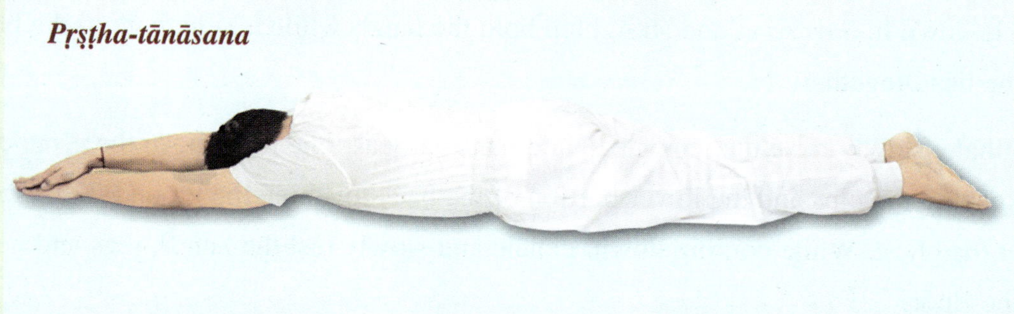
Pṛṣṭha-tānāsana

Benefits:

- It strengthens all the nerves and veins of the back.

Padmāsana

Method:

- Sit down in *Daṇḍāsan* and place the right foot on the left thigh. Similarly, place the left foot on the right thigh. The spine should be kept straight. As per convenience, one may place the left foot first on the right thigh and then the right foot on the left thigh.

- Keep the right palm above the left palm and place them on the lap. Focus the mind on the front portion of the nose or any other point to meditate with concentration.
- In the beginning do it for 1 - 2 minutes and then gradually increase the duration.

Padmāsana

Benefits:

- This is the best *āsana* for meditation. It is helpful in concentration of the mind and upward movement of the *prāṇa*.
- It strengthens the digestive system and is also beneficial in wind related problems.

Baddha-padmāsana

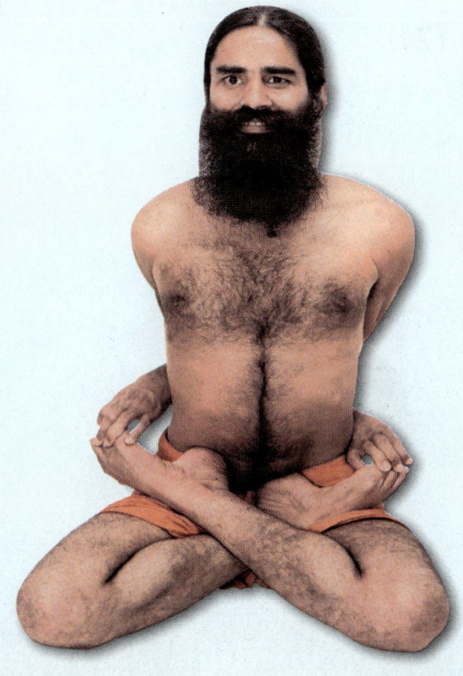
Baddha-padmāsana

Method:

- Sit in *Padmāsana* and hold the thumb of the left foot by brining the left hand from the backside. Similarly, hold the thumb of the right foot by bringing the right hand from behind.
- The spine and back should be kept straight. Close the eyes and try to concentrate your mind.

Benefits:

- It develops the chest of males and females and makes it attractive.
- It is beneficial for hands, shoulders and the entire back.

Yog Mudrāsana (1)

Method:

Yog Mudrāsana (1)

- Sit in *Padmāsana* and keep the palm of the right hand on the navel and keep the left palm on the right hand. While exhaling, bend forwards and rest the chin on the floor. Look in front.
- While inhaling come back to normal position. Repeat this 4 - 5 times.

Benefits:

- It is good exercise for stomach. It improves the digestive powers of the stomach and cures gas formation, indigestion and constipation.
- It reactivates the pancreas and extremely beneficial in controlling diabetes.

Yog Mudrāsana (2)

Method:

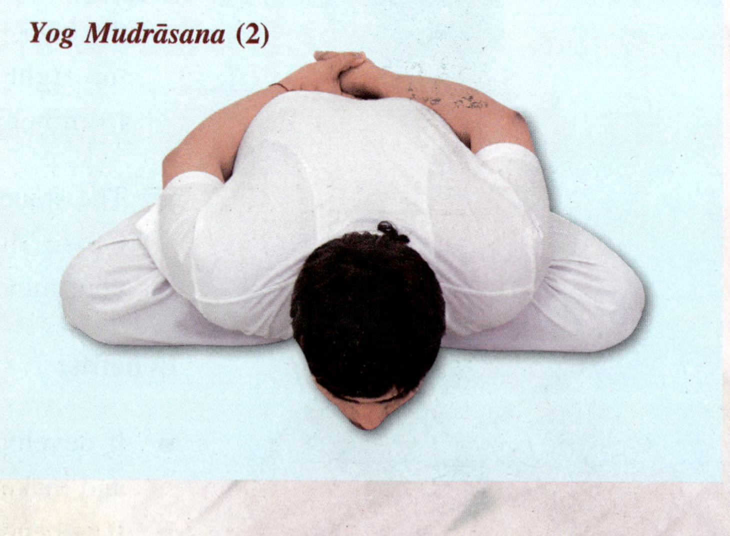

Yog Mudrāsana (2)

- Sit in *Padmāsana* and take both the hands to the rear and hold the left wrist with the right hand from behind.
- While exhaling, bend forward to rest the chin on the floor, looking straight. If the chin does not touch the ground, then bend forward as per the capability.

Benefits: Same as above.

Matsyāsana

Method:

- Sit in *Padmāsana* and lie down backwards while taking support of the hands and resting elbows.
- Bend the neck backwards as much as you can. The back and chest should get raised while the knees remain touching the floor.
- Hold the thumb of both toes respectively with both hands and rest the elbows on the floor. Inhale and hold the breath.

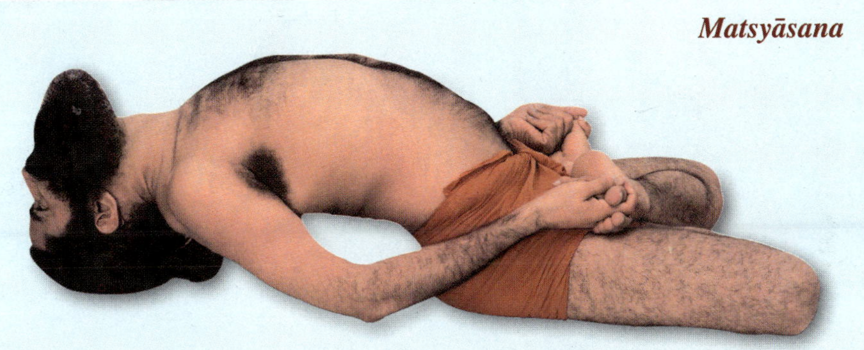

Matsyāsana

- One may either come back to the normal position or lie down in *Śavāsana* by bringing the head and shoulders on the ground and legs stretched.
- This is the reverse of *Sarvāṅgāsana*. Therefore, it should be done after *Sarvāṅgāsana*.

Benefits:

- This is a good exercise for stomach. It activates the intestines and cures constipation.
- It makes the thyroid, parathyroid and adrenal glands healthy.
- It is beneficial in cervical pain and when the rear bone of the neck is enlarged.
- It stops displacement of the navel. It cures lungs related diseases like asthma and other respiratory disorders.

Vajrāsana

Method:

- Fold both the legs and place the feet under the hips in such a way that both the heels are protruding outwards and the toes are touching the hips.
- In this position the thumbs of both the toes shall be touching each other. The back, neck and the head should remain straight. Knees should be touching with the hands resting on the knees.

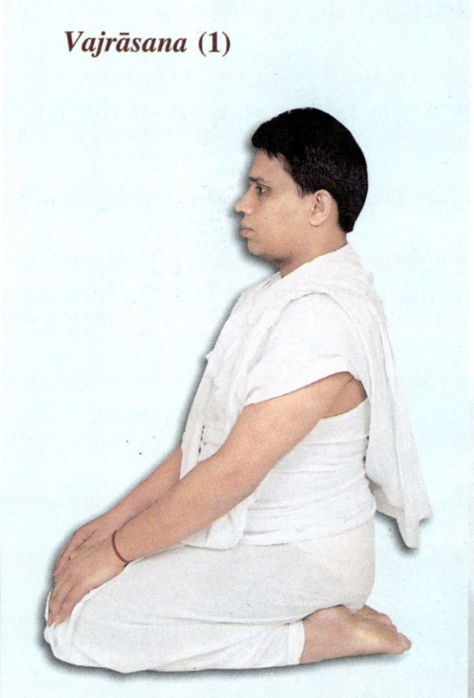

Vajrāsana (1)

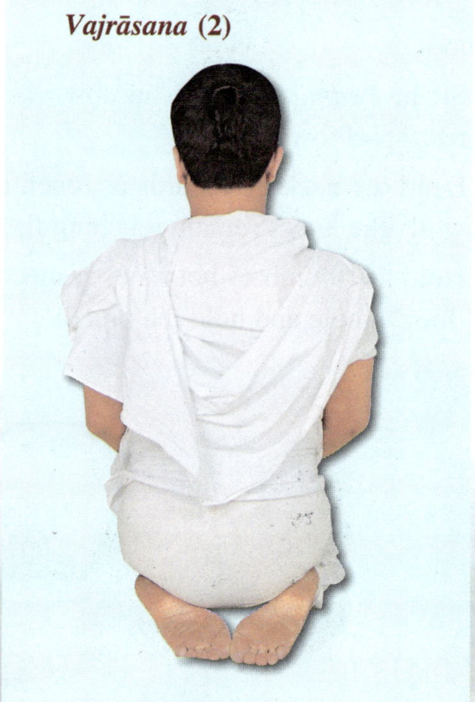

Vajrāsana (2)

Benefits:

- It is a meditative *āsana*. It helps in keeping the mind stable.
- This is the only *āsana* that can be done after meals. This exercise cures indigestion, acidity, gas formation and constipation. The food gets properly digested when undertaken after meals for 5 - 15 minutes. As a part of daily practice, it should be done for 1-3 minutes.
- It helps in relieving pain in the knees.

Supta-vajrāsana

Method:

- Sit as in *Vajrāsana* and keep the hands on the sides. With their support bend the body backwards and rest the head on the ground. The knees should be held together resting on the ground.
- Slowly try to rest the neck, shoulders and back also on the ground. Keep the hands straight on the thighs.
- While regaining the normal position, sit in *Vajrāsana* taking the support of hands and elbows.

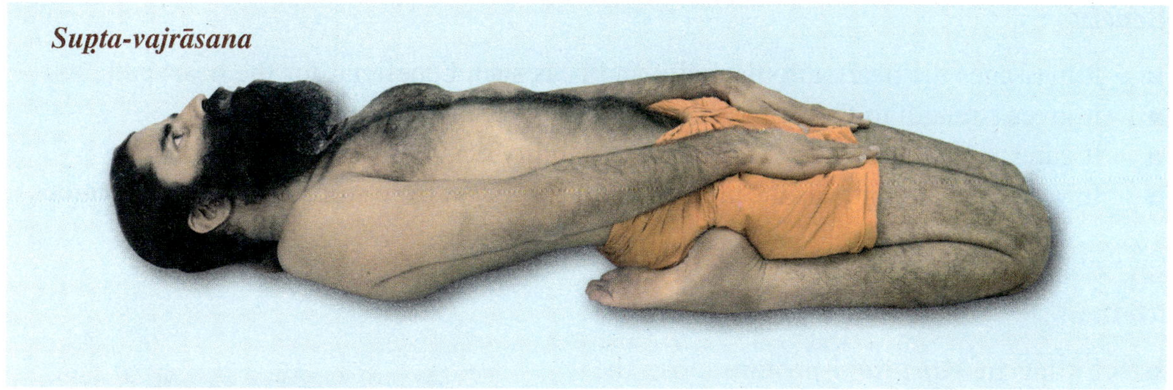

Supṭa-vajrāsana

Benefits:

- This *āsana* helps in stretching the lower part of the stomach, which activates the large intestine, relieving constipation.
- Displacement of navel is removed and is also beneficial for the kidneys.

Śaśakāsana

Method:

- Sit in *Vajrāsana* posture and while inhaling, lift both the hands upwards.
- While bending forward, exhale and stretching the hands forward, keeping the palms down, rest the hands on the ground, till the elbow. The forehead should also rest on the ground.
- Stay in this position for some time and again come back to *Vajrāsana* position.

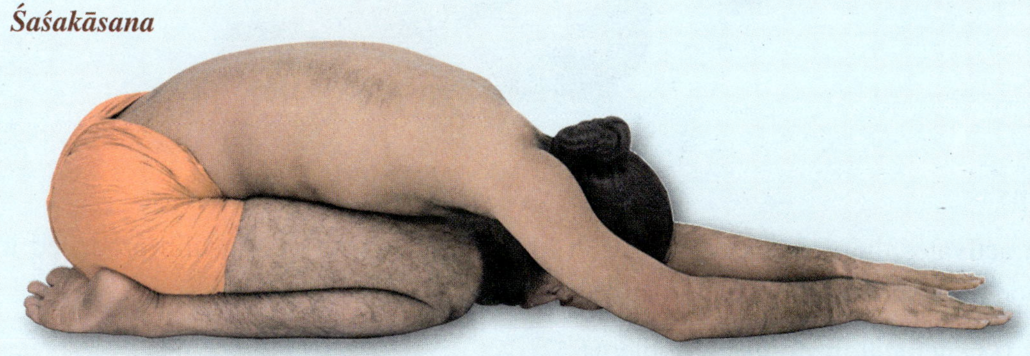

Śaśakāsana

Benefits :

- It massages the heart automatically and is as such beneficial for the heart patients.
- It gives strength to the pancreas, intestines, liver and kidneys.
- It cures mental illness, stress, anger, irritability etc.
- In women, It strengthens the uterus. It reduces the fat from stomach, waist and buttocks.

Maṇḍūkāsana (1)

Method :

- Sitting in *Vajrāsana* posture close the fists of both the hands. While clinching the fists press the thumb inside with the fingers.
- While pressing the navel with both the fists, exhale and bend forward. Keep looking straight.
- Stay in this position for some time and then come back to *Vajrāsana* posture. Repeat this position 3 to 4 times.

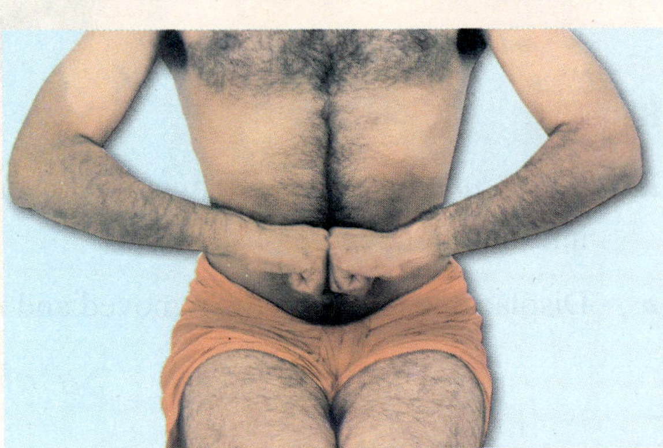

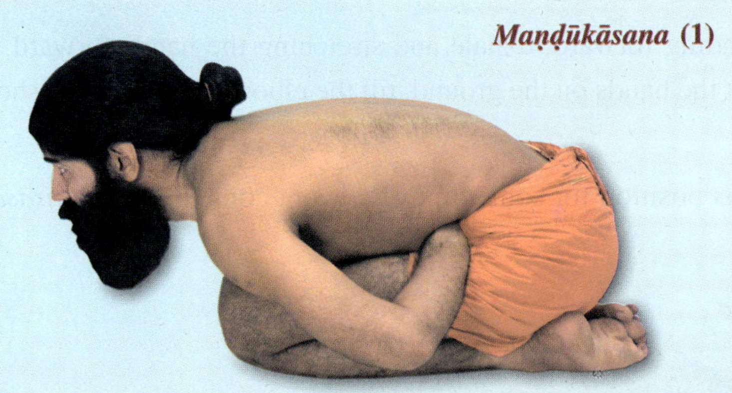

Maṇḍūkāsana (1)

Benefits :

- It activates the pancreas. As a result, there is in quantity of Insulin produced in the body. As such is beneficial in curing diabetes.
- It is beneficial in stomach problems.
- It is beneficial for the heart.

Maṇḍūkāsana (2)

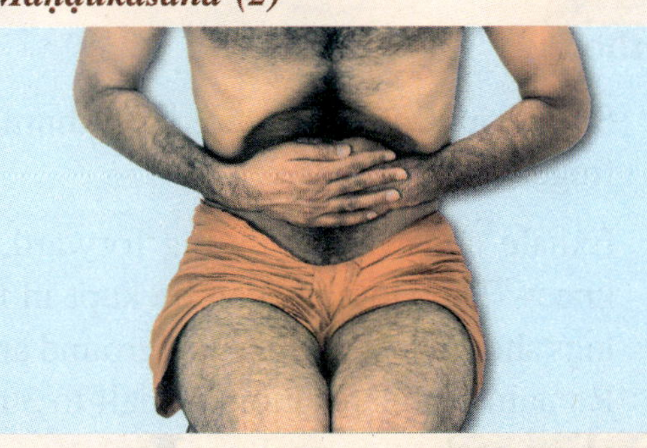
Maṇḍūkāsana (2)

Method :

Sitting in *Vajrāsana* pose, place the left palm on the right palm and keeping them on the navel and press the stomach inwards and while exhaling bend forwards like *Maṇḍūkāsana (1)*. Repeat this position 3 to 4 times.

Benefits :

As mentioned above under *Maṇḍūkāsana* (1).

Kūrmāsana

Method :

- Sitting in *Vajrāsana* posture, place both the elbows on either side of the navel. Keeping the palms upwards, join the hands, while keeping them straight.
- While exhaling bend forwards. Touch the chin with the palms. Look straight. While inhaling come back to the original position or while breathing in and out at a normal pace, remain in that position for 1 minute.

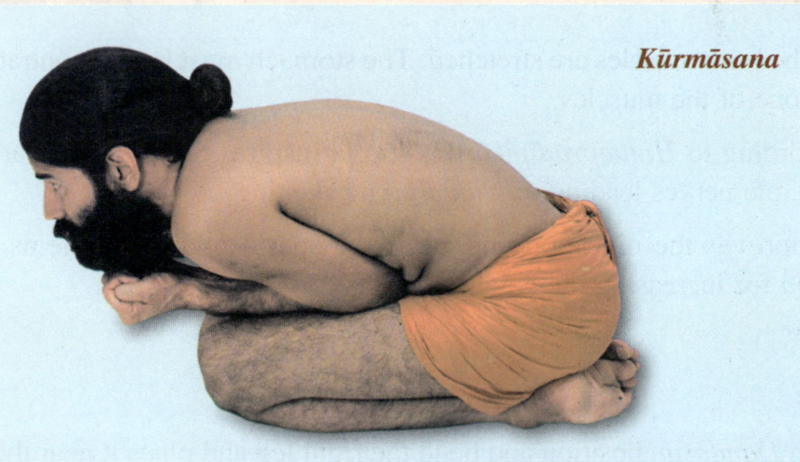
Kūrmāsana

Benefits : As mentioned above

Paścimottānāsana

Method :

- Sitting in *Daṇḍāsan,* hold the thumbs of toes with the help of the thumb and index finger of the hands.
- Exhale and while bending forward, try to touch the head in the space between the knees. The stomach can be kept in the position of *Uḍḍiyāna-bandha*. The knees and legs should be touching the ground and the elbows should also be resting on the ground. Remain in this position for half to 3 minutes, according to your ability. While exhaling come back to normal position.
- After this *āsana* the complimentary *āsanas* viz *Bhujaṅgāsana* and *Śalabhāsana* should be done.

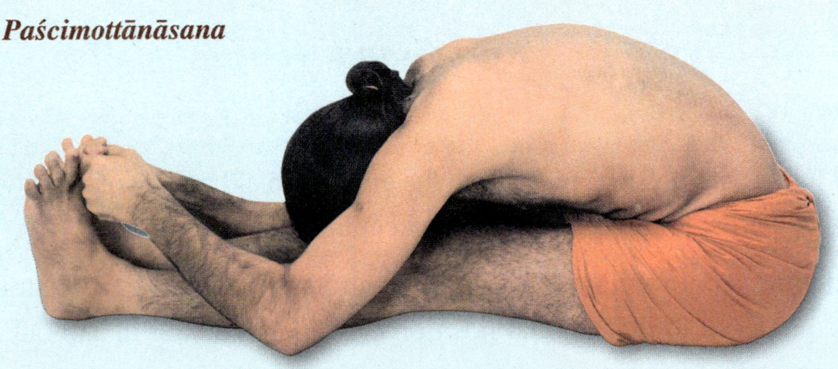
Paścimottānāsana

Benefits :

- All the back muscles are stretched. The stomach muscles are contracted. This improves the tone of the muscles.
- According to *Haṭhapradīpikā* this *āsana* inspires the *prāṇa* towards one of the three principle nerves leading to *kuṇḍalinī* awakening.
- It improves the digestion and cures the sperm related problems. It is an important *āsana* for increasing the height.

Vakrāsana

Method :

- Sit in *Daṇḍāsan* position and bend the right leg and place it near the left thigh, close to the knee. Keep the left leg straight.
- Bring the left hand over the right leg and stomach and place it near the left toe.

- Keep the right hand straight on the ground behind the back. Turn the neck to the right, keeping the eyes straight. The left foot, waist and right hand will remain straight. Repeat it 4-6 times.
- The same should be done in the alternate position.

Benefits :

- This reduces the fat from the waist. It is beneficial for the liver and the spleen.

Vakrāsana

Aṛdha Matsyendrāsana

Method :

- Sit in *Daṇḍāsan* pose and fold the left leg and place the ankle near the hips.
- Place the right leg towards the outside of the left knee, on the ground.
- Keeping the left hand straight, while taking it near the outside of right knee, hold the right toe.
- Fold the right hand behind the back and look backwards.
- The same should be repeated in the alternate position.

Aṛdha Matsyendrāsana

Benefits :

- It is beneficial in diabetes and backache.
- It regulates the blood circulation in all the nerves and veins situated around the spine.
- It cures the stomach disorders and strengthens the intestines.

Pūrṇa Matsyendrāsana

Method :

Pūrṇa Matsyendrāsana

- While sitting in the above mentioned position, fold the left leg and place it close to the navel above the right thigh and fold the right leg and place it near the outside of left knee keeping the right toe straight.
- While keeping the left hand near the outside of right knee, hold the right toe.
- Keep the right hand, on the floor behind back, towards the back.
- Remain in this position for Half to three minutes.
- This *āsana* should be done from both, the right and the left sides.

Benefits : As mentioned above.

Gomukhāsana

Method :

Gomukhāsana

- Sit in *Daṇḍāsan* pose and fold the left leg and place the left ankle near the right hip. Alternatively one can also sit on the ankle.
- Fold the right leg and place it above the left leg in such a way that both the knees touch each other.
- Lift the right hand and bend it back and take the left hand behind the back to hold the right hand. Keep the neck and back straight.
- After doing it for almost a minute from one side do the same from the other side as well.

Benefits :

- It is beneficial in hydrocele and enlargement of the intestines.
- It is beneficial in seminal disorders, excessive urination and gynecological problems.
- It strengthens the liver, kidney and the chest. It cures arthritis and gout.

Paśuviśrāmāsana

Method :

- Sit in *Daṇḍāsan* position and fold the left leg in such a way that the toe is pointing outside and the ankle is touching the hips.
- Fold the right leg and place the toe near the left thigh.
- While inhaling lift both the hands upwards and while exhaling bend forwards, the head and hands should rest on the ground. While inhaling lift the hands and while exhaling bend towards the left side. While bending forwards and lifting up, keep the hands straight touching the ears.
- In the same way change the leg and repeat the exercise from the other side.

Paśuviśrāmāsana

Benefits :

- It reduces the fat accumulated at the back of the waist. It is beneficial in diabetes and stomach problems.

Jānuśirāsana

Method :

- Sit in *Daṇḍāsan* and fold right leg and place the toe near the beginning of the left thigh and place the ankle near the mid portion of the genitals and rectum.

- While holding the toe of the left leg with both the hands, exhale and touch the head with the right knee. After holding on in this position for some time get up while inhaling and repeat the same with the other leg also.

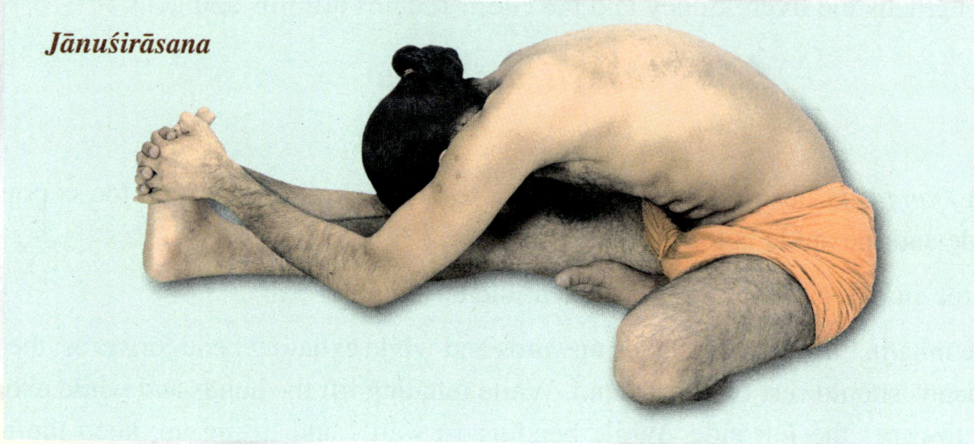

Jānuśirāsana

Benefits :

- Same as for *Paśćimottānāsana*

Exercise for relaxation:

Śavāsana (Yog-nidrā)

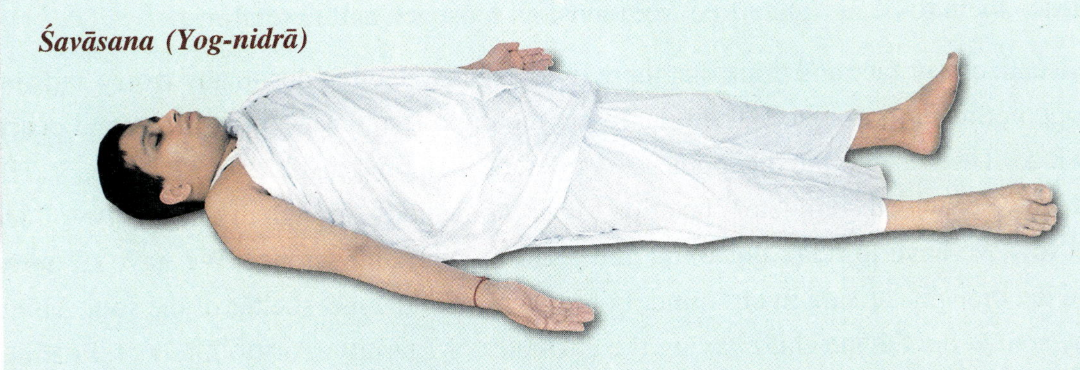
Śavāsana (Yog-nidrā)

Lie down straight with your back on the ground. Keep a distance of one foot between the legs and keep both the hands open, pointing upwards, at some distance from the thighs. Close the eyes, keep the neck straight and relax the whole body. Slowly take four to five deep breaths. Now, visualize each part of the body through your mind with determination and feeling that each organ is in a relaxed and tension free state. Determination is always the main force behind all the works in life and great objectives. Now we need to give complete rest to the body. For this also we have to be determined for relaxing and resting the body.

First and foremost with closed eyes, and with determined of mind, look at the thumbs and fingers of the feet, making them totally loose and relaxed. After toes, visualize the ankles experience their relaxation. Now visualize the calf muscles and think that my calf muscles are absolutely healthy, tension free and in a state of complete rest and experience the tranquility whole body is getting by the mere feeling of relaxation. As we start crying by thinking about sorrows, rejoice with the thought of fulfillment or the pulse starts racing with the mere feeling of prowess, in the same manner the body starts experiencing total tranquility with the mere thought of relaxation. After calf muscles, visualize the knees and experience that they are healthy, tension free and completely relaxed. Within the mind look at the thighs and experience them also to be in a state of total rest. After thighs gradually look at the upper parts of the body viz. waist, stomach and back. Visualizing them with ease, experience a state of total rest, health and freedom from tension. Now with relaxed mind concentrate on the heart and try to listen to the heartbeats. While listening to the symphony of heart and ponder that my heart is absolutely healthy, tension free and at rest; there is no disorder or disease in my heart. Now relaxing the lungs and the heart, visualize the shoulders and experience them to be free of tension and in a state of total bliss. Then, one by one, visualize the arms, elbows, wrists, fingers and even the thumbs of both the hands and experience them to be in a state free from tension, loosened and in total rest.

Now visualize your face and think that there is no negative feeling due to any worry, tension or disappointment on my face. There is divine feeling of happiness, bliss, hope and peace on my face. There is unlimited happiness on my face including my eyes, nose and ears. Till now we have provided complete relaxation to our whole body through divine resolve of our mind. Now we have to relax our mind and make it calm and serene. We have to move beyond the thoughts arising in our mind. For this we have to take shelter of the soul. Think that my soul is the Divine child having the attributes of Eternity, Purity, Intellect, Pristine, Peaceful, Blissful, Enlightenment. I am always complete and immortal. I do not lack any thing, and in fact I am always full of feelings and devotion. I am a part of the Supreme Soul which is Existent, Conscious and Beatitude. I am the divine son of God. I am free from the bondage of nature, body, senses and mind. My real shelter is my God. Increase or decrease of materialistic prosperity does not make me a pauper, poor, orphan, master or a king. I am always in complete harmony. All the changes which are taking place are the attributes of the world, and not those of my soul. In this way think about the divinity of the soul and remove negative thinking, because negative thinking makes a person sad, worried, and stressed. Negative thinking makes a person depressed and always immersed in the ocean of grief. Positive thinking helps a person to always remain happy, balanced, and cheerful even in adverse situations. For this reason, the person should have positive thinking not only at the time of *Yog-nidrā* or *Śavāsana* but all the times. In this way, thinking about the divine soul in a realistic manner, we have given rest to the mind and now we will think about the divine form of God and give total rest to our soul.

Think that your soul has come out of the body and has established itself in the sky, above the body and viewing it as a dead body lying on the ground. This is the reason that this position is called *Śavāsana*. Now devote your conscious soul to The God who is omnipresent in the limitless sky. Imagine that your soul is getting the divine bliss of The God from all sides. Experience the divine happiness of God's creation. With complete devotion to the God any solemn pledge taken is always fulfilled. You think of God's nature and its divinity and concentrating on the wonderful creation of nature think of God's divinity. Think that you are in the valley of beautiful flowers, and the whole atmosphere is full of fragrance of different kinds of flowers, which pleases the mind. There is a kind of divinity all around. Each and every act of God is worth visualization. There is no end to God's greatness. Along with the flowering plants, there are beautiful fruits on the trees; God has filled each fruit with a different flavor. A light breeze is flowing from all sides and giving immense happiness. In this beautiful garden the birds are sweetly singing the infinite glory of God's creation. One can see God's lively appearance from each bud, flower and fruit. When we look at the sky it appears that the stars, the Moon and the Sun are like lamps of the huge universe, which is The God's temple, lighting every thing. The flowing rivers appear as if they are washing the feet of God. How great is The God who is infinite, Endless, Boundless. Oh God! Oh Father! Oh Mother! Creator of the universe, take me, your son, also under your shelter. Bless me with your divine bliss. Oh Lord! always shower your divinity, peace and light on me. I may always remember your divine glory and remain attached to you, and keep busy submerged in your infinite Bliss. Oh God! take me away forever from worldly evil thoughts and grant me your blissful shelter.

In this way, after experiencing the unique bliss of the divinity of God, feel again yourself present in the body. Imagine that you have returned to the body after Yogic sleep. The inhalation-exhalation is continuing. Along with the breath the life giving great energy of life-force entering your body. Experience yourself to be healthy, happy and cheerful and in the way the body was relaxed with determination in the same way and experience a new strength, disease free, divine consciousness and bliss in the body. Look at each part of the body from top to the toe and keep feeling and imagining each part to be fully healthy. For example, if a person has pain in the knee or backache he should imagine that his pain has been completely relieved. By God's grace and practice of *Yog* there is no pain in my knees and back, because *Yog* cures the root cause of these diseases. The pain is being relieved. Similarly, if there is any heart or stomach ailment, think that it has been cured. If there is any blockage in the arteries or the cholesterol level is high, think that the diseases have been cured. Resolve that my body is becoming free from all foreign matter, diseases, and deformities and I am getting healthier. With these thoughts you should experience yourself to be completely healthy both physically and mentally.

At last, experience that both the hands are totally healthy and powerful and thus rubbing them, put both the palms on your eyes and then slowly open the eyes. This is the summarized method of *Yog-nidrā* and *Śavāsana*. If anybody is unable to sleep, then before going to bed, practise *Śavāsana* and relax the body and feel free of tension in the directed method, and thinking of God's divinity, concentrate on respiration and with every breath chant *Oṃ-kāra* in the mind. While inhaling and exhaling meaningful chanting of *Oṃ-kāra* should be done. The meaning of *Oṃ-kāra* is - that The God is Existent, Conscious and Beatitude and is nothing but Truth, Knowledge and Bliss. I am also getting blissful by being in communion with The God. With these thoughts one should meaningfully chant *Oṃ-kāra*. The speed of inhaling and exhaling should be normal. This exercise can be performed by reverse counting from 100 to 1 and with each number, chant *Oṃ*, For example, *Oṃ* 100, *Oṃ* 99, *Oṃ* 98 and so on. Praying in this way will put you to deep sleep and you will get rid of bad dreams. In the daily *Yoga* practice, this *āsana* should be done after every difficult *āsana*. After the end of practice, this *āsana* should be done for 5 to 10 minutes.

Benefits:

- It is easy and best for mental stress, depression, high blood pressure, heart disease and insomnia. These patients should do this *āsana* regularly.
- Weakness of the nervous system, tiredness and negative thinking are cured by practicing this *āsana.*
- The body, mind, brain and soul get complete rest, power, motivation and happiness.
- The concentration power is developed.
- Practising *Śavāsana* in between other *āsanas* relieves the tiredness of the body in a very short span of time.

Makarāsana (1)

Method :

- Lie straight with your stomach on the ground. While folding both the hands inwards keep them on the opposite shoulders.
- Rest the forehead on both the hands. There should be a distance of one foot between the feet.

- Let loose the body like a dead body. While lying down in this position you should think of a dead body and concentrate within the soul through wise thinking and introspection. I am a separate life, pure-hearted, cheerful and flawless soul. This body is perishable. This body is mere collection of the five elements. When thc time comes it assimilates in the same five elements. This body and all other riches remain here. Neither did we bring anything with us nor will we take anything along. In this manner deviate your mind from this mortal world and experience the elation of immersing and submitting yourself to the eternal soul present in this limitless universe.

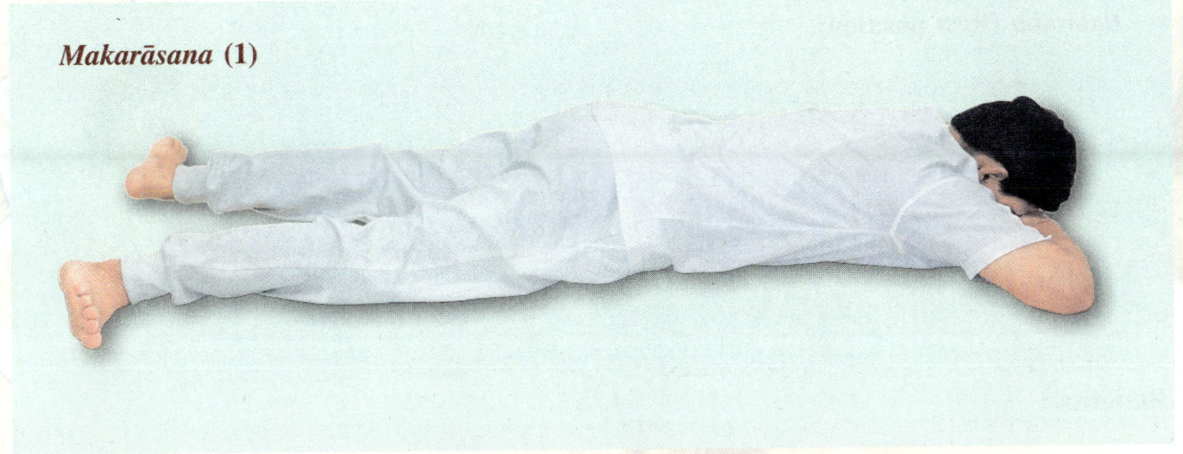

Makarāsana **(1)**

Benefits :

- This is the *āsana* for rest. During rest a person not only feels light physically but also mentally. He is freed from high blood pressure, mental tension and insomnia. In-between the *āsanas* this should be done to take rest. The intestines of the stomach get natural massage, which activates them, and dyspepsia etc. diseases are cured.
- Since the hands are in passive stretching condition it affects the sympathetic nerves and helps in the relaxation of the body.
- The heart is not functioning against the gravitational force, therefore it gets rest.
- The endocrine glands are benefited.

Balāsana (Rest position)

Method :

- Lie down with your stomach on the ground. Keep the left hand under the head on the ground and turn the neck to the right, resting the head on the hands. The left hand will be under the head and the left palm will be under the right hand.
- Fold the right knee slightly, the way a child sleeps, lie down like that and rest. In the same way this *āsana* is done from the other side.

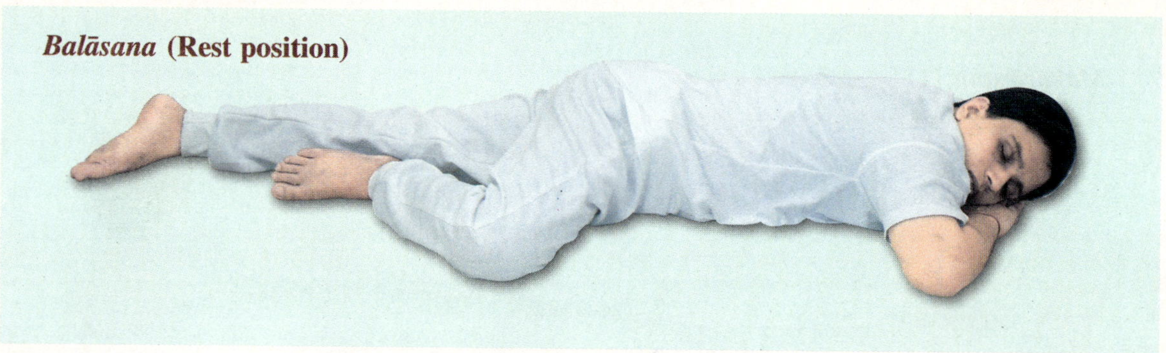

***Balāsana* (Rest position)**

Benefits :

- Just like *Śavāsana*, the tiredness of the entire body and mind is relieved.

Special *āsanas* to reduce weight

Dvicakrikāsana

Method :

- Lie down straight on your back and keep the hands below the hips, stop the breath, raise one leg bend up on the knee, bring the ankle near the hip and rotate as if riding a bicycle. Repeat this exercise from 10 to 25-30 times as per the capacity.
- Similarly repeat the exercise with the second leg. Keep rotating the legs without touching the ground. Make a circular shape with the legs. Repeat from 10 to 25-30 times as per the capacity.

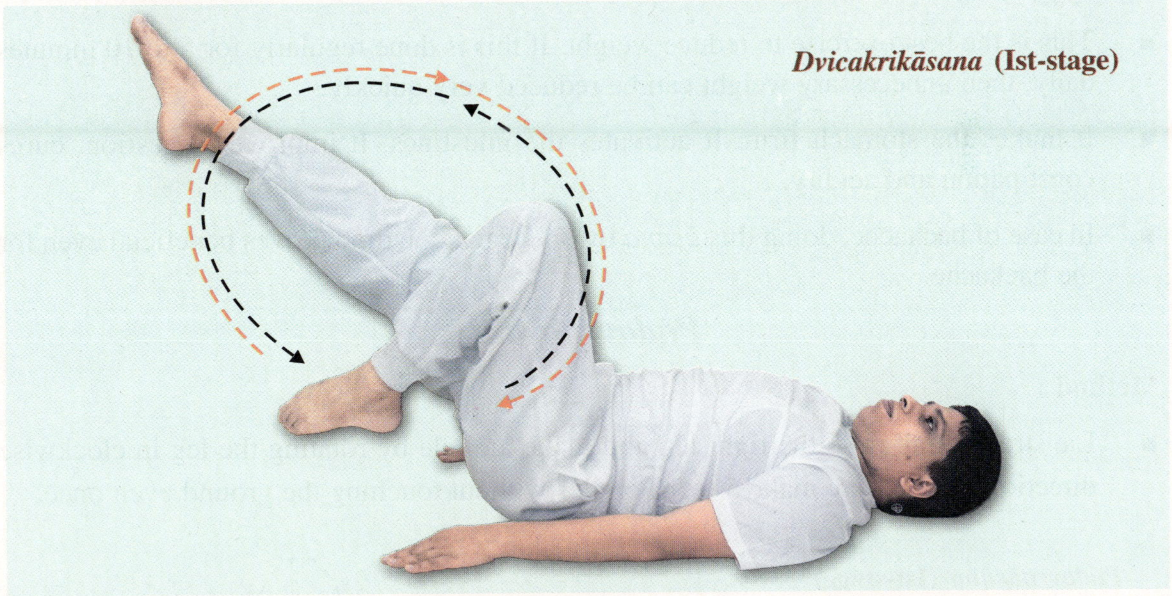

Dvicakrikāsana **(Ist-stage)**

- When tired, lie down in *Śavāsana* and rest for some time and repeat the exercise in the opposite direction and rest again when tired.
- Repeat this exercise, in next level, by rotating both the legs continuously in a cyclic motion. Inhale, fold one leg up to the knee and bring towards the chest, stretch the other leg straight up to the ground. Inhale and rotate the legs as if riding a bicycle. Then repeat this in the opposite direction continuously, like riding a bicycle. Those who do not have backache, heart disease or hernia can do the exercise with both the legs and then rest in *Śavāsana* (see the picture below). Repeat this from 5 to 10 times or as per the capacity.

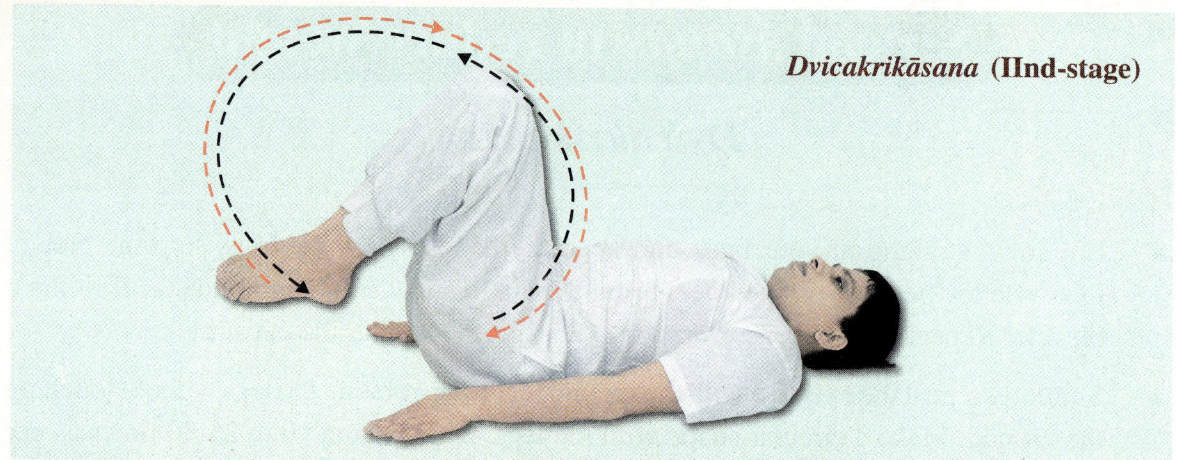
Dvicakrikāsana (IInd-stage)

Benefits :

- This is the best exercise to reduce weight. If this is done regularly for 5 to 10 minutes daily, then unnecessary weight can be reduced very quickly.
- It makes the stomach firm. It activates the intestines. It improves digestion, cures constipation and acidity.
- In case of backache, doing this *āsana* by one leg at one time proves beneficial even for the backache.

Pādavṛttāsana

Method :

- Lie straight and raise the right leg and make a circle by rotating the leg in clockwise direction. In this way make 5 to 10 circles without touching the ground even once.

Pādavṛttāsana (Ist-stage)

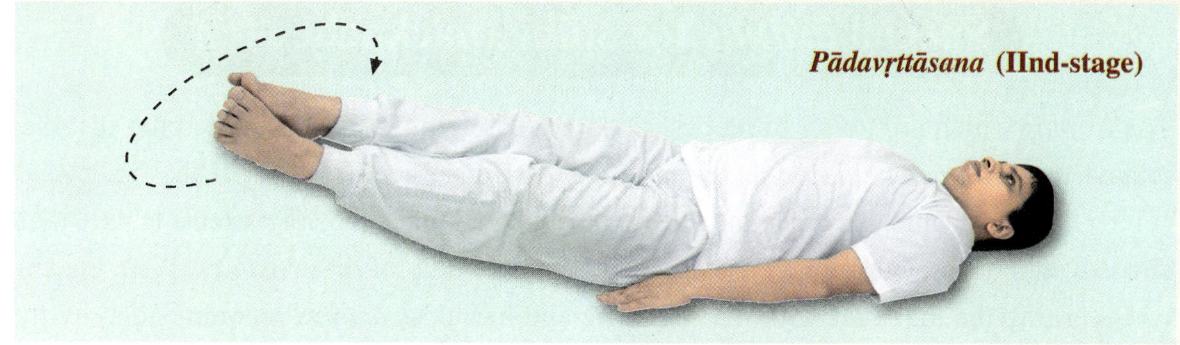

- After rotating in one direction, rotate the leg in opposite direction (anti-clockwise). When tired, rest in *Śavāsana*.
- After doing this exercise with a one leg at a time, do it with both the legs simultaneously. Rotate the legs up-down, right-left, in all four directions as much as you can. With both the legs also rotate in clockwise and anti-clockwise directions.

Benefits:

- This *āsana* is also for reducing extra weight.
- It reduces the fat accumulated at the hips, thighs and waist and gives makes the stomach light and firm.

Aṛdha-Halāsana

Method :

- This āsana is like *Uttānapādāsana*, the only difference is that in *Uttānapādāsana* the legs are raised up to 30 degrees (almost 1 foot) whereas in *Ardha-Halāsan* the legs are raised up to 90 degrees.

Benefits:

- All the benefits of *Uttānapādāsana* are obtained with this *āsana* also. This *āsana* is especially beneficial for reducing weight.

Special *āsanas* for spine (backache etc.)

The *āsanas* which are going to be described here are mainly beneficial to cure diseases related to the backache, cervical, spondylitis, slip disc, sciatica and all the other such spine related ailments. By grace of God we have helped thousands of patients to cure their slip disc and other such spinal cord ailments, with the help of these *āsanas*. With the aim of benefiting the mankind with the scientific and harmless *āsanas* recommended by the sage, these *āsanas* are being prescribed here after practical experience. All these āsanas are also specially beneficial for asthma patients, because the lungs are filled by inHaling air while performing all these *āsanas*. This contraction-expansion of the lungs circulates air and the toxins are exhaled. The dead cells of the lungs get reactivated. In this way these *āsanas* keep the lungs healthy and help getting rid of breathing problems. The glands located in the stomach region also become healthy with these *āsanas*. Kidney problems are eliminated. In this manner these *āsanas* will cure a number of diseases and make a person healthy and an already healthy person will not fall sick due to the diseases, with the practice of these *āsanas*.

Precautions :

The *āsanas* which exert a lot of pressure on the stomach, should not be practiced by patients suffering from ulcer, T.B of the intestine, hernia, liver and spleen enlargement.

Chakrāsana

Method :

- Lie down on your back and fold the knees. The heels should be near the hips.
- Take both the hands on the back side and keep them at the back of the shoulders spread apart, this will maintain the balance.
- Inhale and raise the hips and chest upwards.
- Slowly try to bring the hands and legs nearer; in a manner by which the body takes the shape of a wheel.
- While leaving the *āsana,* relax the body and rest the waist on the ground. Repeat this 3 to 4 times.

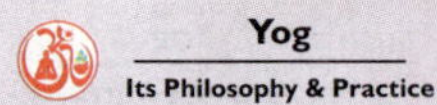

Benefits :

- It makes the spinal cord flexible and stops ageing. It activates the stomach and the intestines.
- It activates the body, gives energy and increases agility.
- It is especially beneficial for hip pain, respiratory diseases, headache and eye problems, cervical and spondylitis.
- It strengthens the muscles of hands and legs.
- In women it cures the problems related to uterus.

Chakrāsana

Setubandh-āsana

Method :

- Lie down straight on the ground.
- Bend both the knees. Raise the hip area and keep both the hands with the support of the elbows under the waist.
- Keeping the hip area raised, straighten the legs. Rest the shoulders and the head on the ground. Remain in this position for 6 to 8 seconds.
- While coming back to normal position slowly rest the hips and legs on the ground. The hands should not be removed from the waist suddenly. Rest in *Śavāsana* for some time and repeat the exercise 4 to 6 times.

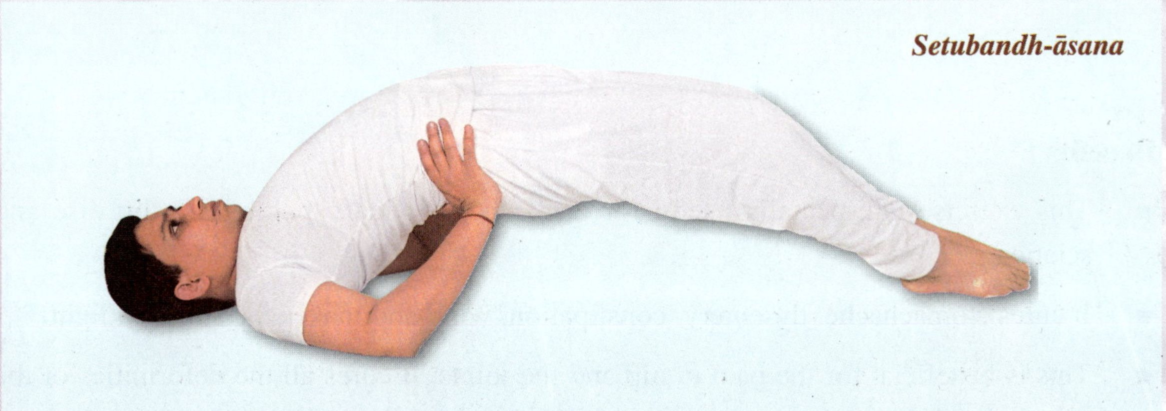

Setubandh-āsana

Benefits :

- This is beneficial in slip disc, backache, neck ache and diseases of stomach. Those who cannot do *Chakrāsana* can get benefited by this *āsana*.

Markaṭāsana (1)

Method :

- Lie down straight and spread both the hands at the shoulder level. The palms should be open, facing the sky. Fold both the legs at the knees and keep them near the hips.
- Now, turn the knees towards the right side, rest the right knee on the ground. Left knee should rest on the right knee and the left ankle should rest on the right ankle. Turn the neck to the left side.
- Similarly, repeat the exercise from left side as well.

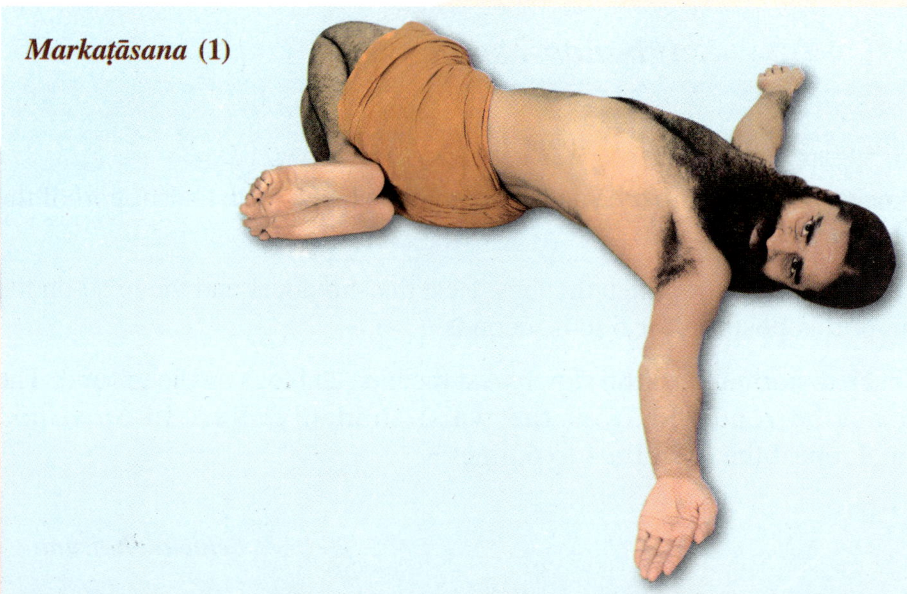

Markaṭāsana (1)

Benefits :

- This exercise is especially useful for backache, cervical, spondylitis, slip disc and sciatica.
- It cures stomachache, dysentery, constipation, wind and makes the stomach light.
- This is beneficial for the pain in hip and the joints. It cures all the deformities of the spinal chord.

Markaṭāsana (2)

Method :

- Lie as in the above position. Fold both the legs at the knee and keep them near the hips. There should be a distance of one and a Half feet between the feet.
- Bend the right knee towards the right side, rest it on the ground. Bend it to an extent that the left knee reaches the right toe and rest the left knee on the right side near the right knee, on the ground. Turn the neck to the left side.
- Repeat the same with the other leg.

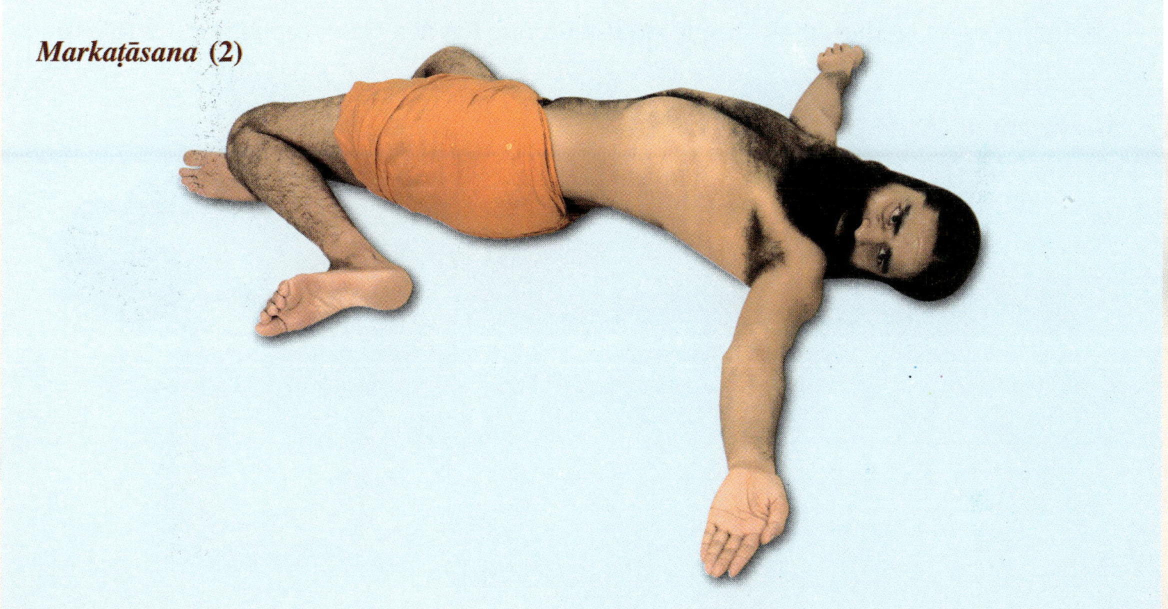

Markaṭāsana (2)

Benefits :

- As mentioned above. This is easier than the previous exercise.

Markaṭāsana (3)

Method :

- Lie down and spread both the hands parallel to the shoulders. The palms should be open, facing the sky.
- Raise the right leg 90 degrees and slowly take it near the left hand, turn the neck to the right side and stay in this position.

- After remaining in this position for some time raise the leg straight upwards up to 90 degrees and slowly rest it on the ground.
- Similarly, repeat this exercise with the left leg.
- In the end, raise both the legs together up to 90 degrees and keep them near the left hand. Turn the neck in the opposite direction and look towards the right side. After some time straighten the legs as before.
- In the same way raise both the legs and keep them near the hand on the right side. Turn the neck towards the left side and look on that side. This is one complete set of exercise. Repeat it from 3 to 4 times. Those who have severe back pain should not attempt with both the legs together, they should do it with one leg at a time, repeating it 2 to 3 times.

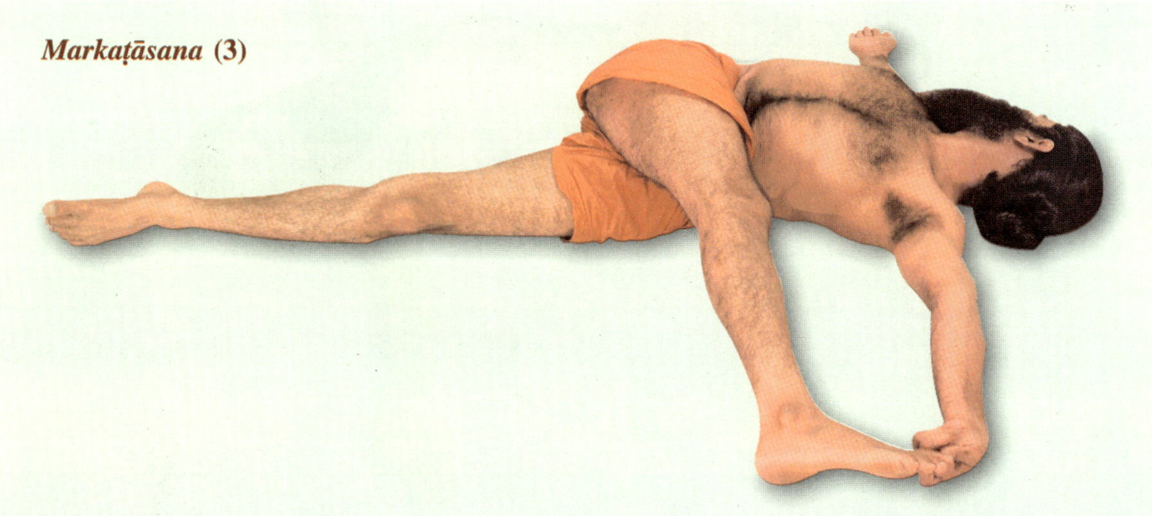

***Markaṭāsana* (3)**

Benefits :

- As mentioned before.

Kaṭi-uttānāsana

Method :

- Lie in *Śavāsana* posture and keep both the legs folded. Spread both the hands on the backside.
- Inhale and raise the waist upwards. The hips and shoulders should rest on the ground. While exhaling bring the back down, press it down, towards the ground and straighten it. Repeat this exercise 8 to 10 times.

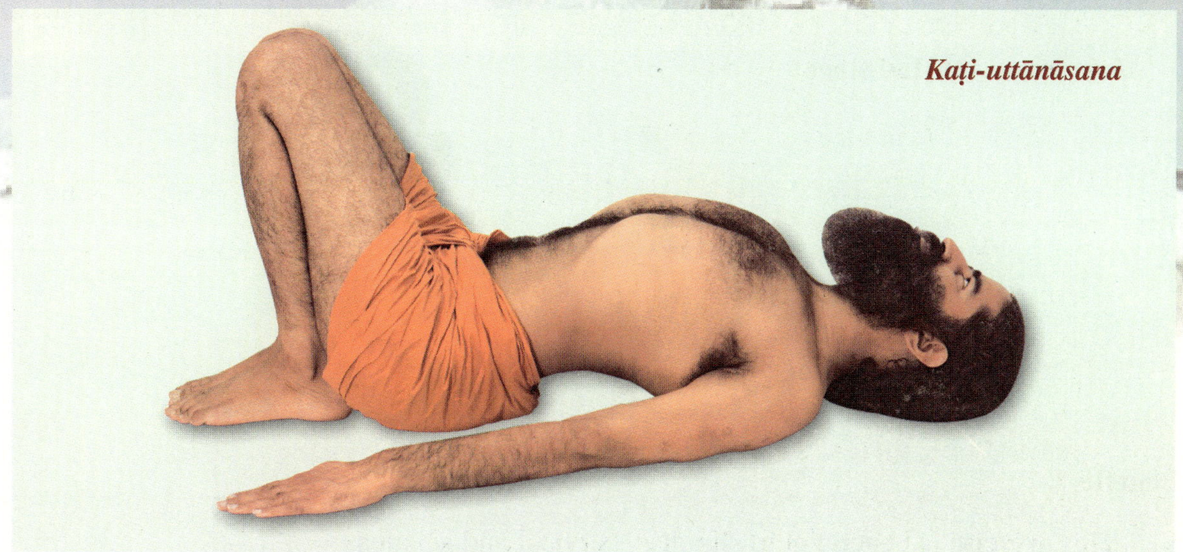

Kaṭi-uttānāsana

Benefits :

- It is beneficial in slip disc, sciatica and back pain.

Makarāsana (2)

Method :

- Lie straight on your stomach.
- Join the elbows of both the hands, making a stand and place the palms under the chin. Lift the chest up. Keep the elbows and legs together.

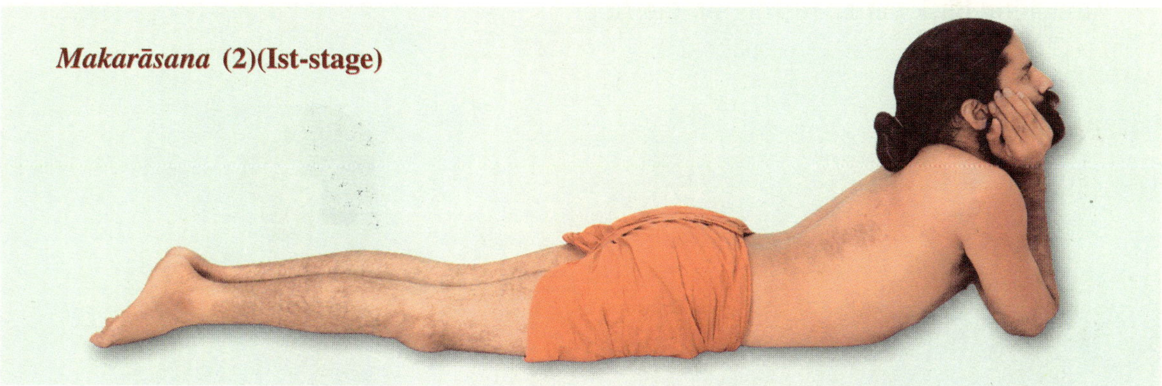

Makarāsana **(2)(Ist-stage)**

- While inhaling, first fold one leg at a time and then both the legs together. While folding, the ankles should touch the hips. While exhaling, the feet should be straight. Repeat it 20 to 25 times.

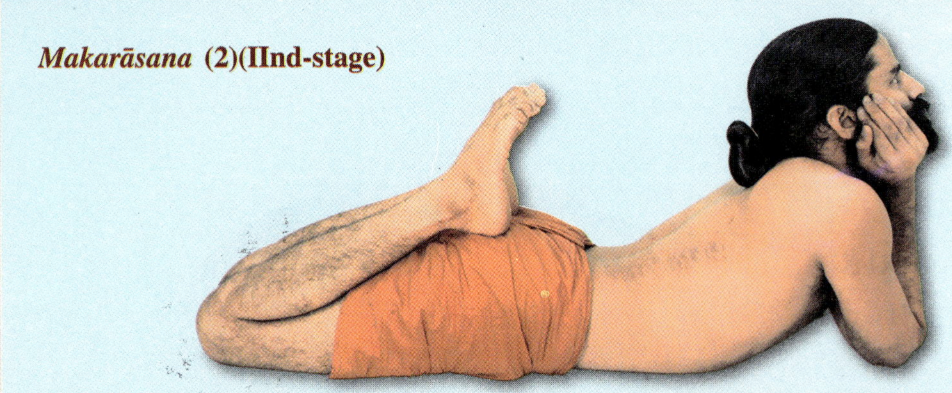

Makarāsana (2)(IInd-stage)

Benefits :

- This exercise is beneficial in slip disc, cervical and sciatica.
- It is especially useful in asthma, lungs related problems, and knee pain.

Bhujaṅgāsana

Method :

- Lie flat on your stomach. Keep the palms on the ground and both the hands near both the sides of the chest. The elbows should be lifted up and the shoulders should be by the sides of the body.
- The legs should be straight and the toes should be joined together. The toes should be stretching backwards, resting on the floor.

Bhujaṅgāsana

- Inhale and slowly lift the chest and head upwards. The part of body below the navel should touch the ground. While lifting the head upwards, bend the neck backwards, as much as you can. Must remain in this position for about 30 seconds.

Purna Bhujaṅgāsana

- Repeat this exercise according to the capacity. After practicing this *āsana*, the same can be done in the form of *Bhujaṅgāsana* or complete *Bhujaṅgāsana.*

Benefits :

- It is important for cervical spondylitis, slip disc, and all spine related diseases.

Dhanurāsana

Method :

- Lie on your stomach. Fold the legs and keep the ankles on the hips. The knees and toes should be touching each other.
- With both the hands hold both the legs from the ankles.
- Inhale and while lifting the knees and thighs stretch them upwards, hands should be straight. After lifting the lower portion, lift the upper part of the stomach, chest, neck and head. Navel and the region around abdomen area should rest on the ground. Remaining parts should be raised. The shape of the body will be like a stretched bow. Remain in this position for about 10 to 30 seconds.
- While exhaling come back to the original position, in the same order. When the breath normalises repeat it. This should be repeated 3 to 4 times.

Dhanurāsana

Benefits :

- It makes the spine flexible and healthy. This *āsana* is useful for cervical, spondylitis, backache and diseases of the stomach.
- Prevents shifting of the navel from its place.
- It is beneficial for menstrual disorders in females.
- It strengthens the kidneys and cures urinary problems. It is beneficial in cases of urination due to fear.

Pūrṇa Dhanurāsana

Method :

- Lie flat on your stomach. Fold both the legs over the back and hold the thumbs of the toes with the hands.
- While inhaling, lift the hands, neck and head and also lift both the legs above the ground, After remaining in this position for some time, while exhaling, rest the body parts on the ground.

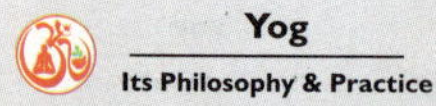

Pūrṇa Dhanurāsana

Benefits :

- As mentioned above

Śalabhāsana (1)

Method :

- Lie with your stomach and place both the hands underneath the thighs.
- Inhale and raise the right leg up; the leg should not bend at knee. The chin should rest on the ground. Remain in this position for 10 to 30 seconds. Repeat this for 5 to 7 times.

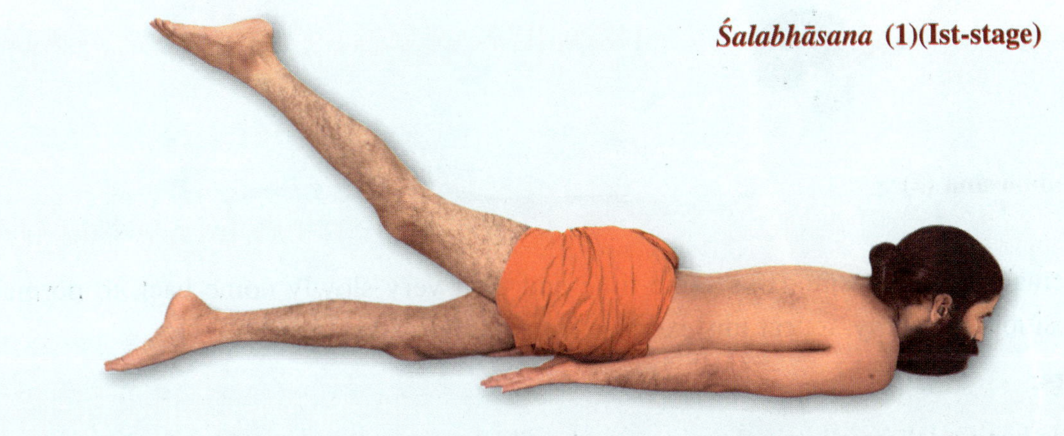

Śalabhāsana (1)(Ist-stage)

- Similarly, after doing it with the left leg, do it with both the legs for 2 to 4 times.

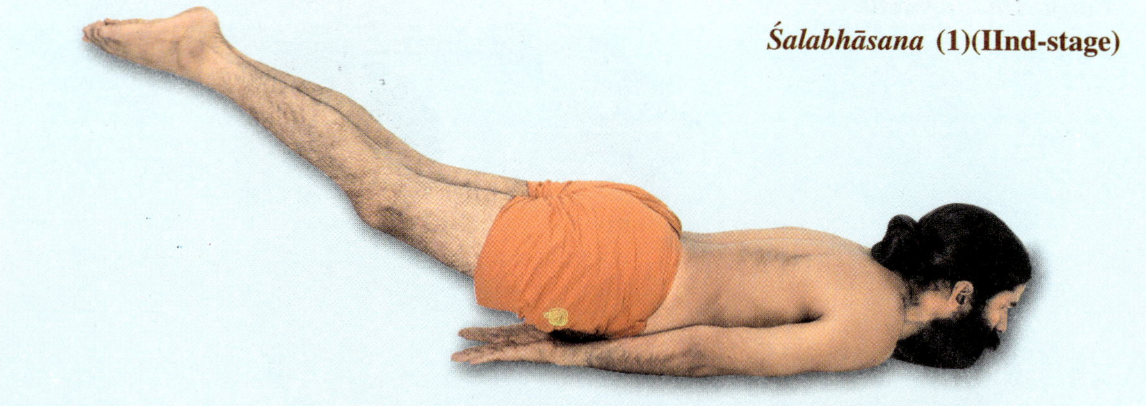

Śalabhāsana **(1)(IInd-stage)**

Benefits :

- It cures all the disorders at the lower end of spine. It is especially beneficial for backache and sciatica pain.

Śalabhāsana (2)

Method :

- Lie on your stomach and straighten the right hand while touching the head and the ear. Keep the left hand on the back.
- While inhaling, lift the head and right hand from the front and from the rear end, lift the left leg above the ground level.

Śalabhāsana (2)

- Remain in this position for some time and then very slowly come back to normal position. Similarly, repeat this exercise from the left side.

Benefits:

- It is beneficial for all spinal and cervical problems, spondylitis and backache.

Śalabhāsana (3)

Method :

- After the previous exercise, take both the hands behind and hold the wrists of one hand with the other. Inhale and at first lift the chest as much as possible and look upwards. Slowly lift the body from both sides. While ex h aling, come back to the original position.

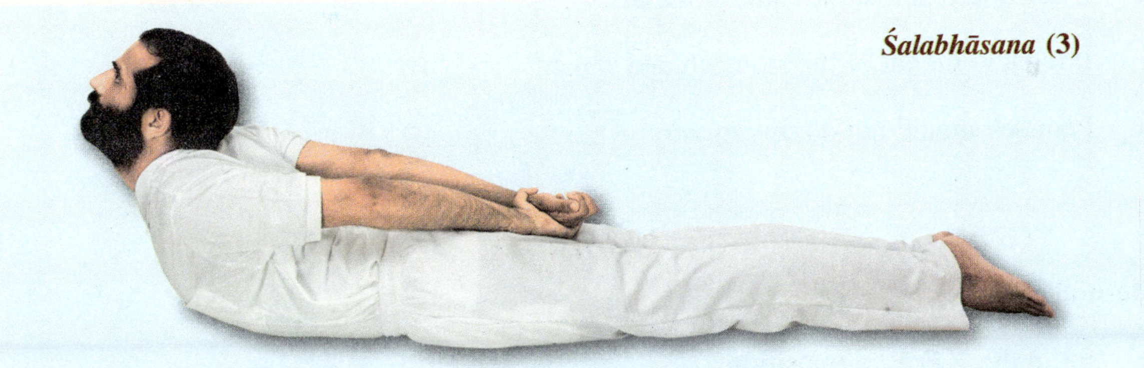

Śalabhāsana (3)

Benefits:

- As mentioned above.

Viparūta Naukāsana (Nābhi - āsana)

Method :

- Lie flat on your stomach and stretch both the hands in the front joined together. The legs should also be joined together and be straightened backwards. The toes should be stretched backwards.
- Inhale and lift the body from both the ends. The legs, chest, head, and hands should be raised above the ground. Repeat 4 - 5 times.

Viparūta Naukāsana (Nābhi - āsana)

Benefits:

- It is beneficial for all diseases of the spine.
- It strengthens the navel area.
- It expels gas from the body.
- It cures sexual diseases and weakness.
- It reduces the fat of the stomach and waist.
- Females should not do this *āsana*.

Uṣṭrāsana

Method :

- Sit in the *Vajrāsana* position.
- Lift the ankles (with the toes touching the ground) and keep both the hands on them such that the fingers are inwards and the thumbs are outwards.
- Inhale and bend the neck and head backwards and lift the waist. While exhaling, sit down on the ankles. Repeat this 3 - 4 times.

Uṣṭrāsana

Benefits:

- This *āsana* is very useful for the respiratory system. The cells in the lungs are activated, which helps the patients of asthma.
- It cures cervical spondylitis, sciatica and all other spinal problems.
- It is useful for thyroid.

Aṛdhçhaṇdrāsana

Method :

- Sit in *Uṣṭrāsana* position and stand on the knees. Keep both the hands on the chest.
- Inhale and bend the head and neck backwards and lift the waist and stretch.
- When the head is bent backwards and rests on the ankles, it is called *Pūrṇa Çhaṇdrāsana*

Aṛdhçhaṇdrāsana

Benefits:

- The benefits of this *āsana* are the same as those of *Uṣṭrāsana*. Those who cannot do *Uṣṭrāsana* can benefit from this *āsana*.

Trikoṇāsana

Method :

- Stand straight keeping a distance of about one and a Half foot between the feet. Both the hands should hang parallel to the body, palms inside.
- Inhale and bring the left hand near the left toe or near the ankle and lift the right hand upwards and bend the neck to the right side and look at the right hand. Then while exhaling, come back to the original position and repeat the exercise on the other side also.

Trikoṇāsana

Benefits:

- The lower back area becomes flexible. The fat on the sides is reduced. With the pressure on the backside, the muscle formation improves. The chest is develops.

Sūrya-Namaskāra

Sūrya namaskāra helps the entire body become disease-free, gain strength and energy. It reactivates all the body parts and enables regulation of hormonal secretions of all the internal glands. If possible perform this exercise at sunrise. According to capacity 11 to 21 repetitions can be done.

Method :

1. Stand facing the Sun, fold the hands in the position of *namaskāra* and keep them in front of the chest.

***Sūrya-Namaskāra* (1 & 12)**

***Sūrya-Namaskāra* (2 & 11)**

2. Inhale, stretch the hands in the front and take them backwards. Look towards the sky. To the extent possible bend backwards from the waist.

3. Exhale and while bending the hands in the front, rest them near the feet on the ground. If possible touch the ground with the palms and try to touch the knees with the head.

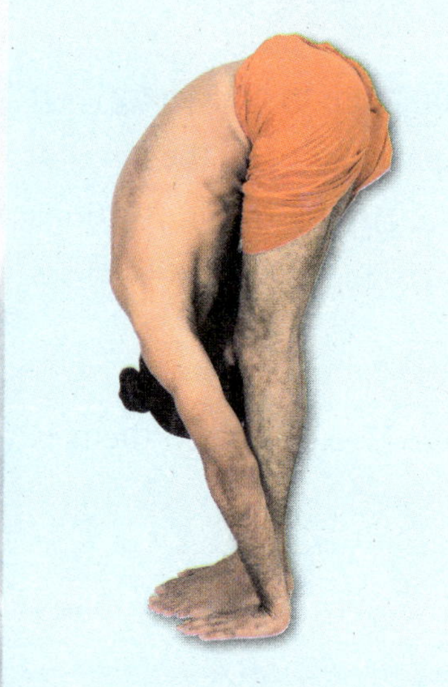

***Sūrya-Namaskāra* (3 & 10)**

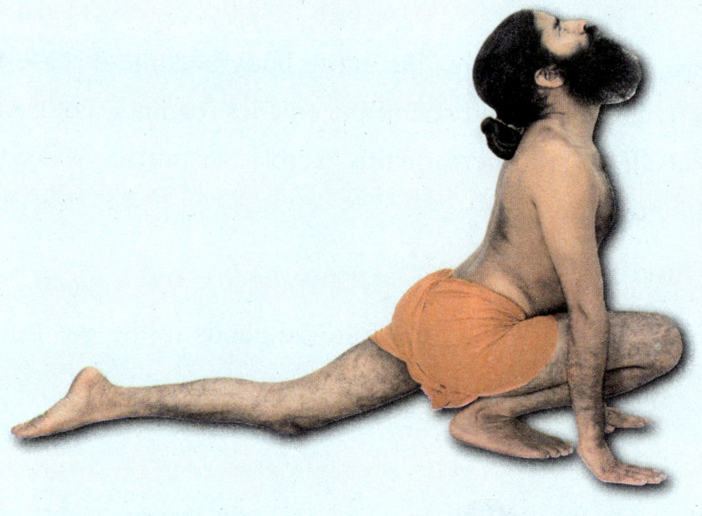

***Sūrya-Namaskāra* (4 & 9)**
Right foot forward in method no. 4
Left foot forward in method no. 9

4. Now bend forwards and place the hands on both sides of the chest. Raise the left foot and take it back, as is done in *Bhujaṅgāsana*. Let the right foot be in between both the hands. Knee should be in front of the chest and rest the heel on the ground. Look towards the sky and hold the breath inside.

***Sūrya-Namaskāra* (5 & 8)**

Sūrya-Namaskāra **(6)**

5. Exhale and take the right leg backwards. The neck and head should be in between the hands. Lift the hips and waist and bend the head down and look at the navel.

6. Keeping the hands, legs and toes steady, touch the knees and chest on the ground. In this way, when two hands, two legs, two knees, chest and head touch the ground, it becomes *Sāṣṭāṅgāsana*. Breathe normally.

Sūrya-Namaskāra **(7)**

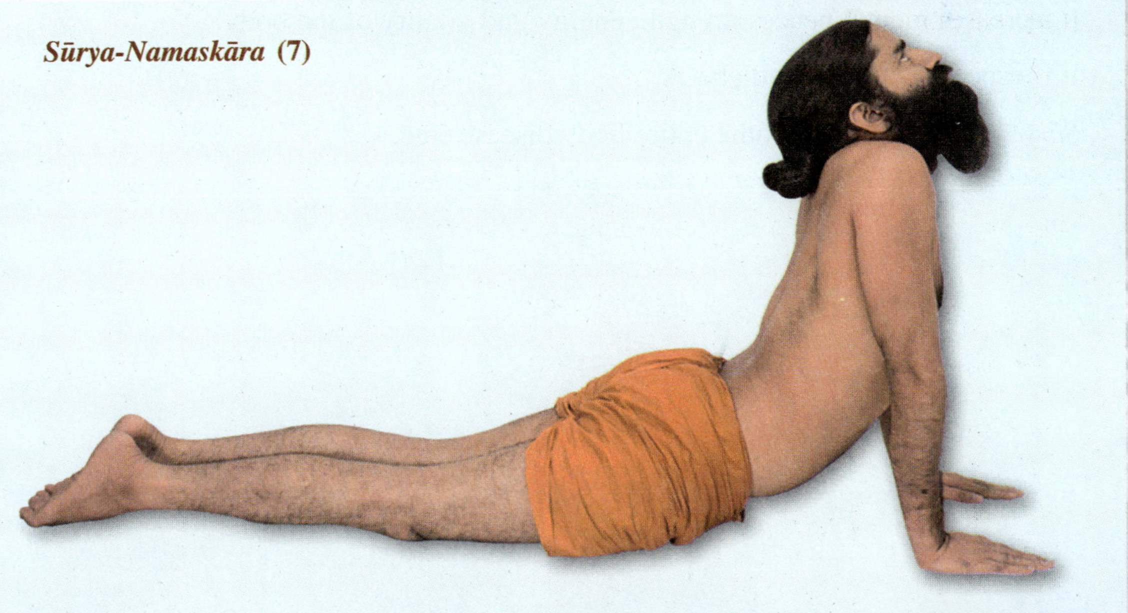

7. Inhale and lift the chest and look at the sky, resting the body up to the waist on the ground, and keep the legs and hands straight.

8. As mentioned in step 5.

9. As mentioned in step 4. Change the position of the legs. In this case keep the left leg in between both the hands.

10. As mentioned in step 3.
11. As mentioned in step 2.
12. As mentioned in step 1.

Benefits:

- *Sūrya namaskāra* is a complete exercise. All the body parts and joints become strong and disease free.
- It makes the stomach, intestines, heart and lungs healthy.
- It makes the spinal cord and waist flexible and cures their deformities.
- It regulates the blood circulation in the entire body and in this way it removes the impurities of blood and also cures skin diseases.
- The muscles of hands, legs, shoulders and thighs become stronger and toned up.
- It increases mental peace, strength, energy and vitality of the body.
- It is especially useful in diabetes.
- *Sūrya-namaskāra* makes the entire body disease free.

Other Miscellaneous Āsanas

Śīrṣāsana

Method :

- Make a cushion out of a long cloth or dhoti. Interlock the fingers of both the hands and rest the hands upto elbows on the ground. Keep the cushion in between the hands.
- The front portion of the head should rest on the cushion and knees should rest on the ground. Now controlling the body weight on the neck and elbows, straighten the legs to the ground level.
- Now while bending one knee, lift it straight, after this lift the second leg and bend up to the knee.
- Now one by one try to lift the legs, do not hurry in the beginning. Slowly the legs will be straight. When the legs are straight, then in the beginning join them and bend them slightly forward otherwise there is a chance of falling backwards.

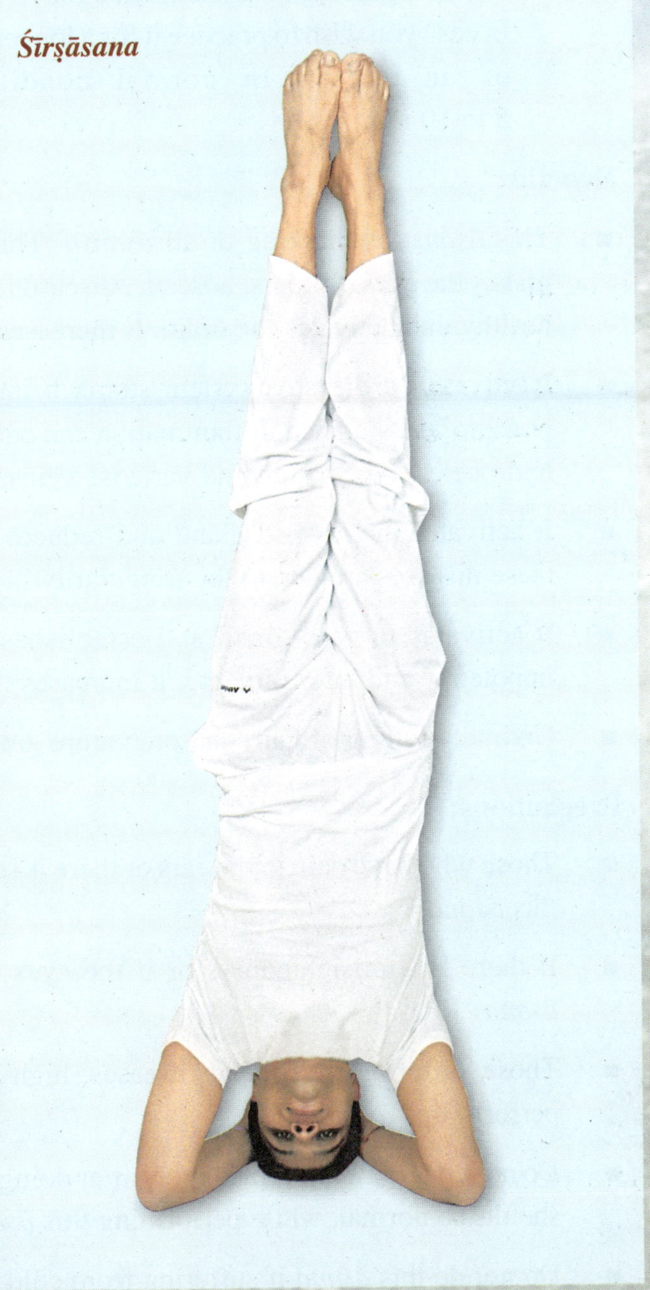
Śīrṣāsana

- Keep the eyes closed, and breath normally.
- Follow the same steps in the reverse order to come back to the original position. As you may like, do *Śavāsana* or stand up straight after *Śīrṣāsana*, so that the blood circulation which flowed towards the brain becomes normal.

Time: In the beginning do this exercise for 15 seconds and slowly extend it to 30 minutes. In case you wish to practice it for a longer time you should do it under the supervision of an expert. In normal conditions it is sufficient to do it for 5 to 10 minutes.

Benefits:

- This *āsansa* is the king of all *āsansa*. This provides pure blood to the brain, which makes the eyes, the ears, nose etc. disease free. It makes the pituitary and pineal glands healthy and activates the brain. It increases memory, sharpness and concentration.
- It activates the digestive system, stomach, intestines, and liver and increases the digestive power of the stomach. Inflammation and enlargement of the intestines, hernia, hysteria, hydrocele, constipation and varicose veins, etc. are cured by its practice.
- It activates the thyroid gland and reduces both obesity and weakness because both these diseases are due to the irregularity in functioning of the thyroid gland.
- It activates thyroid gland and establishes celibacy. It cures night-fall, gonorrhea, impotency and infertility, etc. It increases the glow and vitality on the face.
- Untimely falling of hair, and premature graying of the hair are cured by its practice.

Precautions:

- Those who have pain in the ears or there is secretion form ears, they should not perform this *āsana*.
- If there is shortsightedness or if the eyes are unduly red, then do not perform this *āsana*.
- Those suffering from heart diseases, high blood pressure and back pain should not perform this *āsana*.
- Do not do *Śīrṣāsana* immediately after doing any heavy exercise. The body temperature should be normal, while performing this *āsana*.
- Do not do this *āsana* if suffering from cold and coryza.

Ekapāda-grīvāsana

Method :

- Sit in *Daṇḍāsan* and fold the left leg from the knee and keep it in front of the groin. Then lift the right leg and place it firmly on the neck towards the backside. Now keep both the hands in front in *namaskāra* position looking in the front. Try to remain in this position for one and Half to two minutes and then come back to the original position. Repeat the exercise with the other leg also.

Ekapāda-grīvāsana

Benefits:

- The shoulders and chest become strong with this exercise.
- The parts of the leg become flexible and strong. The leg muscles become strong.
- Many stomach problems are cured and fat is reduced.

Siddhāsana

Method :

- Sit in *Daṇḍāsan* and fold the left leg and place the ankle in between the genitals and the rectum. The ankle of the right leg should be kept on the upper portion of the genitals. The heel of the right leg should be above the heel of the left leg. The toes should rest between the thigh and the calf muscle.

- The knees should rest on the ground. Both the hands should be in *Jñāna (Gyāna) Mudrā* (tips of the index finger and the thumb touching each-other, remaining three fingers should be straight) and resting on the knees. The spine should be erect. With eyes closed, concentrate the mind in between the eyebrows.

Siddhāsana

Benefits:

- It has been practiced by high level experts, therefore, it is called *Siddhāsana*. It protects celibacy and makes a person celibate.
- It cools down the lust for sex and removes the instability of the mind. This is the best asana for awakening the *kuṇḍalinī*.
- It is beneficial for piles and sexual diseases.

Kukkuṭāsana

Method :

- Sit in *Padmāsana*, put the hands in between the thighs and the calf muscles and rest them on the ground.
- Inhale and put the pressure on the palms to lift the body up to the elbows above the ground. When tired slowly come down.

Kukkuṭāsana

Benefits:

- The nerves of hands and shoulders become strong.

Uttāna Kukkuṭāsana

Method :

- Sit in *Padmāsana* and keep the hands in the front.
- Position the body above the elbows but below the armpits, making it stable on the arms, inhale and then raise the entire body duly supported on the hands.

Uttāna Kukkuṭāsana

Benefits:

- As mentioned above.

Supta Garbhāsana

Method :

- Sit in *Padmāsana* and lie down on your back. Like *Kukkuṭāsana* take out the hands from in between the thighs and calf muscles.

Supta Garbhāsana

- Tie the hands at the back. Keep the breathing normal. This can also be done by holding the neck or ears with the hands.

Benefits :

- It is useful for hands, legs, waist and stomach.

Garbhāsana

Method :

- Sit in *Padmāsana*, take out the hands from in-between the thighs and the calf muscles and hold the ears. The weight of body will be on the hips.

Benefits:

- It improves digestion. It is useful for the whole digestive system.

Tolāṅgulāsana

Method :

- Sit in *Daṇḍāsan*, balancing the body weight on the hands, inhale and lift the entire body, including the hips, above the ground.

Benefits :

- It gives extra ordinary strength to the nerves of hands and feet.

Mayūr-āsana

Method :

- Join both the hands in the front and turn the fingers backwards. Sit on the knees.
- Inhale and place the elbows on both sides of the navel slowly straighten the legs backwards. The whole body weight will be on the elbows. At the completion stage, the head and legs will be above the ground at the same level.

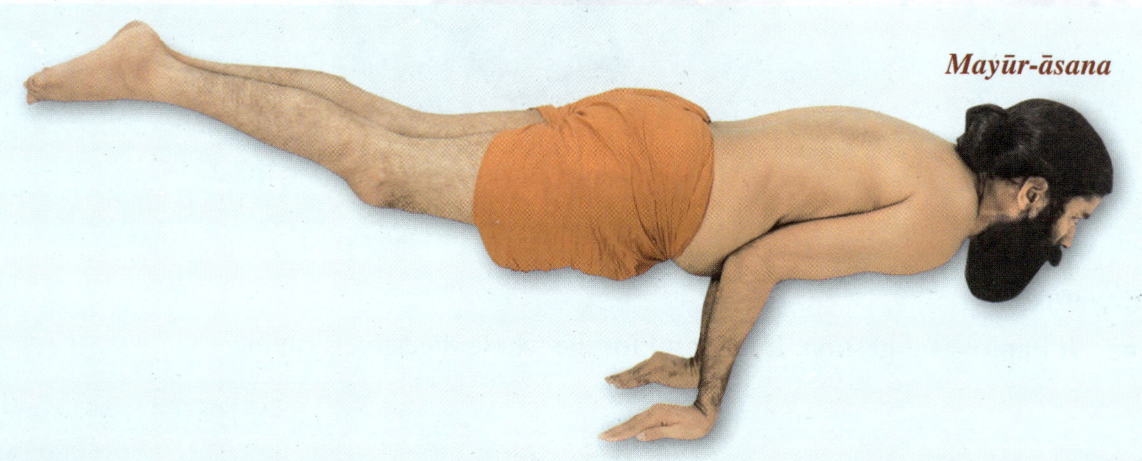
Mayūr-āsana

Benefits:

- It benefits spleen, liver, kidneys, pancreas and stomach. It brings glow on the face.
- It is beneficial for the patients of diabetes. It cures constipation.
- It improves digestion power of the stomach.

Parvatāsana

Parvatāsana

Method :

- Sit in *Padmāsana* and raise your-self up straight with support of knees.
- Keep both the hands above the head in the *namaskāra* position.

Benefits:

- It increases the concentration of the mind.

Utkaṭāsana

Utkaṭāsana

Method :

- The toes should be resting on the ground and rest the hips on the ankles. Keep both the hands on the knees and spread the knees parallel to the ankles.

Benefits:

- It is useful for celibacy and cures piles also.

Siṇhāsana

Method :

- If possible, sit in *Vajrāsana* facing the Sun and spread the knees apart. The fingers of the hands should face backwards and kept straight in between the legs.
- Inhale and take out the tongue. Look in between the eyebrows and exhale. While exhaling, roar like a lion. Repeat 3 - 4 times.
- After doing *Siṇhāsana* while taking the saliva inside the mouth, massage the throat lightly. This prevents soarness of throat.

Siṇhāsana

Benefits:

- It is useful for tonsils, thyroid and other throat problems.
- It is beneficial in ear-problems and unclear pronunciation.
- It is beneficial for the children who lisp.

Mārjārāsana

Method :

- Take the position by resting both the palms and knees on the ground.

Mārjārāsana **(Ist-stage)**

- Inhale and lift the head and the chest and bend the waist down-wards. Remain in this position for sometime, exhale and lift the back and bend the head down. Repeat 5 to 6 times.

Mārjārāsana **(IInd-stage)**

Benefits:

- It is useful for pain in lumbar region of the body and fissures in the rectum. It strengthens the lungs.
- It cures the problem of prolapse (displacement) of the uterus.

Vṛścikāsana

Method :

- Sit and keeping a distance between the hands, rest the elbows on the ground.
- Now like *Śīrṣāsana* rest the head in between the hands and lift the legs. When the legs go up try to lift the head. In the beginning some difficulty will be experienced. After practice, a scorpion like shape begins to form with the head and legs. In the completion stage try to keep the legs over the head.

Vṛścikāsana

Vṛścikāsana
(Final position)

Benefits :

- It improves the digestion power of the stomach and cures all the stomach problems.
- It cures urinary problems and increases glow on the face.

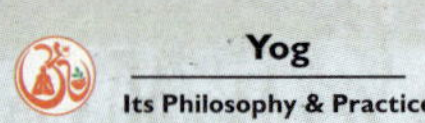

Prasṛta-Hasta Vṛścikāsana

Method:

- Lie down on your stomach. Raise both the legs by applying some force, fold them and keep them above the head This *āsana* is very difficult and therefore, in the beginning there may be difficulty in performing it.

Benefits:

- as mentioned above.

Prasṛta-Hasta Vṛścikāsana

Pādāṅguṣṭhāsana

Method:

- Keep the right heel in between the genitals and the anus.
- Keep the left leg above the right thigh. Rest both the hands on both sides, balance the body on the heel and toe and lift the hands making *namaskāra* position. Try and remain in this position at will. Keep the breathing normal.
- After doing with one leg repeat the *āsana* with the other leg.

Benefits:

- It is useful for celibacy. When practiced for long time, *kuṇḍalinī* awakens and the semen moves upwards. It increases strength in the body, intellect, radiance and glow.

Pādāṅguṣṭhāsana

Brahmacaryāsana

Method:

- Sit in *Vajrāsana* position and turn the toes outwards with the help of the hands. The heels should be touching the hips.
- Both the knees should be touching each other and keep the hands straight on the knees. The back should be straight and breathing should be normal. As per capacity do it for 5 - 30 minutes.

Brahmacaryāsana

Benefits:

- This *āsana* is beneficial for celibacy and justifies its name. It completely cures all problems related to semen, night-fall, gonorrhea, diabetes, etc.

Gorakṣāsana

Method:

- Keep both the heels and toes joined together in the front.
- Sit down keeping the middle portion between the genitals and the anus on the heels. Both the knees should rest on the ground. Keep the hands in *Jñāna (Gyāna) Mudrā* on the knees.

Benefits:

- It is the complementary to *Brahmacaryāsana*. After practicing the previous *āsana*, do this *āsana* in which the position of the feet gets reversed, which regulates the blood circulation in the muscles and makes them healthy.
- Since in this *āsana mūla-bandha* is done naturally, it is therefore completely helpful in celibacy. It stops the wavering of the senses and calms down the mind. That is why it is called *Gorakṣāsana*.

Gorakṣāsana

Ākarṇa-dhanuṣṭaṅkārāsana

Method:

- Sit in *Daṇḍāsana* position. Fold the right leg and keep it on the left leg.
- Hold the thumb of the right foot with left hand and vice versa.
- Inhale and bring the right foot close to the left ear. Remain in this position for some time. Come back to the *Daṇḍāsana* position. Similarly, repeat the exercise with the other leg.

Ākarṇa-dhanuṣṭaṅkārāsana

Benefits:

- It relieves the joint-pain of hands and feet and strengthens its glands.
- This is beneficial in Parkinson's disease.

Bhūnamanāsana

Method:

- Sit in *Daṇḍāsana* position and spread the legs on both sides as much as you can.
- Hold the thumbs of feet with the respective hand. While exhaling touch the ground with the chest and stomach. The chin should also be touching the ground. Remain in this position as per your capacity and then return to the original position.

Bhūnamanāsana

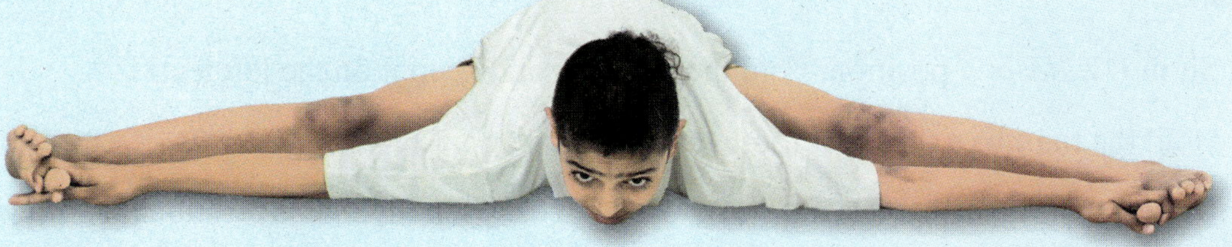

Benefits:

- It makes thighs, legs, waist, stomach and back disease free and stabilizes the semen.

Skandha-pādāsana

Method:

- Sit in *Daṇḍāsana* position and put the left leg, with the help of hands, on the neck.
- Keep the hands in front of the chest in *namaskāra* pose. Keep the waist and head straight.
- Similarly do the exercise with the other leg.

Benefits:

- It provides strength to the nerves of hands, legs, and neck.

Skandha-pādāsana

Dvipādagrīvāsana

Dvipādagrīvāsana

Method:

- Sit in *Daṇḍāsana* position and keep the legs one by one on the neck.
- Balancing the body weight on the hips, keep the hands in namaskāra position. Try to remain in this position for as long as the stamina permits.

Benefits:

- Same as *S̃kadhapādāsana*.

Bakāsana

Bakāsana

Method:

- Firmly place the palms on the ground and rest the knees on the arms above the elbows.
- Inhale and slowly try to lift the legs above the ground balancing the weight on the palms. With practice you could get in a position looks like the bird - Crane.

Benefits:

- It gives special strength to the nerves of the hands and makes them disease free. It increases the radiance on the face.

Upadhānāsana (Takiyāsana)

Method:

- Sit in *Daṇḍāsana* position, fold the left leg and place it on the neck with the help of the hands.
- Rest the right elbow on the ground and touch the hand to head and lie down on the ground.
- The right leg should lie straight on the ground. Keep the left hand straight on the left thigh.
- In the same way change the leg and do the *āsana* with the other leg.

Upadhānāsana (Takiyāsana)

Benefits:

- It strengthens the nerves of the hands, feet and the neck.

Hasta Pādāṅguṣṭhāsana

Method:

- Stand straight, lift the left leg and keep it on the right thigh and hold the thumb of the left foot with the right hand.
- Keep the left hand on the waist such that the thumb is facing towards the back and the fingers facing towards the stomach.
- Balancing the body weight on the right leg, stretch the left leg forward at an angle of 90 degrees (while holding the thumb of the left leg with the right hand). In this position the hand will also be straight. After doing this exercise with one leg, do it with the other leg.

Benefits:

- It cures the diseases of the feet and hands. It is a good exercise for people suffering from Parkinson's disease.

Hasta Pādāṅguṣṭhāsana

Dhruvāsana

Dhruvāsana

Method:

- Stand straight and lift the right leg and keep it on the left thigh in such a way that the toe is facing downwards and the heel touching the base of the thigh.
- Make the *namaskāra* pose with both the hands. Remain in this position for as long as you can and repeat the exercise with the other leg.

Benefits:

- It removes the wavering of the mind. It develops the nervous system and makes it stable.

Koṇāsana

Koṇāsana

Method:

- Stretch the legs about one & a half to two feet apart and stand straight.
- Inhale and touch the left toe with the right hand while bending on the right side and lift the left hand straight upwards as much as possible. The heels and toes should rest on the ground. The body should bend only from the sides. One should not bend forwards or backwards. Remain in this position for 4 - 6 seconds and repeat this 4 - 6 times.
- Change the hand and touch the right toe with the left hand.

Benefits:

- It is especially useful in curing the pain in the waist, ribs and weakness of lungs. It is also useful for the women. It reduces the fat from the waist and gives it a good shape.

Garuḍāsana

Method:

- Stand straight, bringing the right leg from the front coil it around the left leg. Coiling both the hands in the same way form the namaskar pose. Repeat it from the other side as well.

Benefits:

- This is especially beneficial for hydrocele, prostrate and kidney diseases.
- It cures pain and any abnormality in the hands and feet.
- It cures urinary problems.

Vṛkṣāsana

Method:

- Stand straight and rest both the hands on the ground, about six inches apart.
- Balancing the body weight on the hands, slowly raise the legs above the ground and stabilize them straight like a tree.

Benefits:

- It increases the body strength, glow and semen.
- It cures disorders of eyes, seminal disorders and cough. It makes the arms attractive and shapely.
- It enhances blood circulation in the heart and lungs and makes them healthy.

Tāḍāsana

Tāḍāsana

Method:

- Stand straight and breathing deeply, raise both the hands from the sides. As the hands are raised so the heels should also be raised simultaneously. The body weight will be on the toes and the body will be fully stretched upwards.

Benefits:

- Due to deep breathing it provides strength and expansion to the lungs.
- It is the best exercise to increase the height. It develops and activates the nerves of the entire body.

Pakṣyāsana

Method:

- Stand straight and place the left leg on the neck and shoulder.
- Spread both the hands on both sides parallely. The right leg should be absolutely straight. Keep the hands in *namaskāra* pose.
- After doing it with left leg repeat it with right leg.

Benefits:

- This *āsana* makes the body active and light. It develops the nerves of the thighs. It cures brain related problems.

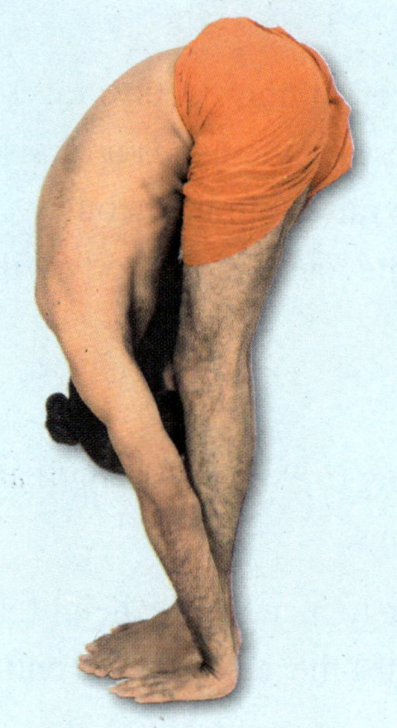

Pāda-hastāsana

Pāda-hastāsana

Method:

- Stand straight and while inhaling, raise the hands and bend forward. Touch the head with the knees. The hands will be placed on the backside, near the calf muscles lowered as much as possible to the ground level.

Benefits:

- It renders the waist and stomach healthy. It is very beneficial for increasing the height.

Naṭarājāsana

Method:

- Stand straight and turn the right leg backwards. Take the right hand from above the shoulder and hold the thumb of the right foot.
- The left hand should be raised straight up. After doing it with one leg repeat with the other leg.

Benefits:

It develops the nerves of the hands and legs. It strengthens the nervous system.

Naṭarājāsana

Vātāyanāsana

Method:

- Stand straight, fold the left leg and place it on the base of right thigh in such a manner that the toe is on the thigh and the heel on base of the groin.
- Folding the right leg, rest the left knee on the ground. The hands should be in *namaskāra* pose. In the same way repeat it with the other leg.

Benefits:

- It is beneficial in knee problems. The body becomes light. It increases the water content of the thighs. It is considered beneficial for patients of hernia.

Vātāyanāsana

Haṭha-yoga & Ṣaṭkarma

Lord Shiva is considered to be the creator of *Haṭha-yoga*. *Swāmī Gorakṣa Nātha,* Shri *Matsyendra Nātha*, *Mīnā Nātha*, *Caurańgī Nātha*, *Svātmā Rama* and others up to *Bhartṛhari* and *Gopīchanda* have kept this tradition alive. With *Haṭha-yoga* we can make our body pure, healthy and pious and make it worthy of *Rajyayog*, as has been stated by the author of *Haṭha-yoga Pradīpikā* :-**"*Kevalaṃ Rājayogāya Haṭha-vidyopadiśyate*"** means *Haṭha-yoga* is preached only to enter into the realms of *Rajyayog*, because *Rajyayog* guides on how to purify our innerself leading us to *Dhyān* and *Samādhi*. But if we are unhealthy, our consciousness is lying dormant, then it is almost impossible to reach the stage of concentration and deep meditation. Therefore, *Haṭha-yoga Pradīpikā* further says :

"Haṭhaṃ vinā Rāja-yogaṃ Rāja-yogaṃ vinā Haṭham
Na sidhyati tato yugmāniṣpatteḥ samabhyaset "

(*Haṭha-yoga Pradīpikā* :2.76)

Without *Haṭha-yoga,* we cannot master *Rajyayog* and without Rajyayog, *Haṭha-yoga* is incomplete. Therefore the devotee should practice both *Haṭha-yoga* and Rajyayog together in a coordinated manner. Generally people think that *Haṭha-yoga* means the *yoga,* which is done beyond our capacity to perform, however, the meaning is totally opposite of what is being understood. The Shastras define *Haṭha-yoga* as:-

"Hakarah Kirtitah Suryashthkarah Chandra Uchayate
SuryaChandramsoryogaad Hathyogo Nigadyate "

'Hakāra' represents Surya nadi and *'ṭhakāra'* denotes Chandra nadi. Haṭha-*yoga* is derived by the combination of Surya and Chandra nadis. Both these are present in our body. We get the power of life from these two *nāḍīs*. It is sufficient to mention here that every person has two types of powers- one is the power of the fire - strength, courage, bravery, semen and the second is the power of *soma* - devotion, peace, tolerance, well-being, love and sympathy. These powers bring success in all the dealings of an individual. These two powers, when used jointly, enable achievement of The Divine Power, is a yogic action. These two powers give rise to a science called the science of breathing the science of nadis, which has been described below in brief.

Ṣvara (Science of Breathing)

"Yathā brahmāṇḍe tathā piṇḍe " means all powers of the outside universe are located within us. We need not obtain power from outside, we need to recognise the powers within us and to utilize them properly and in an appropriate manner. The Sun and the Moon are the basis of life support in the outside universe. These two regulate and administer the world. These are the representatives of power of the fire and power of the *soma*. Exactly in the same way there are *Surya* and *Chandra Ṣvaras* within us. *Chandra Ṣvaras* represents *soma*. This awakens piety, politeness, strength, bliss and will-power in an individual. The *Surya Ṣvara* is full of valour, semen, prowess, capacity to fulfill the desires. When these two powers become even and balanced, a thirdpower is created or awakens, which is established in between these two powers, is called *sušhuṃna*. These *Ṣvaras* in *Haṭha-yoga* are also known by the names of *Gaṅgā*, *Yamunā*, and *Sarasvatī*.

"Iḍā Bhagavatī Gaṅgā , Piṅgalā Yamunā nadīī
Iḍā-Piṅgalayormadhye bāla-raṇḍā ca Kuṇḍalīī "

(*Haṭha-yoga* :3.110)

Iḍā means the left *nāḍī*, which is called Goddess *Gaṅgā*. *Piṅgalā* is the right *nāḍī*, which is called *Yamunā*. In between these two nadis lies the *sušhuṃna nāḍī*, which is also known by the names of *bal-randa, saraṣwatī* and *kundali*. Saint *Kabīīra Dāsa* says:-

"Cānda sūraja to bane masālacī , sūrata suhāganī nāca rahīī
Iḍā Piṅgalā tānā bharanīī , Sukha-mana tāra se bhīīnī cadariyā
Ghaṭa meṅ Gaṅgā , ghaṭa meṅ Yamunā , ghaṭa meṅ Ṭhākura-dvārā "

Now we shall throw some light on the *Ṣix-karmas* included in *Haṭha-yoga.*

Six- *kaṛmas*

The teachings of Six-*kaṛmas* were given by saints to their pupils to initiate them into the purification of the body and beginning of *Rạjyayog*. These activities rejuvenate the human body and make it disease free, endow with longer life, healthy, strong, and radiant.

"Ṣaṭkarma-nirgata-sthaulya kapha-doṣa-malādikaḥ
Prāṇāyāmaṃ tataḥ kuryād anāyāsena sidhyati "

The activities of these six-*kaṛmas*, while purifying the *physical* body are extremely helpful in the purification of the *astral* body also. By practicing these activities, 20 types of *kaph diseases*, all *vāt diseases, piṭta diseases,* leprosy, abdominal diseases, diseases of the lungs, heart and kidney related diseases, are all cured. Therefore, for the benefit of entire mankind, these activities, as told by The *Ṛiṣhis*, are being described below in brief:-

"DhautirBastistathā NetisTrāṭakaṃ Naulikaṃ tathā
Kapālabhātiścaitāni Ṣaṭ karmāṇi pracakṣate "

(*Haṭha-yoga* 2:22)

"DhautirBastistathā Netiḥ NaulikasTrāṭakastathā
Kapālabhātiḥ Ṣaṭ-karmāṇi samabhyaset "

(*Gorakṣa-saṃhitā*)

Dhōutī , *Baṣti*, *Neti*, *Trāṭaka*, *nōli* and *Kapāla-bhāti*, are six activities that have been taught to the followers of the *yogic* path. All aspirants of *yog* should practise them regularly. They are being described in detail hereunder:-

1. *Neti* : Accepting different types of fluids through nose is called *Neti*.

Types of *Neti*:

(a) Jal Neti, (b) *Sūtra Neti,* (c) *Ghṛta Neti,* (d) *Tail Neti,* (e) *Dugdha Neti*

Jal Neti

(a) *Jal Neti* :

Method : Add 10 gms of rock salt in one liter of water, heat it to make it lukewarm and pour it into the vessel to be used for *Neti*. Morning time is suitable for *Neti*. In case of a particular disease, it can be done twice a day. Put the pipe of the vessel in the right nostril and keep the left nostril slightly lowered. Open the mouth slightly and breath through the mouth. The water will start flowing out of the left nostril on its own. Similarly, do it with the other nostril. If there is no phlegm, *Neti* can be performed slowly without salt, using only cold water. Those who are suffering from *coryza* and *catarrh* should do it with lukewarm, salted water only. Those who do not have phlegm should start doing it with lukewarm water and slowly switch over to water at normal temperature. *Neti* cures cold and catarrh but some people catch cold by doing *Neti*. After *Neti, Kapāla-bhāti* should also be done so that the water entering or already stuck up in the empty sacs may come out, then the person will not catch cold and catarrh.

Sūtra Neti

b) *Sūtra Neti*:

Method: *Sūtra-Neti* is done with a thin rope made threads of cotton. The rope should be soaked in water before inserting it in the nose. After soaking in water, it should be bent slightly from the end where wax is applied, so that it can easily enter the nostril. Now slowly put the *Neti* in the right nostril and when it reaches inside the mouth, take it out slowly with the help of the hand.

Note: In case *Sūtra-Neti* is not available, a catheter of the size 4/5 can be used for this purpose. *Sūtra-Neti* creates a typical mild pain in the nose and throat, therefore, after *Sūtra-Neti, ghṛta-Neti* or *Tāil-Neti* should be done.

c) *Ghṛta Neti, etc*:

Method: Sit on a chair or lie down on a hard bed or a cot and keep the head slightly suspended at the backside. With the help of a dropper or a small spoon, pour 8 to 10 drops of luke warm ghee in the nostrils. In the same way *Tāil-Neti* is also done. Drinking milk from the nostril is called *Dugdha -Neti*. After attaining proficiency in *jal-Neti*, *Dugdha -Neti* is done. In *Dugdha -Neti,* the milk is not allowed to fall from the nostril as in case of *Jal-Neti,* instead the milk is slowly swallowed inside.

Benefits:

In *Haṭh-yoga Pradāpikā, Neti* is said to purify the forehead, improves eyesight and cure all the diseases of the body-parts above the throat speedily.

"Kapāla-śodhanī caiva divya-dṛṣṭi-pradāyinī
Jatrūrdhva-jātarogaugham Netirāśu nihanti ca "

Neti definitely cures coryza and catrrh, and other *kaphaja* diseases. It is extremely beneficial in eye problems, graying of hair, headache and other diseases. The purpose of *Neti* is not only cleansing the nose but also protecting the phlegmatic membrane (and making it strong) from external pollution, dust particles, smoke, heat, cold, bacteria and other germs. Some people have very sensitive synovial membrane, which gets afflicted by atmospheric stimulus. This is called allergy. *Neti* reduces the sensitivity of synovial membrane and cures all the problems. In some people, the bone in the nose increases. In this situation sinusitis can be cured with *Neti* at its initial stage.

2. Dhōutī: *Dhauti* is performed for cleaning of the stomach. *Dhōutī* means - 'To wash'. It has normally four classifications - *Vāman Dhōutī, gajkaraṇī, VaṣṭraDhōutī* and *Daṇḍa Dhōutī.*

a) *Vāman Dhōutī* (Vomiting):

Method: This action should be undertaken after finishing all the morning chores. For this, prepare 1 to 2 liters of lukewarm water with small quantity of salt added to it and try to drink this water as much as possible, then bend about 90 degrees forward, put the two middle fingers of the left hand in the throat, this will cause vomiting and the water will come out. In this manner, by touching the inner throat with the fingers, throw out entire quantity of water. Those who have redness in eyes should not do this action forcibly. To much bending down should be avoided and the legs should be kept close to each other. This action is also known as *bādhī kriyā.*

Benefits: The phlegm in the stomach, *piṭta* (bile) and undigested food, etc. come out with *Vāman Dhōutī.* Those who have phlegm problem, respiratory problems, asthma, acidity, etc. should do this activity. When the disease is on the decline, reduce the activity also. *Dhōutī* removes abnormal bile and also helps in removing any fever in the body through perspiration. This also stops dizziness and allied problems. This should normally be done once a week.

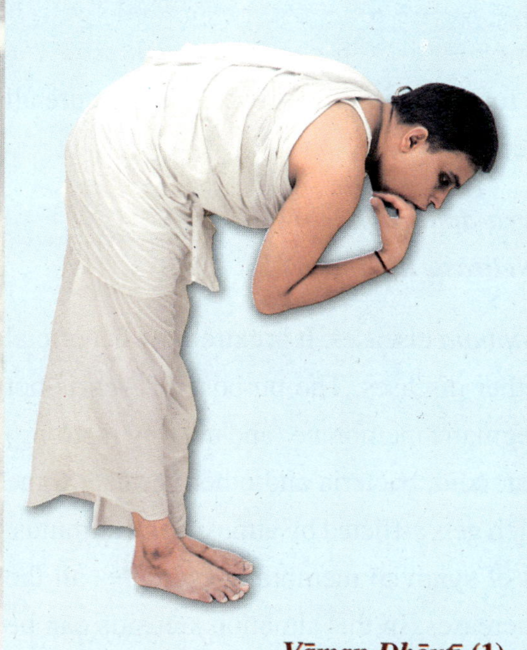

***Vāman Dhōutī* (1)**

***Vāman Dhōutī* (2)**

b) *Gajakaraṇī or Kuñjara Kriyā*

The only difference between *Vāman Dhōutī* and *gajakaraṇī* is that in the former, water comes out intermittently, whereas in the latter, entire water comes out at one go. *Gaja* or *kuñjara* means elephant. As an elephant fills water in its trunk and throws it all at one time like a fountain, this action takes place in the same way. Therefore, it is called *gaja-karaṇī*, meaning doing like an elephant.

Method: Drink as much water as you can and after drinking, bend forward at an angle of about 90 degrees. Contract the throat, mouth and neck and inhale as in *ujjāyī* or push the air in the stomach, like we do when drinking water in gulps. Now contract the abdomen. This will contract the stomach and water will start coming out like a waterfall. One can put slight pressure also on the abdomen with the left hand.

Benefits: As mentioned above.

c) *Vaṣtra Dhōutī*

Method: Take a muslin cloth, 22 feet in length and about four fingers wide. Roll it and leave it in a vessel containing boiled clean water, for 4 to 5 minutes. Sit on your feet and keep the edge of the cloth on the front portion of the tongue. Slowly swallow the cloth along with the saliva as we do while eating the food. In between, keep drinking water so as to facilitate swallowing of the cloth easily. In the beginning vomiting sensation will occur. When you feel like vomiting, shut your mouth. In the beginning, only 3 to 4 feet of cloth will go inside. With practice, you will be able to swallow the whole cloth, slowly. After swallowing the cloth stand up and do *uḍḍiyāna baṇdha* and right *nōuli* 2-3 times. After doing *nōuli* action, sit down and slowly take out the cloth. While taking out, if the cloth gets stuck in between, then re-swallow a part and then take it out. After taking it out, wash it properly with soap, etc and keep it safe after drying.

Vaṣtra Dhōutī (1)

Vaṣtra Dhōutī (2)

Precautions:

While swallowing the cloth, do not press it under the teeth.

While swallowing the cloth, at least one-foot length should be left outside.

After about 20 minutes of the beginning of swallow action, it is necessary to take it out, otherwise, the front portion of the cloth, which has in the meantime reached the end of the stomach, can get digested and is very likely to cause harm. Therefore after 15 to 20 minutes, whatever length of cloth has been swallowed should be pulled out.

Those who get excessive acidic belches or have any type of ulcer in the stomach, should not do practise this activity.

Benefits:

VaṣtraDhōutī removes the phlegm covering the inner walls of the stomach, which helps in creation of digestive juices resulting in enhanced appetite.

It is especially beneficial for patients suffering from phelgm. This activity is very good in cases of chronic stomach swelling.

d) *Daṇḍa Dhōutī*

Method: Boil a 3-feet long and 6 mm. round soft rubber tube in water, so that it is disinfected. The edge, which is to be introduced in the mouth, should be first rubbed slightly on a stone. Now drink 1-2 glasses of lukewarm salted water, as per capacity. Now stand leaning forward. Put one edge of the tube in the mouth and try to swallow it slowly. Swallow it only to such an extent that its front edge reaches the stomach. The other edge will be hanging outside. As soon as the pipe reaches the stomach, the water will automatically start coming out due to syphon action. Thus, throw all the water, taken inside earlier.

Precaution: The pipe should be stretched and checked before use. Otherwise there may be a chance of breaking while inside the stomach.

Benefits: When the faecal matter accumulates on the digestive juices secreting glands in the stomach, secretion of the digestive juices is hampered. Due to this, a reverse action causes the walls of the windpipe excite and get loosened, resulting in expulsion of the phlegm. Therefore one feels higher levels of hunger and patients suffering from asthma are specially benefited. As a result the stiffness caused in the windpipe due to asthma gets normalised and also helps in stopping asthmatic fits.

Rejuvenation Measures - *Śaṅkha Dhōutī* or *Shaṇkha Prakṣhālan*

The shape of our intestines is like a conch shell. Purification of the conch shell shaped intestine is called *śaṅkha* purification or *varisar* action. This activity has been experimented on several patients and it was found that it really rejuvenates the person. This process is capable of curing very serious and chronic diseases. There is hardly any disease including stomach problems, obesity, piles, hypertension, diabetes and diseases related to tissue elements, which cannot be benefited by undertaking this activity. We have found in *yoga* camps that half of the benefits are achieved due to the other *yoga āsanas* and activities and the remaining half benefit is achieved due to this process. We clean our clothes everyday. If we do not wash our clothes even for one day they get dirty. Our abdomen contains around 32 feet long intestines, which are never cleaned even once in our lifetime. As a result, a subtle layer of toxic and contaminated matter accumulates on its inner walls. Due to the formation of this dirty layer, absorption and secretion of juices does not take place properly, resulting in dyspepsia, indigestion, acidic belches, etc. Putrefaction of this matter causes stinking in the stomach. It causes gastric trouble. The juices are not produced properly. When the main instrument gets deformed, the subsidiary organs like stomach, pancreas, etc are also affected and cause different types of diseases.

Our body is an instrument. A great wonder out of the many wonders of the world, it is the greatest surprise as to who has created this unique instrument? Just as we undertake complete servicing and overhauling of the musical instruments, motor car, watch and other machines, which enables them to work properly, in the same way, we should undertake servicing and overhauling of our own bodily instrument, so that it remains healthy, long-living and strong.

Items required for this process:

One tumbler (for drinking water), lukewarm water which contains appropriate quantities of lime juice and rock salt, semi-solid *khiçhdi* made out of rice and *mōong* pulse, 100 gms of *ghēe* per head made out of cow milk. Incase *ghēe* made out of cow milk is not available, then you may use *ghēe* made out of buffalo milk. A mat or a blanket for doing the *āsana*, light bed sheet to cover, and a toilet near by, are required.

Prior Preparation: Practice of *āsanas* should be started at least one week before the day on which this activity is to be performed. The night prior to the day on which this activity is to be undertaken, easily digestible light meals should be taken at around 8 P.M. In the evening, drink milk mixed with 50-100 gms. raisins as this will facilitate the purification process. Go to bed before 10 P.M. On the next day, if possible, get free from the morning chores, viz. brushing teeth, evacuation of bowels, taking bath etc. It does not matter whether you have been able to evacuate bowels or not.

Three Types of water:

(a) **Water containing Lime juice and rock-salt:** Adding appropriate amounts of lime-juice and rock-salt in water. All healthy persons, except patients of high blood pressure, *kaphaja* and *vātika* problems, have to drink this water.

(b) **For the patients of** *kaphaja* and *vātika*: Patients suffering from physical pains like joint pains, gout, swelling, cervical spondylitis, slipdisc, etc and *kaphaja* problems should take warm water having rock-salt only.

(c) **For patients of hypertension and skin diseases:** Those people who are suffering from hypertension or any skin disease should drink hot water containing lime juice only before undertaking the said activity.

Method:

- Sit in *Utkaṭāsana* (on your feet) and drink quickly, without bothering for the taste, one or two glasses of the water prepared, as per the directions. Then do two repetitions of the five *āsanas* prescribed for this activity and then drink water as per desire. After drinking water, repeat the exercises in the same order. In this way, repeating the exercises and drinking water in between will result in passing bowels. Do not try hard to pass the bowels in the toilet. Pass the bowels in the quantity as it comes. While sitting in the toilet, do *ashvinī mudrā* (contracting and expanding the anus), this will clean the stomach and piles and other diseases will also be cured. After coming out of the toilet, again drink water and do the exercises. In this way keep drinking water and keep doing the exercises and pass the bowels. After you have been to the toilet 8-10 times, you will see that yellow water stops flowing out. The water, which you have been drinking, the same water is coming out of the anus. Then drink 4-5 glasses of water or as desired and do *Vāman Dhōutī*. After doing *Vāman Dhōutī,* lie down in *Śavāsana* for 30-40 minutes and take rest. Cover the body with light cloth, preventing excessive exposure to wind as it is undesirable. After 30-40 minutes of rest, consume the pre-prepared light *khicarī* made from equal quantities of rice and *Mōong* pulse (halved pieces of whole pulse grain having its peel over it) and containing pre-heated quantity of *ghēe*, as per pleasure. It is recommended to consume at least 50 gms of *ghēe*, while a healthy person may consume as much as he likes. This activity purifies the entire body. After purification, the body should be lubricated in the same way as greasing is done for vehicles after their washing and cleaning. After this action, the *ghēe*, which is consumed, performs lubrication action on all the glands and they become soft. Due to lubrication, the excretory matter, etc

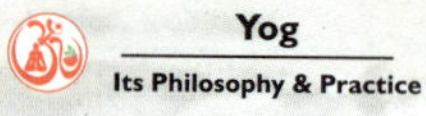

does not stick to them. The ghee thus consumed does not harm people suffering from any disease. After eating *khicharī*, if possible, do *yoga nidrā*. *Yoga nidrā* is similar to *Śavāsana*. *Dhyān* has a special importance in this process. We now describe the five *āsanas* necessary for *Sāṇkhya Ṗrakṣhālan.*

(a) *Ūṛḍhawa Tāḍāsana*

Method:

- Stand straight and interlock the fingers of both the hands and keep them on the head. Keep the legs close.
- Inhale and stretch the hands upwards and simultaneously lift the heels. While exhaling, come down. Keep the hands on the head. Repeat it 5 times.

Ūṛḍhawa Tāḍāsana

(b) *Tiṛyak Tāḍāsana*

Method:

- Stand in the above mentioned position, take the hands up, interlock the fingers and stretch them straight upwards. The palms should face the sky and the feet should be kept about one foot apart.

- While inhaling, bend to the right as much as possible, without bending backwards or forwards, and the arms should not be leaning at the elbows. While exhaling, take the hands above the head. In the same way do it on the left side. Do these five times on each side.

Tīŗyak Tāḍāsana

(c) *Kaṭiçhakŗāsana*

Method:

- Keep the legs about one foot apart, stand straight. Spread both the hands along the shoulders, keeping the palms straight facing the ground.
- Turn the right hand from the front and keep it on the left shoulder. Fold the left hand from the backside and keep it on the waist. The palm of the hand, which is on the waist, should face upwards.

Kaṭiçhakŗāsana (First Method)

- Now while turning the neck to the left, look at the right ankle from the rear side. If you are unable to see it, then just try doing it. After doing from one side, repeat from the other side. Similarly, perform this 5 times from each side.

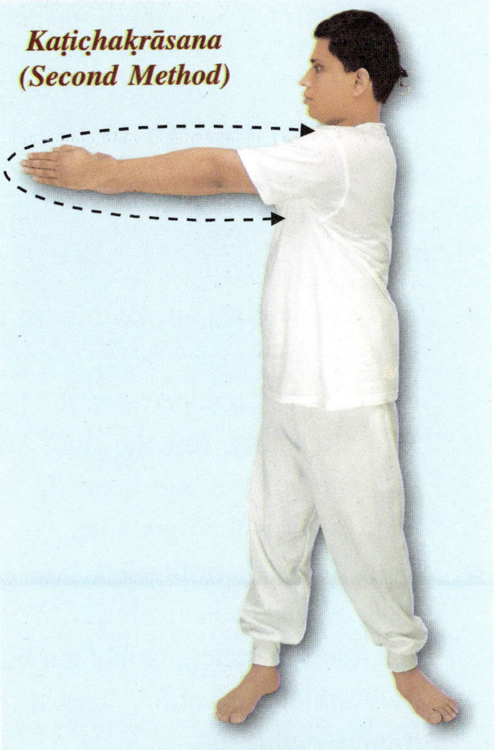

Kaṭichakrāsana (Second Method)

Second Method:

- Stand up and bring both the hands in front of the chest. While inhaling, turn the hands towards right side as much as possible. The distance between the hands should be equal to the chest width and the sight fixed between the hands. While exhaling, come back to the middle position. In the same way, do it from the other side also.

(d) *Tiṛyak Bhujaṅgāsana*

Method:

- Lie down on your stomach and keep both the hands on either side of the chest and close to the shoulders. The elbows should be touching the sides and raised.
- While keeping a distance of about one foot between the legs, keep the toes stretched backwards.

Tiṛyak Bhujaṅgāsana

- While inhaling, lift the chest. When the portion up to the navel area is raised, look at the left heel from above the right shoulder. While exhaling, come down. Repeat it from the left side.

(e) *Udarā-karṣaṇa or Śaṅkhāsana*

Udarā-karṣaṇa or Śaṅkhāsana

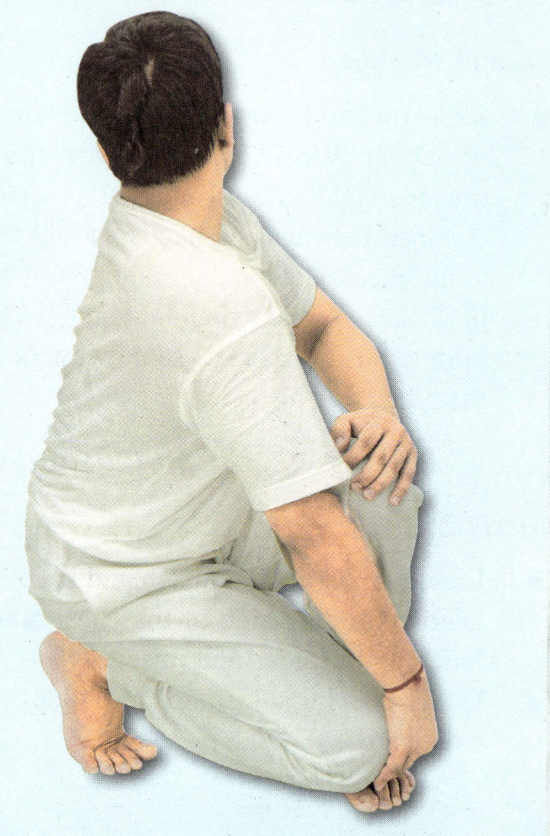

Method:

- Sit on your feet and keep both the hands on the knees. Keep a gap of about 1 - 1 1/4 feet between the legs.
- While inhaling, rest the right knee near the left toe and bend the left knee towards the right side.
- Turn the neck to the left side and look at the back. Remain in this position for sometime and get back to the middle position. Repeat this from the other side.

Benefits:

- This activity cures all types of diseases, as has already been informed earlier.
- The body becomes clean and pure and light like a flower, full of radiance.
- All stomach diseases like constipation, dyspepsia, gas, acidity, sour belches and piles, etc. are definitely cured.
- It is extremely beneficial for obesity, diabetes, respiratory diseases, heart diseases, appendicitis, headache and all the diseases related to mouth, throat, tongue and eyes.
- It cures menstrual disorders in case of ladies. Joint pains, arthritis, etc *vata* related diseases, untimely graying of hair, wrinkles on the face and black pigmentation marks, etc are all cured.
- It is extremely beneficial for all diseases related to intestine, kidney, pancreas and spleen. On the whole, the benefits of this activity are unlimited.

Precautions:

- In the beginning, this should be practiced under the guidance of an instructor. Performing this *āsana* could be tiring and hence painful.
- Warm water and salt are used in performing this activity. Performing this *Āsana* causes increased thirst and internal heat. In this condition, consumption of cold water is harmful, as it causes tiredness and weakness to the body. The practitioner feels uncomfortable. It is, therefore, necessary that, in the beginning, the temperature of water should be just warm and the quantity of salt should be excessive. This problem is solved by successive decrease in the quantity of salt the next time. If drinking water results in vomiting, then drink less water and do not perform *Tīṛyak Bhujaṅgāsana*.
- Initially, regular bowels will be passed followed by yellow water, and after yellow water, normal water like bowels will be passed. After that again yellowish water will come out. At this juncture, this activity should be stopped.
- After eating *khicharī*, do not drink water till 3 hours. Even after three hours if you want to drink water, take small-quantity of warm water. Cold water should not be taken on that day. Because drinking cold water can cause problems in the throat, as also catarrh and cold, etc.
- Take rest for the whole day, do not roam about in the open. After the activity, take rest but do not sleep.
- Do not take bath after the activity. If it is summer time then hot water bath can be taken in the evening.
- After the activity, do not sit under the fan and during the winter season, sitting under the sun is prohibited.
- Do not wash the hands and feet with cold water for the whole day. This can cause swelling. On a cloudy day or if it is raining, this activity should not be done.
- Children, mother of a newly born baby, and extremely weak persons should not do it.
- For three days from performing this activity, milk and milk products like sweets, buttermilk, curd, etc. (except *ghēe*), should not be consumed.
- The *khicharī* should be made semi-solid by adding rice and pulse in equal quantities. While cooking, only rock salt and turmeric powder is to be added. Do not use anything else. On the day this activity is to be undertaken, only *khicharī* and *ghēe* should be consumed, do not eat any thing else. Even after this activity also, those who are obese, people suffering from chronic diseases of the abdomen, and diabetics, should consume *khicharī* only, for the next three days. Do not add *ghēe* to the *khicharī* in the same

quantity as done earlier. Normally, on the second day, a little quantity of vegetable made from gourd, or any similar green vegetable, etc can be taken. It implies that only easily digestible food items should be eaten and that too in small quantity. After three days, gradually start taking normal meals.

Time of practice:

Diabetics should perform this activity once every 40 days. Patients of piles, chronic constipation and psoriasis should also do this once in 40 days. A healthy person should also do this once in six months or once a year so that the body may not catch any disease.

Laghu Śaṅkha Prakṣālana

This activity is especially beneficial for patients of chronic constipation, obesity and diabetes. In this case also, appropriately hot water is consumed and *āsanas* are practiced. During this case, only 7-8 glasses of water should be taken, not more. This will enable passing the bowels 3 - 4 times and the stomach will be cleaned. After this, if desired, *Vāman Dhōutī* can also be done.

Note: The benefits are as mentioned before. Any special diet control need not be followed. After the activity, take *kicharī* with a small quantity of *ghēe*. In the evening, *ҫhapati* and vegetable can be taken. On the day this activity is undertaken, it is better not to consume milk and buttermilk on that day.

Gaṇeśa kriyā (Basic purification)

Dip the index finger of the left hand in castor oil. Immerse it about one inch deep in the rectum and turn it on all sides for excretion of stool. Wash the hands and repeat it again the same way. In this way, remove the entire quantity of excreta left in the rectum. This process is done after passing the bowel only. The fingers should not have out grown nails. Cut the nails with the nail cutter and smoothen it nicely.

Benefits: This action strengthens the internal and external muscles of the rectum, which prevents constipation, etc. The remaining stool left in the rectum, after passing the bowels, can be taken out easily with this action, so one does not suffer from piles etc. This activity is extremely beneficial for the patients suffering from piles. They should do this exercise everyday.

3. Basṭi

Sucking the water or air through the rectum opening and purifying the large intestine is called *Basṭi*. It is of two types- *Jal Basṭi* and *Pavan Basṭi*. To learn this process, it is necessary to attain expertise in *nōuli maḍhyamā, uḍḍiyāna banḍha,* and *vāma-Dakṣiṇa nōuli.*

(a) *Jal-Baṣti*

Method:

- Stand in clean water, which is up to the navel level, and then perform this activity. This action can also be done by filling a large water tub and sitting in *Utkaṭāsana*.
- Sit in *Utkaṭāsana* and take a 6-7 inches long, half inch round wooden tube with a hole. Both the edges of the stick should be smoothened and rounded off with some lubricating liquid, and inserted in the anus. The other end of the stick should remain submerged in the water.
- Exhale and perform *madhyamā nōuli while doing uḍḍiyāna baṇdha and mūla baṇdha.* Thus, the water will get sucked till such a time that you do not breath.
- Before inhaling, close the other end of the stick with the finger. Again exhale and suck the water as before. Repeating this for 5-6 times will fill the large intestine with enough water.
- Now remove the stick, stand up and do *nōuli* action. With this the water will spread in the intestine and clean it.
- When *nōuli* is turned from the right side there will be a desire to pass the bowels, and then pass the bowels.
- This process can be done without the wooden pipe by standing in the water as mentioned before and doing *uḍḍiyāna baṇdha* and *mūla baṇdha* and suck the water upwards. When these are performed properly the anus opening becomes wide automatically and the water gets sucked in. Add a little lime-juice in the water. This process should be done in the morning, after passing bowels.

Benefits:

- *Baṣti* purifies the large intestine, which cures constipation, etc. The heat of the stomach is removed, which cures diseases relating to semen like night-fall, etc. This action is more beneficial than enema. In enema, water is passed inside with pressure, so in this case, the large intestine remains inactive. It results in the expansion and weakening of the large intestine. However, in *Baṣti,* the intestine sucks water on its own strength, which enables strengthening of the intestine instead of weakening it.

(b) *Pavan-Baṣti*

Method:

Sit on the feet, and as mentioned before, exhale and perform *mūla bandha, uḍḍiyāna baṇdha* and *madhyamā nōuli,* air will get sucked inside. In this way, sucking air inside and then throwing it out is called *Pavan Baṣti.*

Benefits:

- Same as detailed above. But in the previous case i.e., *Jal Baṣti* process, stool comes out, while in this case, only polluted air comes out. Therefore this process is beneficial for wind related problems and piles. It also increases the power of digestion.

4. *Trāṭaka*

Method:

- Sit in any one of the meditative positions namely *Padmāsana*, *Siddhāsana,* etc.
- Light a *dīyā* of *ghēe* and keep it at a distance of 3-4 feet in front of the eyes. If *ghēe* is not available mustard oil can be used.
- Now without blinking, set your gaze at the flame. *Dīyā* should be kept at a place where air movement is negligible.
- When tears start pouring out or the eyes start burning, stop gazing. If tears start rolling, then after some time, dip your head and eyes in a vessel containing cold water and open your eyes. Fill water in your mouth and open and close your eyes in the vessel. This will remove the burning sensation of the eyes. The duration of practice should be increased gradually. If the practice lasts three hours, then the results are miraculous. This also creates different types of *yogic* accomplishments. The time spent for gazing at the flame (known as external *Trāṭaka*) should match the time that we should spend remembering the Supreme Soul, God, while concentrating on the light of *Divya* between the eyebrows. This enables accomplishment of *Ḍhārṇa,* which, further enables entry into the state of *Ḍhyān.* This activity can also be done by marking a black spot on a white paper. *Trāṭaka* is also done by gazing at the Moon and the rising Sun. The guidance of an expert should be taken in order to fully accomplish this activity.

Benefits:

- This eliminates the instability of the mind, which gives easy entry into the field of Yogic stages.
- It improves the eyesight.
- You don't see dreams when *Trāṭaka* is performed in the evening on a flame of *Divya* and even if the dreams come they are very few in number. Therefore, *Trāṭaka* gives happiness of a sound sleep and protects from bad dreams.

5. *Nōuli*

Madhyamā Nōuli :

Method:

- Stand up keeping a distance of one to one and a half-foot between the feet, with the hands on the knees. Press the knees with the hands. Look at the ground.

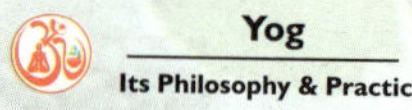

- It is difficult to perform *nōuli* in the beginning therefore firstly *Agnisāra kriyā* must be done in order to gain expertise in performing *nōuli*. Exhale fully and pull the stomach inwards to such an extent that the stomach touches the back. Then push the stomach out. Repeat this exercise according to your capacity. This will soften the stomach and help in doing *nōuli* process.
- Now for doing *nōuli*, keep bending as before. While pressing the knees, contract the stomach from both sides and pushing out the center portion, try to push out both the muscles in the front.
- When you feel like inhaling, inhale and then again repeat the exercise, as done earlier.

Vāma Nōuli:

Method:

- Stand as in the previous position and perform *madhyamā nōuli*. When *nōuli*comes in the center, bending to left put pressure on the left hand, this will bring forward the left large muscle of the stomach. The right side should remain relaxed, in this case.

Vāma Nōuli

Dakṣiṇa Nōuli:

Method:

- *Dakṣiṇa (right) nōuli* is similar to *vāma nauli*, and the process is also similar to left *nōuli*.

Nauli Circulation:

Method:

- When *nauli* has been performed in both directions, then push the *nōuli* out and massage the thighs with both hands, i.e. move the palms on the thighs up and down. When you do this, you will notice that the *nōuli* starts rotating from right to left. Learning it may take some time. After doing from the right side, do it from the other side.

Benefits:

- *Haṭha-yoga Pradīpikā* describes *nōuli* action to be the best among all the activities. ***"Haṭha-kriyā mauliriyaṃ ca Nauliḥ "***
- It definitely cures dyspepsia, constipation, gas, diarrhoea, sprue-syndrome, obesity of the abdomen, etc.
- It is also beneficial in gynecological problems, painful menstruation, etc.
- This is an important activity for *kuṇḍalinī yog*, which enables the union of *ṗrāna-apān.*

Caution: People suffering from slip-disc, heart problem and ulcer, should not attempt this activity.

6. *Kapāla-bhāti:*

Method:

- Sit in *Padmāsana* or *Siddhāsana* and keep both the hands on the knees. Inhale and push the lower portion of the navel area towards the backside repeatedly, while it automatically bulges out. In the end, exhale completely and do *mahā banḍha*. Repeat this activity as before. In one minute, 60 pushes should be given. Later on it can be increased to 120 times. For a beginner, 25-30 pushes per minute are sufficient.

Benefits:

- This exercise is the purifier of the forehead, hence known as *Kapāla-bhāti*. '*Bhā dīptau*' means one, which provides luster to the forehead. It is beneficial for the lungs and heart. Complete digestive system including liver, intestines and pancreas, etc become healthy and the blood circulation increases.

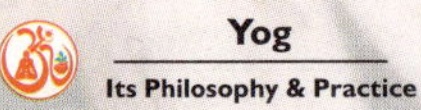

Chapter on *Mudrās*

In the practice of yog (*yog-sādhana*), in addition to the eight steps of *yog* (*aṣṭāṅga-yog*), Mudrās are also very important. *Mudrās* are the developed forms of *āsanas*. In *āsanas*, senses are primary and *prāṇa* is secondary, whereas in *Mudrās* senses are secondary and *prāṇas* are primary. The scriptures have described the importance of *Mudrās* and it is said that:

"Nāsti Mudrā-samaṃ kiñcit siddhidaṃ kṣiti-maṇḍale "

which means there is no other action on this earth gives the same results as of *mudrā*. For convenience, various *Mudrās* are being described under two categories:

- Hand *Mudrās* that regulate the elements.
- *Mudrās* that help in awakening the *kuṇḍalinī* and elevating the *prānas*.

Hand *Mudrās* that regulate the elements

This whole universe has been constituted by five elements. Our body has also been made from the union of five elements. The five fingers in our hand represent the five elements. The thumb represent fire, index finger air, middle finger space, ring finger earth and the little finger water. The body remains healthy if the five elements are in balance whereas any disturbance in this balance results in diseases. According to the science of *Mudrās,* the coordinated action of these five elements controls the internal glands, body parts and their functions are regulated and the dormant powers of the body are awakened.

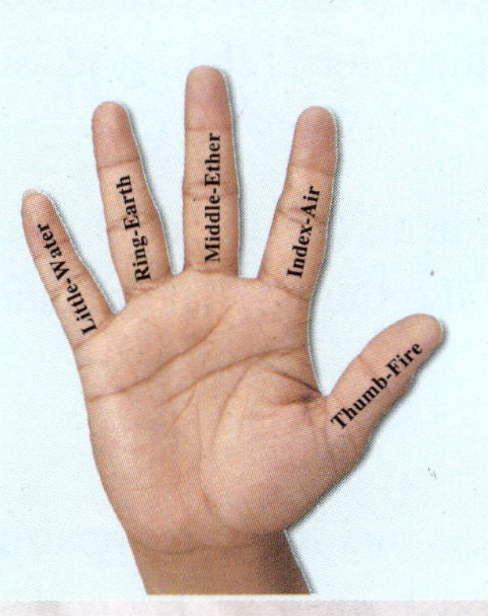

The hand *muḍrās* become effective instantly. The hand by which these *Muḍrās* are made, the part of the body opposite to it starts showing signs of effect immediately. These *Mudrās* can be performed in any way- while standing, sitting or walking. It is more beneficial to perform them sitting in *Vajrāsana*, *Padmāsana* or *Sukhāsana.* Practising these *Muḍrās* daily for 10 minutes in the beginning and later on doing them for 30-45 minutes will give complete benefit. If you cannot do them at a stretch then do them in 2-3 installments. While performing any *Muḍrā*, the fingers that are not being used, should be kept straight.

1. ***Ḉyān or Dhyāna Mudrā*:** Touch the tips of the thumb and the index finger with each other, keeping the remaining three fingers straight.

Benefits:

- It helps develop the stages of *Ḍhārṇa* and meditation. Concentration improves and negative thoughts get reduced.
- It increases the memory power, therefore, its regular practice makes the children become intelligent and bright.
- The brain nerves become strong. Headache, insomnia, and stress are removed. It destroys anger. For better results, perform *prāṅa mudrā* after this *mudrā*.

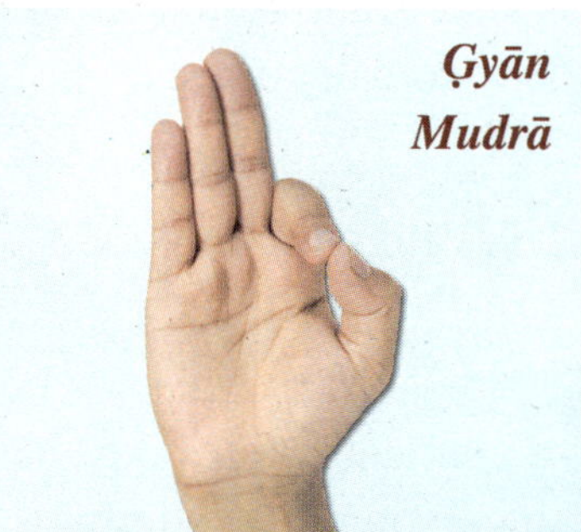

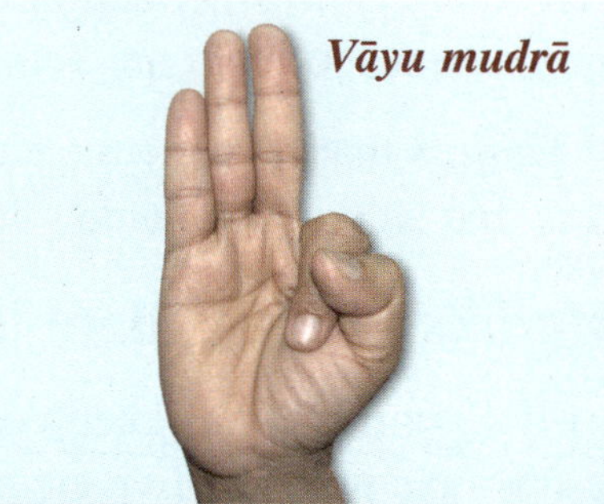

2. ***Vāyu mudrā*:** Joining the index finger with the root of the thumb and putting slight pressure on it with the thumb results in *vāyu mudrā*. The remaining three fingers should be kept straight.

Benefits:

- Regular practice of this *mudrā* eliminates all *vāyu* related problems - gout, arthritis, joints pain, paralysis, parkinson, sciatica, knee pain and gas formation like diseases. Provides relief in the pain of the neck and spine. The disorders relating to blood circulation are removed.

3. ***Śūnya mudrā* :** The middle finger represents the space element, this finger is touched at the root of the thumb and light pressure applied with the thumb. The remaining fingers should be kept straight.

Benefits:

- This *mudrā* cures secretion from the ears, ear pain, deafness and hearing impairment problem, etc. if practiced at least one hour daily, continuously over a long period. It cures weakness of bones and heart diseases. The gums become strong and benefit is obtained in throat diseases and thyroid problems.

Precaution: Do not do this *mudrā* while eating and strolling.

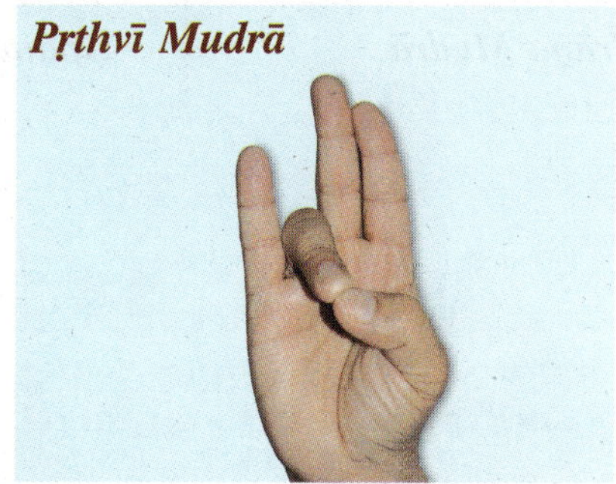

4. ***Pṛthvī Mudrā*:** Join the tips of ring finger and thumb and keep the remaining three fingers straight, this makes *Pṛthvī mudrā*.

Benefits:

- Regular practice of this *mudrā* cures weakness of the body, leanness (underweight), and obesity etc. This *mudrā* improves digestive power, develops vitality and *sattvic* qualities, and removes the deficiency of vitamins. It makes the body active, bright and glowing.

5. ***Prāṇa Mudrā*:** This *mudrā* is made by touching the tips of the little finger, the ring finger and the thumb. The remaining two fingers should be kept straight.

Benefits:

- This *mudrā* enables awakening of *prāṇa śhakṭi* lying dormant, and the body becomes active, healthy and energetic. It cures eye problems and improves the eyesight. It enhances body's immunity to diseases, removes the deficiency of vitamins, and removes fatigue as also rejuvenates the body. Due to this there is no problem of hunger and thirst during long hours of fasting. In case of insomnia, it provides benefits if done in conjunction with *Jñāna mudrā*.

6. ***Apāna Mudrā*:** This *mudrā* is made by touching the tips of the thumb, the ring finger and the middle finger and keeping the remaining two fingers straight.

Benefits:

- Any foreign matter in the body gets thrown out and the body is purified. Practicing this *mudrā* cures constipation, piles, vāta-doṣa, diabetes, obstructions in passing urine, problems related to the kidneys, teeth troubles, etc. it is a beneficial *mudrā* for the stomach. It helps in heart related problems and causes perspiration.

Precaution: This *mudrā* is diuretic.

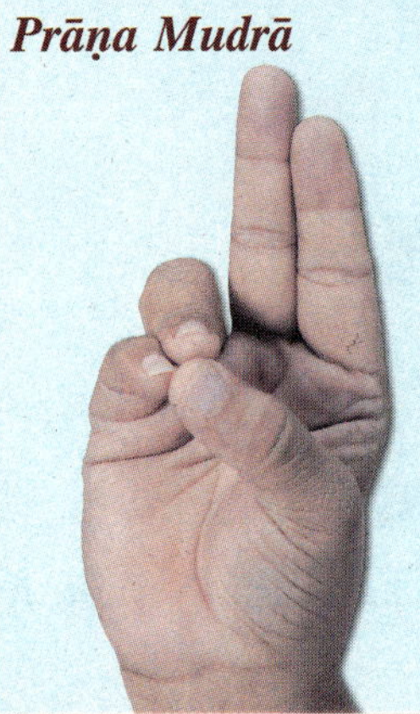
Prāṇa Mudrā

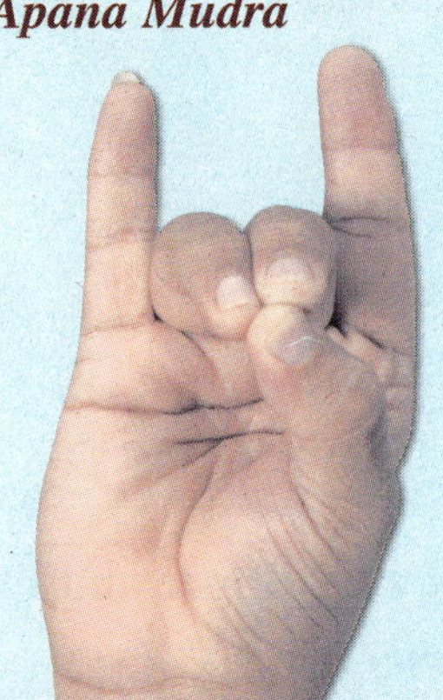
Apāna Mudrā

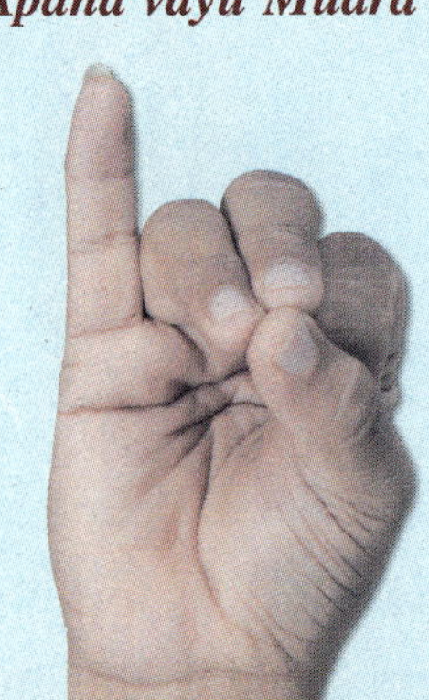
Apāna vāyu Mudrā

7. ***Apāna vāyu Mudrā*:** Performing *Apāna mudrā* and *Vāyu mudrā* together is known as *Apāna-vāyu mudrā*. The little finger remains straight.

Benefits:

- It cures heart and *vāta-doṣa* related problems and makes the body healthier. Those who are suffering from a weak heart should practice it daily. In the event of a heart attack, performing this *mudrā* gives relief. It releases any gas accumulated in the stomach. It is beneficial in headache, asthma and high blood pressure. Performing this *mudrā* 5-7 minutes before climbing up the stairs provides comfort.

8. ***Sūrya Mudrā*:** Keep the tip of the ring finger at the root of the thumb and press it with the thumb.

Benefits:

- This *mudrā* balances the body, reduces weight and obesity and increases heat in the body, which helps in proper digestion. It reduces stress, enhancement in body strength, and reduction of cholesterol content in the blood. Practicing this *mudrā* cures diabetes and liver problems.

Caution: This *mudrā* should not be performed by a weak person. Do not perform it for longer periods during summer time.

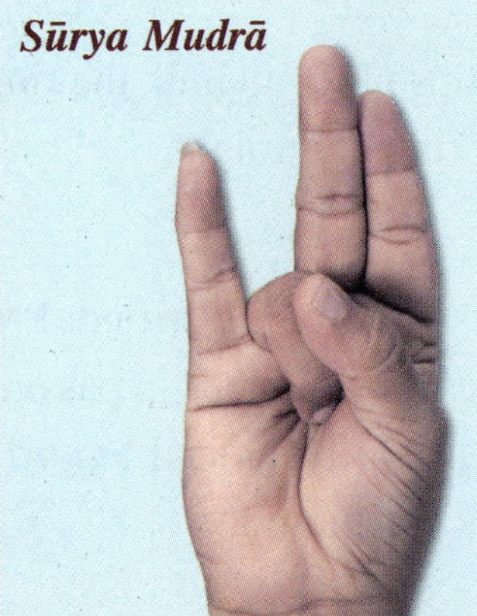
Sūrya Mudrā

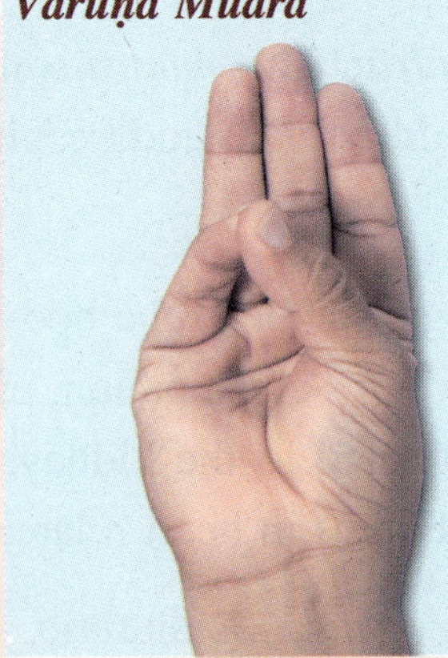
Varuṇa Mudrā

9. *Varuṇa Mudrā* : Touch the little finger with the thumb.

Benefits:

- This *mudrā* removes dryness of the body and makes the skin soft and shinning. It cures skin diseases, blood disorders, pimples, and diseases arising out of deficiency of the water element. It makes the face beautiful.

Caution: People having *kapha-prakṛtī* (constitution) should not practice it in excess.

10. *Liṅga Mudrā*: Interlock the fingers as shown in the picture and keep the thumb of the left hand upright.

Liṅga Mudrā

Benefits:

- This *mudrā* increases heat in the body. It is beneficial in cold-catarrh, asthma- cough, sinusitis, paralysis, and low blood pressure. This dries the phlegm.

Precaution: While practicing it consume plenty of water, fruit, fruit juices, *ghēe* and milk. Do not practice this for unduly long duration.

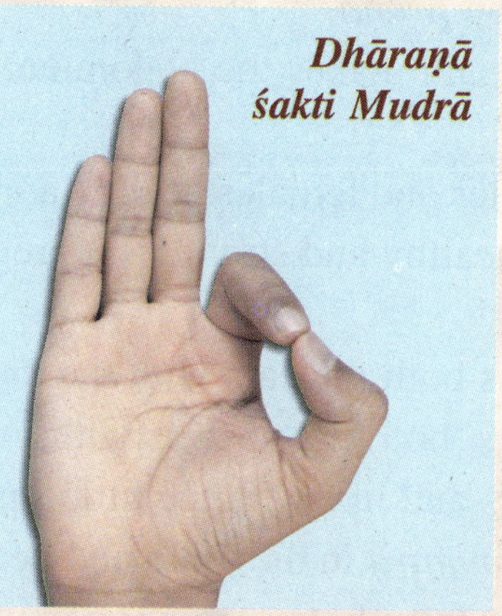
Dhāraṇā śakti Mudrā

11. *Dhāraṇā śakti Mudrā*: This *mudrā* enables us to retain our breath in the lungs for a longer time. When you do *pūraka* (inhaling), then press the first part (upper most portion) of the thumb with the tip of the index finger. This helps in performing internal *kuṃbhaka* for a longer time. If you press the middle portion of the thumb then *kuṃbhaka* can be done for still longer time. In case the root of the thumb (part-3) is similarly pressed then *kuṃbhaka* can be done for a very long time, easily.

Benefits:

- More *prāṇa vayu* is available by retaining the breath in the lungs for a longer time, blood and body will become stronger and the total amount of air breathed in and exhaled during the whole day can be reduced to a large extent, which increases longevity.

Mudrās helpful in *kuṇḍalinī-jāgaraṇa* and upward movement of *prāṇa*

1. ***Bhūcarī mudrā*:** Sitting in *Padmāsana* or *Siddhāsana* or in any other meditative *asana* and looking in the open sky, at a distance of roughly three inches from the nose tip and stabilizing the mind is *Bhūcarī mudrā*.

Benefits:

- It increases concentration and makes the mind suitable for meditation.

2. ***Khecarī Mudrā***: Folding the tongue in the reverse side and touching the palate is called *Khecarī Mudrā*. This *mudrā* should be practised under the guidance of an instructor.

Benefits:

- In *yog śhaṣṭras* the benefits of this *mudrā* have been described copiously. In the *yog* tradition, it is considered that regular practice of this *mudrā* enables the *yogi* start getting the taste of the nectar. With the practice of *Khecarī Mudrā*, the nectar juice (sweet juice) is secreted from the nectar gland. The practitioner does not feel hungry, thirsty and sleepy.

3. ***Aśvinī Mudrā***: Sitting in *Padmāsana* or *Vajrāsana* or any other meditative *āsana,* contracting and expanding the anus is called *Aśvinī mudrā*. This can be practiced while lying, sitting, or in any other position, at any time, anywhere (however on an empty stomach). Performing this *mudrā* after doing *bāhya kumbhaka* is more beneficial. Begin with 20-25 times and increase it to 50-100 times.

Benefits:

- It is beneficial in celibacy and upward movement of the *prāṇa*.
- It cures gas, constipation, piles and urinary problems and makes the abdominal area healthy.
- Practicing this *mudrā* makes the sex organs of both males and females healthy and free from any disease. The uterus of the females remains healthy and strong. If a pregnant woman practices it then the delivery is comfortable.

4. ***Yoni Mudrā***: Sit in *Siddhāsana* and inhale. Now press both the ears with the thumbs of both the hands, both the eyes with the index fingers, both the nostrils with middle fingers, both the holes of the nose with the ring fingers and lips with the little fingers. In this way close all the openings and chant *Oṃ-kāra manṭra* in the mind and keeping the mind stable, resolve firmly that the energy is rising from below, moving upwards, piercing through the *chakrās* is reaching The Lotus having thousands of petals. This is also called *Parāṅgmukhī mudrā*.

Benefits:

- The *prāṇa* and *Apāna vāyu* combine together to help awaken the *kuṇḍalinī*. The condition of appearance of the *cakras* evolves and divine light is sighted.

5. ***Unmanī Mudrā***: Sit in *Padmāsana* and look in between the eyebrows and concentrate in the *ājñā cakrā*. Do not allow any thoughts to come to your mind and concentrate only on the *Ājñā cakrā*.

Benefits:

- This *mudrā* is very helpful in concentration of the mind and meditation. The mind and all the senses become still, results into *pratyāhār* (withdrawal of the senses from respective sense objects) condition and stillness of the intellect, leading to the state of establishing *samādhi*. The light of knowledge emerges and one feels attaining of *Riṭaṃbhrā Prajya*.

6. ***Śakti-cālinī Mudrā*:** Just as the urinary organ is pulled inside to stop the urge of urination, in the same way, sitting in *Vajrāsana* and pulling inwards and releasing the urinary organ is called *Śakti cālinī Mudrā*. In the beginning it should be done 20-25 times and slowly increased to 50-100 times regularly.

Benefits:

- Laziness, carelessness and stupidity are cured. Upward movement of the *prāṇa* takes place soon and the *kuṇḍlinī* awakens resulting in opening of the path of *cakās-vigyan*. Practice of this *mudrā* by females keeps their reproductive organs- uterus, etc. strong and healthy.

7. ***Vīparīta-karaṇī Mudrā*:** Lie straight on your back. Join both the legs and lift them up keeping them straight and raise your back with the support of the hands. With both feet and the legs touching, do not raise them straight pointing to the roof but slightly lowered. In *Sarvāṅgāsana* the legs are raised at 90 degrees straight. Whereas in this *mudrā* the legs are approximately at an angle of 45 degrees as in the position of *Ardha-sarvāṅgāsana*. Then perform *jālandhara baṇdha* and concentrate your sight at the thumbs of the feet. Breathe normally. Begin with 1 minute and then slowly increase the duration of practice to 10 minutes.

Vīparīta-karaṇī Mudrā

Benefits:

- Regular practice of this exercise, all the benefits of *Sarvāṅgāsana* become available, the digestive system is strengthened. Appetite increases, the body remains healthy, the face remains bright and premature graying of hair is prevented. Intellectual power increases. All the diseases like swelling of the feet, early swelling in case of filaria, goiter, blood related diseases like boils, pimples, itching, etc are cured. Its special use can be made in *Sāṇkhya Prakṣhālan* when during the activity, water does not flow out of the anus, then application of this *āsana* enables quicker movement of water from small intestine to the large intestine and water starts coming out slowly, which cleans the stomach.

8. ***Yoga mudrā*:** Its practice helps maintain the body healthy, happy, fit-n-fine, and flexible. Nerves are purified and the *prāna śhakti* improves. The inner-self is purified. It helps in the attainment of stages of *Dhāraṇā, Dhyāna,* and *samādhi*. For the method and picture, please refer *Yoga-Mudrāsna* 1 and 2, given on page 52.

9. ***Mahamudrā*:** Keep the left heel in the space between the anus and the genitals firmly and stretch the right leg. Then gradually, along with *pūraka* perform *mūla baṇdha* and *jālandhara baṇdha* and hold the thumb of the right toe and place it firmly on the left knee and perform *kumbhaka* as per capacity. The breath inhaled during *kumbhaka* needs to be expanded in the *koshta* and imagine that the *prāṇa* is awakening the *kuṇḍalinī* and entering into the *Suśhumna nāḍī*. After that, lift the forehead from the knee and while doing *rechaka* (exhaling) slowly, go back to the original position. In the same way repeat it with the other foot. Increase the number and duration of *prāṇāyāma.*

Benefits:

- According to *Gorakṣ* system, diseases like tuberculosis, leprosy, boils around the anus, indigestion and other stomach problems and even gonorrhoea are cured by practicing this *mudrā*. Practicing this for a longer time helps the *prāṇas* to enter *suśhumna,* their upward movement and awakening of *kuṇḍalinī.*

10. ***Tribaṇdha Mudrā*:** Sit in *Padmāsana* do *pūraka* and mix the outgoing breath with the *saman-prān* and lift the *apān-prān* from the *mūladhār* and while performing *jālandhara baṇdha, uḍḍiyāna baṇdha and mūla baṇdha* try to push the internal air into *sushumna*. Remaining in this position, place the palms on the floor on both sides of the body, raise and lower the hips slowly on the floor. Repeat it several times.

Benefits:

- The *prāṇa* starts entering the *Suṣumṇā naḍī* soon. The *kuṇḍalinī* awakens quickly and starts moving upwards, the *cakrās* also start enlightening slowly.

11. ***Brahma Mudrā*:** Sit in *Vajrāsana*, rotate the neck, head and shoulders up-down, right-left, and in a circular motion in both directions. Repeat each exercise 5-10 times.

Benefits:

- Vertigo, cervical spondylitis and stiffness and pain in the neck are cured. With the practice of this *mudrā*, throat problems do not occur, headache is cured and the nerve-cells of the brain become strong.

12. *Agnisāra kriyā*: Sit in *Vajrāsana* or stand up and exhale and move the stomach inwards and outwards. Till such a time that you can do *bāhya kumbhaka,* contract and expand the entire abdominal area. Repeat it at about 20-40 times. Do not move the shoulders. Take and release long and deep breath 4-5 times and again repeat the above exercise in the same way. Perform this entire activity 4-5 times or as per your capacity.

Benefits:

- Indigestion does not take place even after sitting in *sādhnā* for a long time. The digestion takes place smoothly. It cures all stomach related problems like constipation, gas, belching ulcer, etc. It increases appetite.
- Obesity, diabetes and urinary problem are cured. Burning sensation in the urine gets reduced. This activity also stops excessive urination.

Acupressure Treatment

The system of putting pressure, as prescribed, on the special points located in the human body, to cure the disease is called *acupressure*. The meaning of the word acupressure means pressure. Putting requisite pressure on the specified special points, different diseases are cured miraculously by this system.

Principle of Acupressure

According to this system, every disease is cured by treating the body as a single unit comprising of the physical and emotional forms. In acupressure system, from physical and emotional point of view, the human body is considered to be an integral unit

The second important principle is that all the main centers of the blood circulating nerves, nervous system and glands are located in the palms and soles of the feet. In this system, pressure is exerted on the pressure points located at different parts and from there the energy is circulated to all the nerves, nervous system and glands, which get energized and cured. Unbalanced-uncontrolled food, laziness-carelessness and violation of rules related to sleep and celibacy result in the accumulation of foreign matter in the body and absence of the *āsana* and *prāṇāyāma* etc., the organs and the muscles start becoming weak and the bones of the hands-feet and the spine start shifting from their positions. Functional activity of the entire nervous system slows down. Blood circulation in the body-parts is reduced. The chemical elements, toxic substances, foreign matter deposited in the blood, start accumulating around displaced joints. The more the number of such accumulations the more is the number of diseases that start erupting in the body. As soon as the functioning of the body parts decline, the related pressure points located on the palms and the soles of the feet also start getting blocked and some kind of minute chemical crystals deposit on the points, due to which there is improper blood circulation in the related parts. With acupressure, pressure is applied on those points so that the crystal deposits are destroyed, which regulates blood circulation and the affected parts become healthy. According to another point of view, our body is a combination of five elements. These five elements - earth, fire, wind, water and space/sky are regulated by an electrical force, which is called bio-electricity or bio-energy. According to the famous acupressure practitioner F.M.Thestan (The Healing Benefits of Acupressure), all those points located in the hands, feet and various parts of the body which when pressed cause pain, energy of the related part leaks out of the body from these points. As a result, the concerned body parts develop some defect or disease. When we apply pressure on these points, leakage of electricity stops. With the stoppage of leakage, circulation of the electrical force in the related body parts becomes normal and the defects or diseases developed in the body parts are cured.

Main effects of Acupressure on the human body

- With the acupressure system the foreign matter is removed out of the body and necessary elements are produced by the internal immune system.
- This method, by awakening the electrical forces of the body, produces power, energy and activeness.
- It creates flexibility in all the muscular tissues of the body.
- It cures the deformities (pain, etc) in the bone system and the spine which is an important part of the human body.
- Acupressure completely helps in removing the deformities of the nervous system.
- With this system, functioning of all endocrine glands like thyroid, pituitary, pineal, pancreas, etc can be regulated.
- With acupressure, adequate improvement in the normal functioning of the internal organs of the body can be brought about.

Acupressure - Indian Knowledge

Acupressure is the improved version of the ancient Indian deep massage system, which means curing the diseases by putting pressure on hands, feet, face and some special centers of the body. Knowledge of acupressure has not been imported in India from China or any other country. In fact, Chinese travelers who came to visit India took the ancient Indian *Āyurvedic* texts with them to China and propagated to the whole world that acupressure was their own science. It is unfortunate to accept this science as of foreign origin. Acupressure has extensive description in the Indian texts. It is imperative to know why the Indian women have been wearing for ages anklets, toe-rings, bangles, pendants, lockets, *ṭīkā* (ornament put on the forehead), earrings, nose-pins, etc? Men and women have been wearing rings in their fingers for a long time. All this has been possible as a result of acupressure only.

Treatment of major diseases with acupressure

Even though acupressure has a special utility in all the diseases, it is a harmless system and can be adopted along with other systems of medication. But few diseases, which can be successfully treated with acupressure, are, as described below:

- World Health Organization (WHO) has accepted the utility of acupressure and acupuncture systems of treatment and found them more effective in the treatment of all problems related to spine-sciatica, cervical-spondylitis, etc, frozen shoulders, pain in the knees, bed wetting, ulcer, dysentery, constipation, headache, migraine, deformity of nerves and veins, gas formation, acidity, swelling and pain in the throat, tonsils, sinusitis, bronchitis, asthma, eyes, ear and throat diseases, tooth-ache, paralysis and meniere's disease, etc.

- The acupressure treatment system has been successfully used on thousands of patients at the *Brahmakalpa* Hospital managed by the ashram, to cure the above-mentioned diseases. Many times the patients have been benefited with astonishing results. In cases of severe cervical spondylitis, where the patients were unable to even move their necks, we have treated them to full recovery within 5-10 minutes. Age-old chronic shoulder pain, in which case it was not possible to even move or raise the hand, it was completely cured within 5-10 minutes. In our opinion, in all types of bodily pains, joint-pain, backache or deformities of nerves and veins etc, acupressure gives relief so fast that cannot be achieved by any other system.

- Even in case of heart pain, acupressure gives quick relief and blockage in the arteries or any other problem can be cured by acupressure.

- This system is also effective in cases of stomach problems, diabetes and brain related ailments.

- Along with curing the diseases, acupressure is found to be very useful in disease-diagnosis. With this system, by applying pressure on different reflex centers, it can be found easily as to which parts of the body or glands are not performing their work properly. Many a times, diagnostic tests carried out in the laboratories are also unable to detect the exact cause of the disease. In such a situation, by testing the reflex centers, it can be found out within seconds as to what part of the body is suffering from which type of ailment. Therefore, in this situation, the reflex centers are also called the mirrors of the diseases.

Examination of the reflex centers and method of applying pressure

- Acupressure can be performed with the help of the thumbs, fingers, or any other suitable equipment made of wood or plastic, etc as per the convenience.
- Do not put either excessive or very little pressure on the points, instead, pressure should be applied using reasonable force. While doing this, if anybody feels unbearable pain at the pressure points, then it should be understood that the part related to that reflex center suffers from any defect or disease. Those reflex centers which when pressed do not cause excessive pain; imply the corresponding parts are healthy.
- When pressure is applied on the reflex centers, the crystals of toxins and foreign matter deposited in the arteries of the hands and the feet slowly leave their place moving with the blood flow and finally leave the body through sweat or the kidney system. For this reason, while doing acupressure, after pressing the desired points, in the end the reflex centers of both kidneys should definitely be pressed for 1-2 minutes. With the pressure as the crystals leave their place the gravity of the disease also gets reduced in the same manner. As the intensity of the disease reduces, the pain at the reflex centers due to pressure also gets reduced and the patient himself also experiences relief in the disease. After doing it regularly for a few days, the disease is cured completely and the pain due to application of pressure either does not remain or is reduced considerably.
- In most of the patients at the beginning, when reflex centers are pressed and the crystals start leaving from their place, those points experience severe pain or even swelling. In this situation one should not worry as this a natural phenomena. When this happens, fomentation with lukewarm water mixed with salt should be done on those points, which relieves the pain and swelling.

Time of Acupressure

Normally acupressure can be done at anytime. However if acupressure is to be applied for stomach, intestines, liver and pancreas, etc then it should be done on empty stomach or two to three hours after the meals. After the meals since the entire body's energy is being utilised in digesting the food, hence performing acupressure before meals is the best. Incase of taking small amount of milk or fruit, after a short gap, acupressure can be done.

Duration of Pressure

Depending upon the type of disease, pressure on the specified points should be applied from 30 seconds to 2 minutes at each reflex center. While applying pressure on any point, full care should be taken about the tolerance of the patient else many a times the patient may also faint. The same point should not be continuously pressed. Instead turn-by-turn different points should be pressed in rotation. Normally pressure should be applied twice a day in the morning and evening. Incase of excessive pain, acupressure can also be applied thrice a day.

Number of Pressure Points

Chenchuyu Su Eh (Modern Acupressure) authored by Dr. *Chu Li Yen* is considered to be the most authentic text published on this subject in China. This includes a list of 669 acupressure points. In some other charts, 1000 acupressure points have been shown. However in daily application, mainly around 100 points are of greater important.

The acupressure points (healing centers) situated in different parts of the body that are useful in various diseases have been shown in the pictures that follow. These pictures have been compiled (with thanks) from a book called "Natural Acupressure Treatment" written by Dr. *Atar Singh.*

Width-wise division of body in three parts

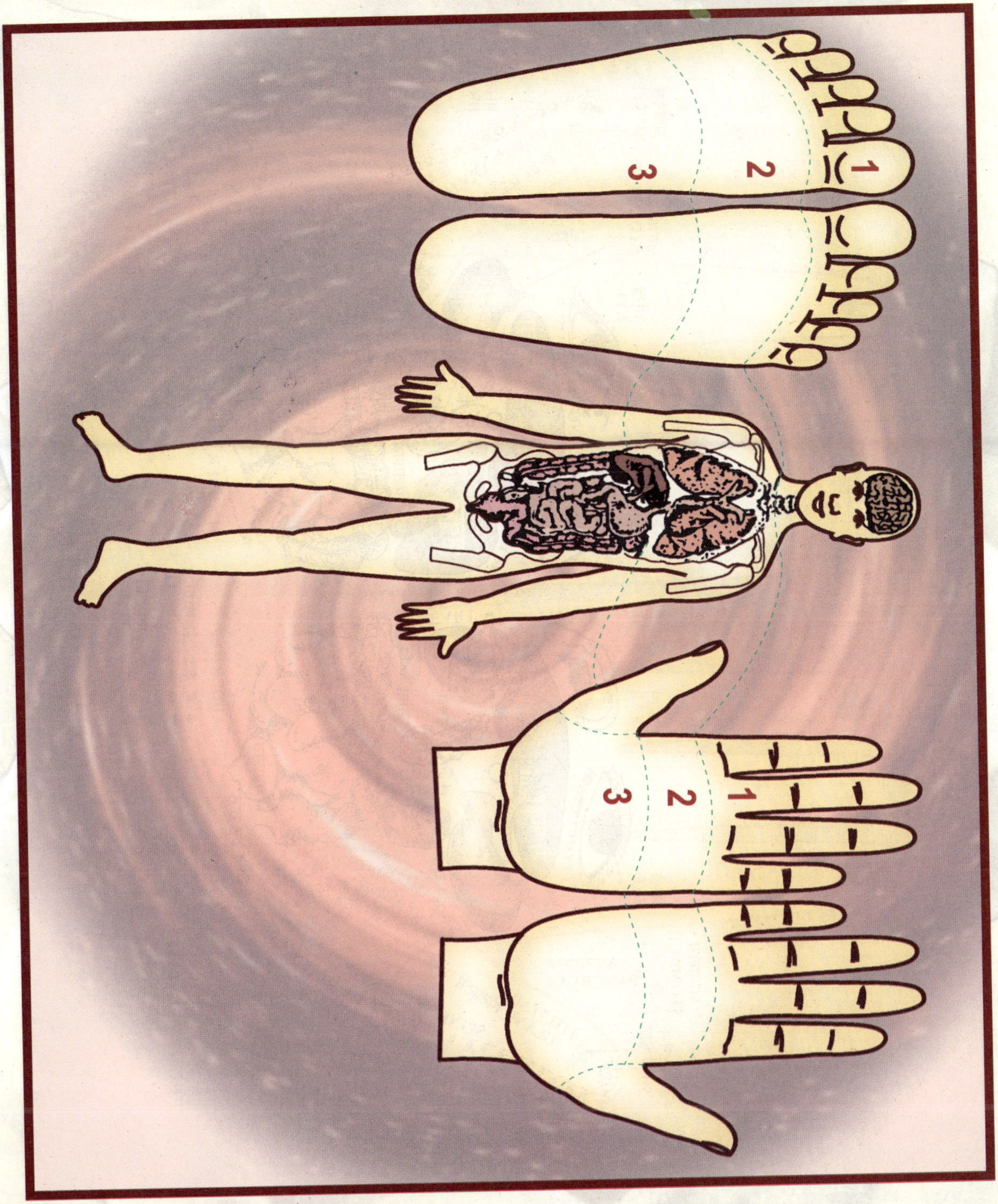

Main pressure points of acupressure located in hands

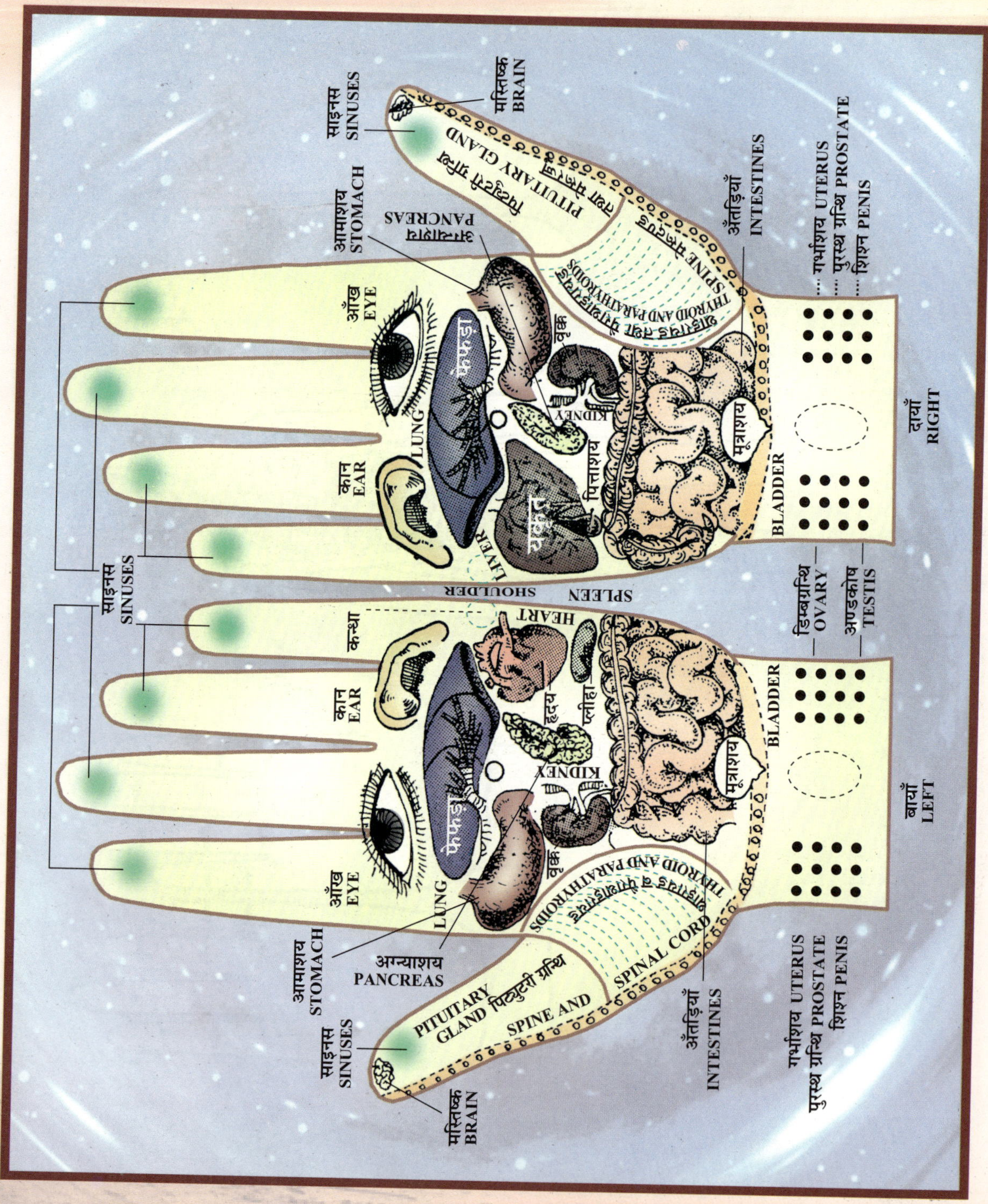

Main pressure points of acupressure located in feet

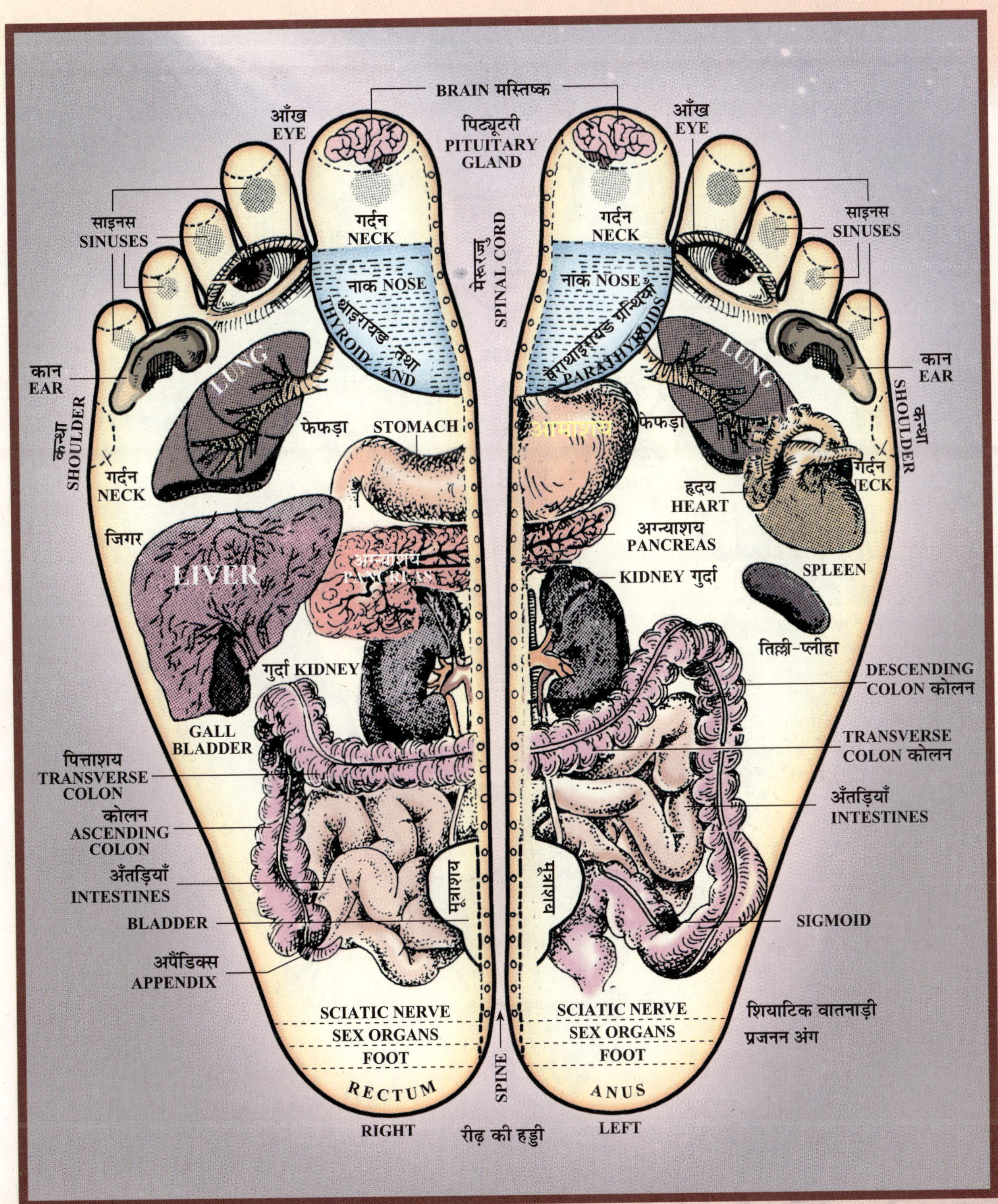

Brain, nervous system, spinal cord, sinuses, voice, eyes, ears, neck, throat, shoulders, hips, knees and legs related pressure points in feet and hands

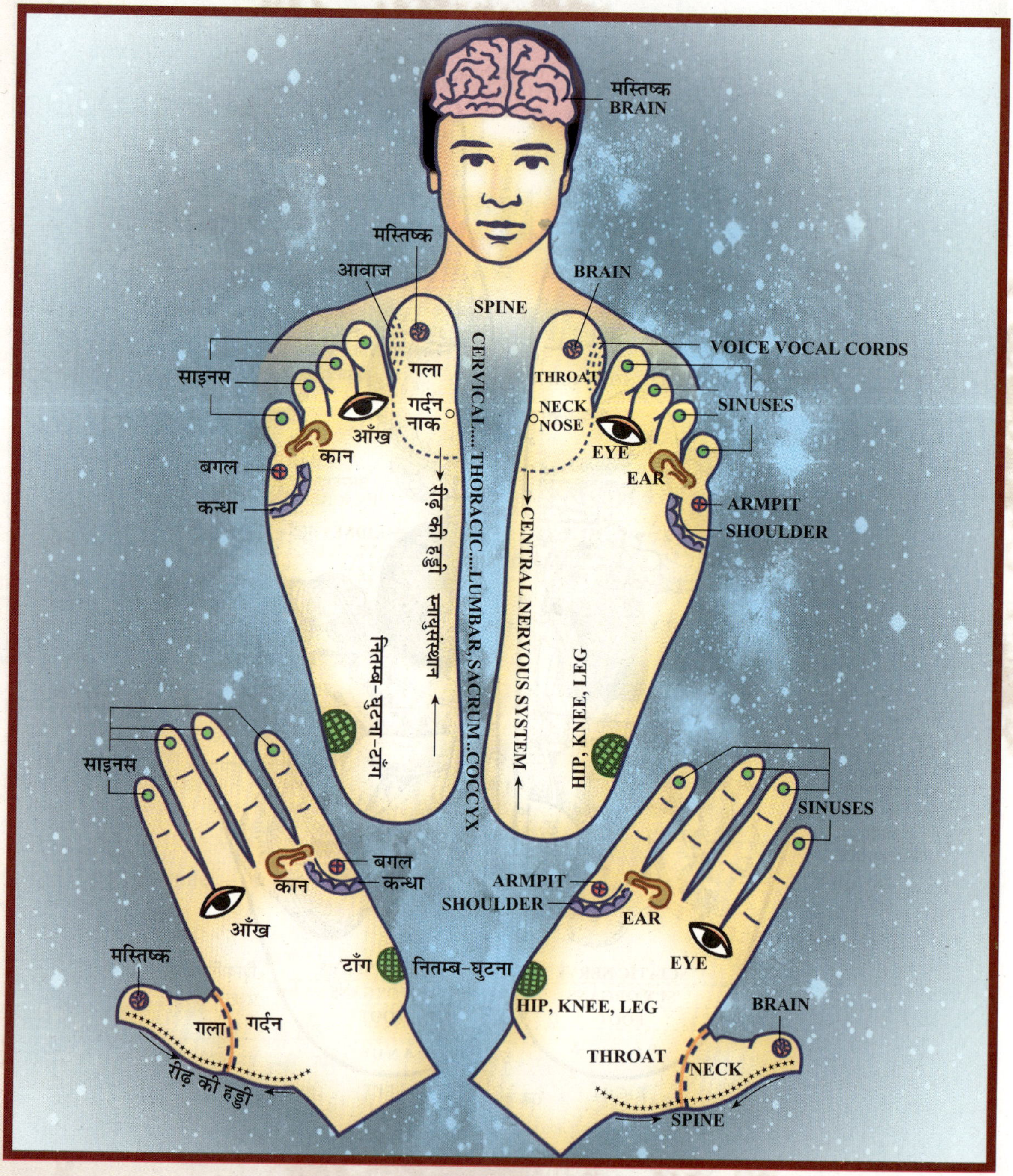

मस्तिष्क
BRAIN
मस्तिष्क
आवाज
SPINE
BRAIN
VOICE VOCAL CORDS
साइनस
गला
THROAT
SINUSES
गर्दन
नाक
NECK
NOSE
आँख
कान
EYE
EAR
बगल
ARMPIT
कन्धा
SHOULDER
CERVICAL.... THORACIC....LUMBAR, SACRUM..COCCYX
रीढ़ की हड्डी
स्नायुसंस्थान
CENTRAL NERVOUS SYSTEM
नितम्ब-घुटना-टाँग
HIP, KNEE, LEG
साइनस
SINUSES
बगल
कन्धा
कान
ARMPIT
SHOULDER
EAR
आँख
EYE
मस्तिष्क
टाँग
नितम्ब-घुटना
HIP, KNEE, LEG
BRAIN
गला
गर्दन
THROAT
NECK
रीढ़ की हड्डी
SPINE

Endocrine glands and related pressure points located in feet and hands

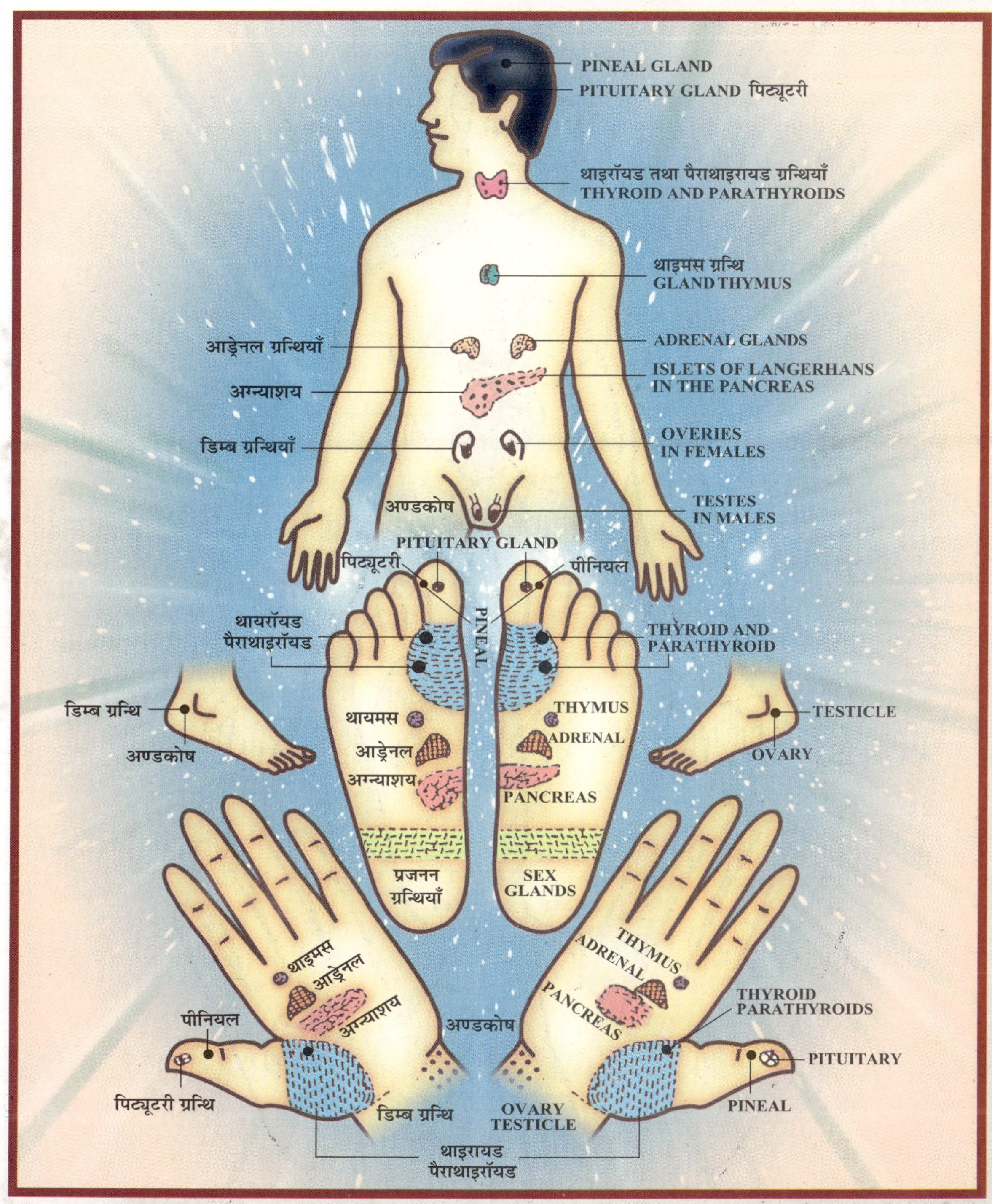

Position of heart and spleen in the body and related pressure points located in feet and hands

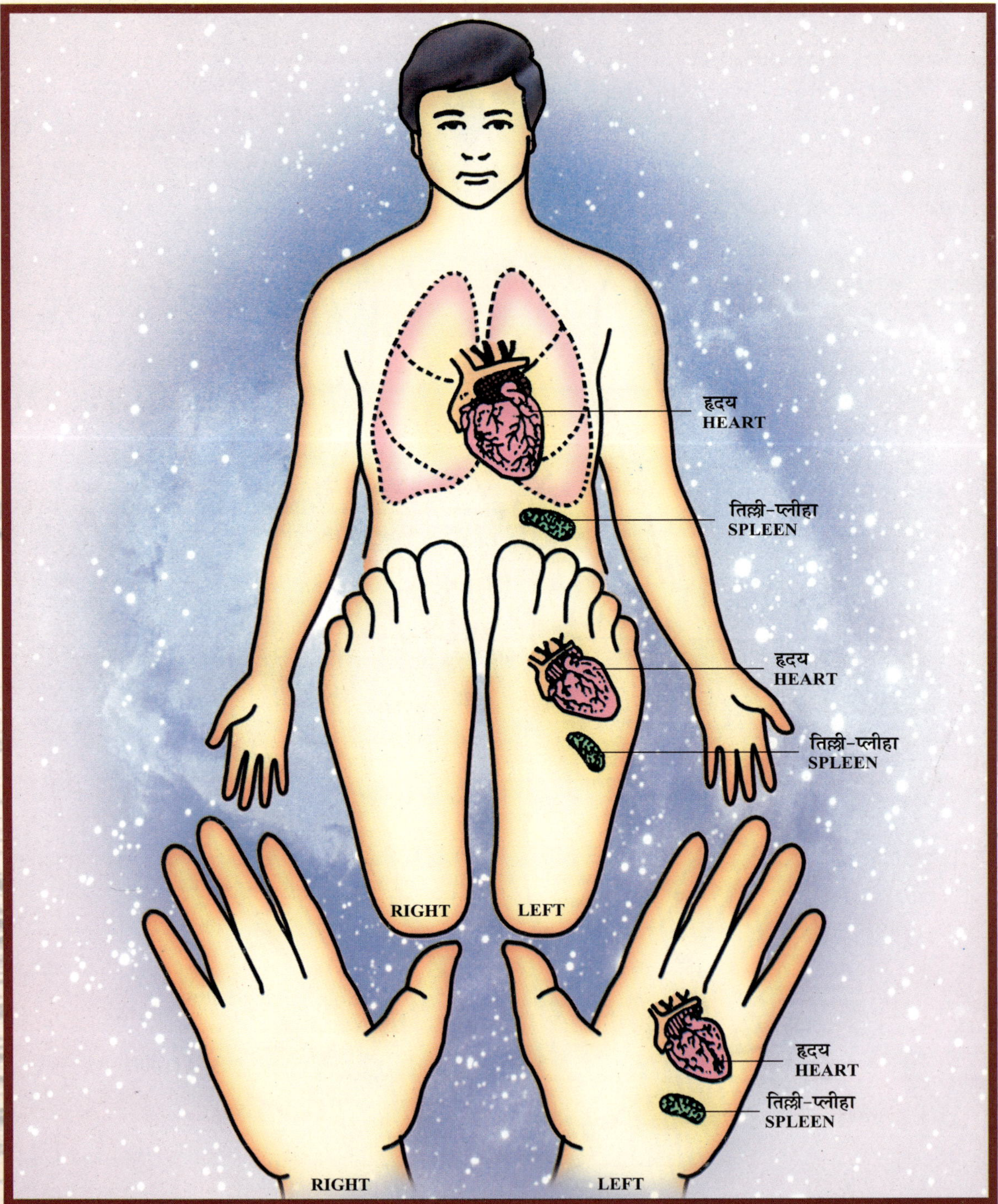

हृदय
HEART

तिल्ली-प्लीहा
SPLEEN

हृदय
HEART

तिल्ली-प्लीहा
SPLEEN

RIGHT
LEFT

हृदय
HEART

तिल्ली-प्लीहा
SPLEEN

RIGHT
LEFT

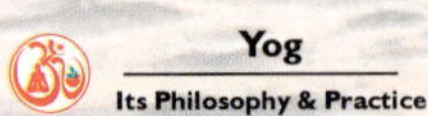

Position of different parts of respiratory organs and related pressure points located in feet and hands

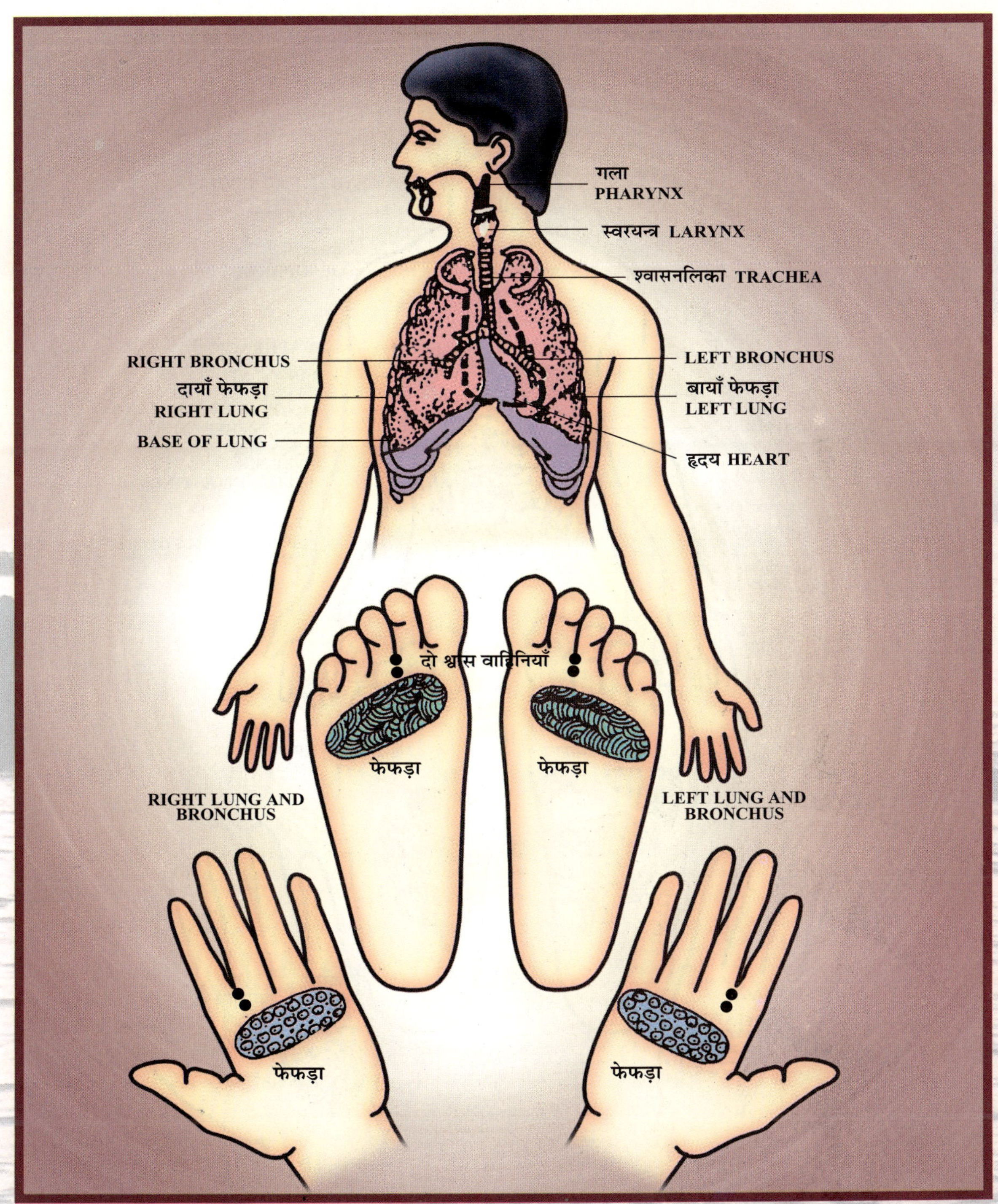

Position of organs of digestive system and related pressure points located in feet and hands

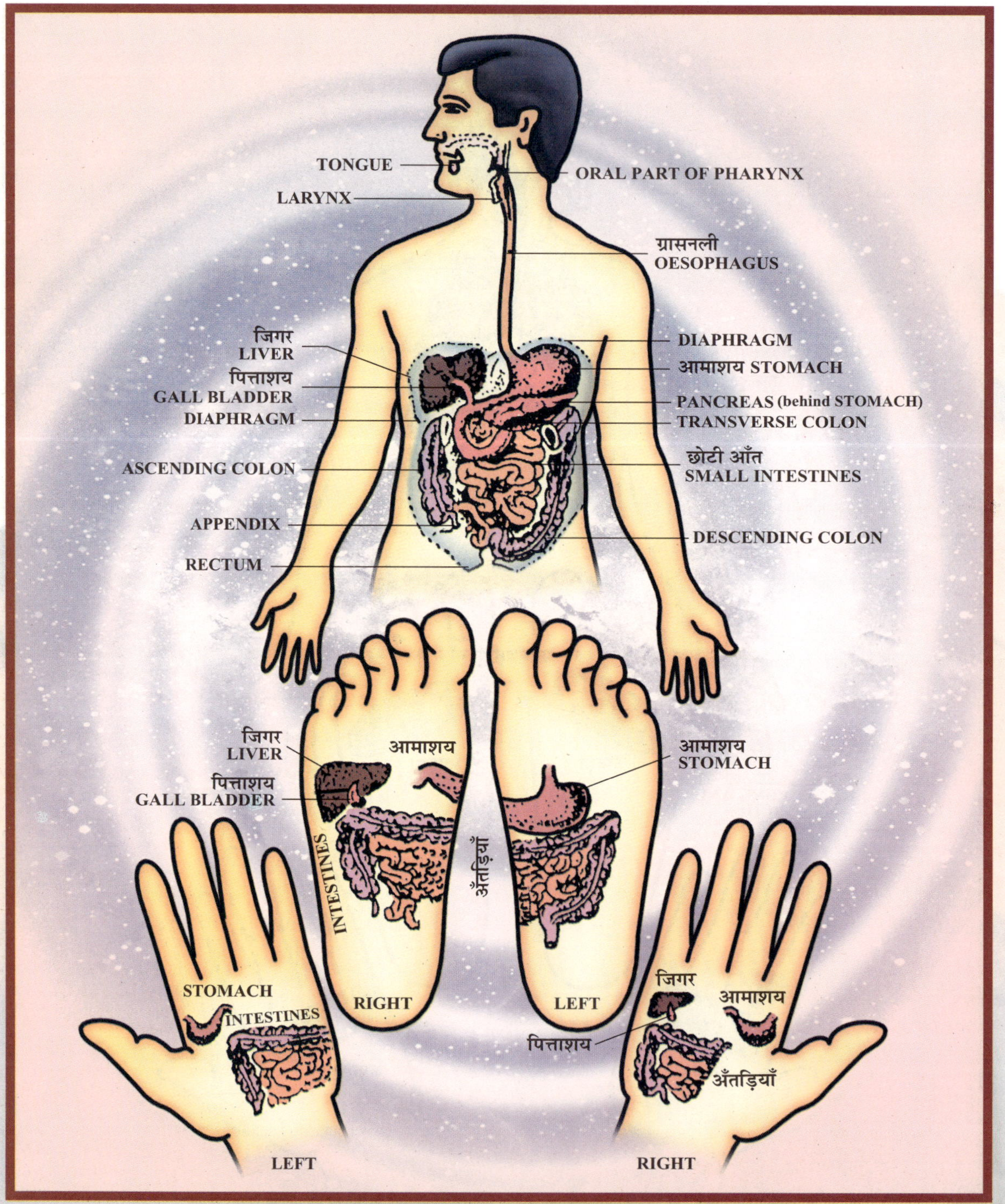

TONGUE
ORAL PART OF PHARYNX
LARYNX
ग्रासनली
OESOPHAGUS
जिगर
LIVER
पित्ताशय
GALL BLADDER
DIAPHRAGM
DIAPHRAGM
आमाशय STOMACH
PANCREAS (behind STOMACH)
TRANSVERSE COLON
ASCENDING COLON
छोटी आँत
SMALL INTESTINES
APPENDIX
DESCENDING COLON
RECTUM

जिगर
LIVER
आमाशय
पित्ताशय
GALL BLADDER
INTESTINES
अँतड़ियाँ
आमाशय
STOMACH
RIGHT
LEFT

STOMACH
INTESTINES
LEFT
जिगर
आमाशय
पित्ताशय
अँतड़ियाँ
RIGHT

Position of organs of urinary system and related pressure points located in feet and hands

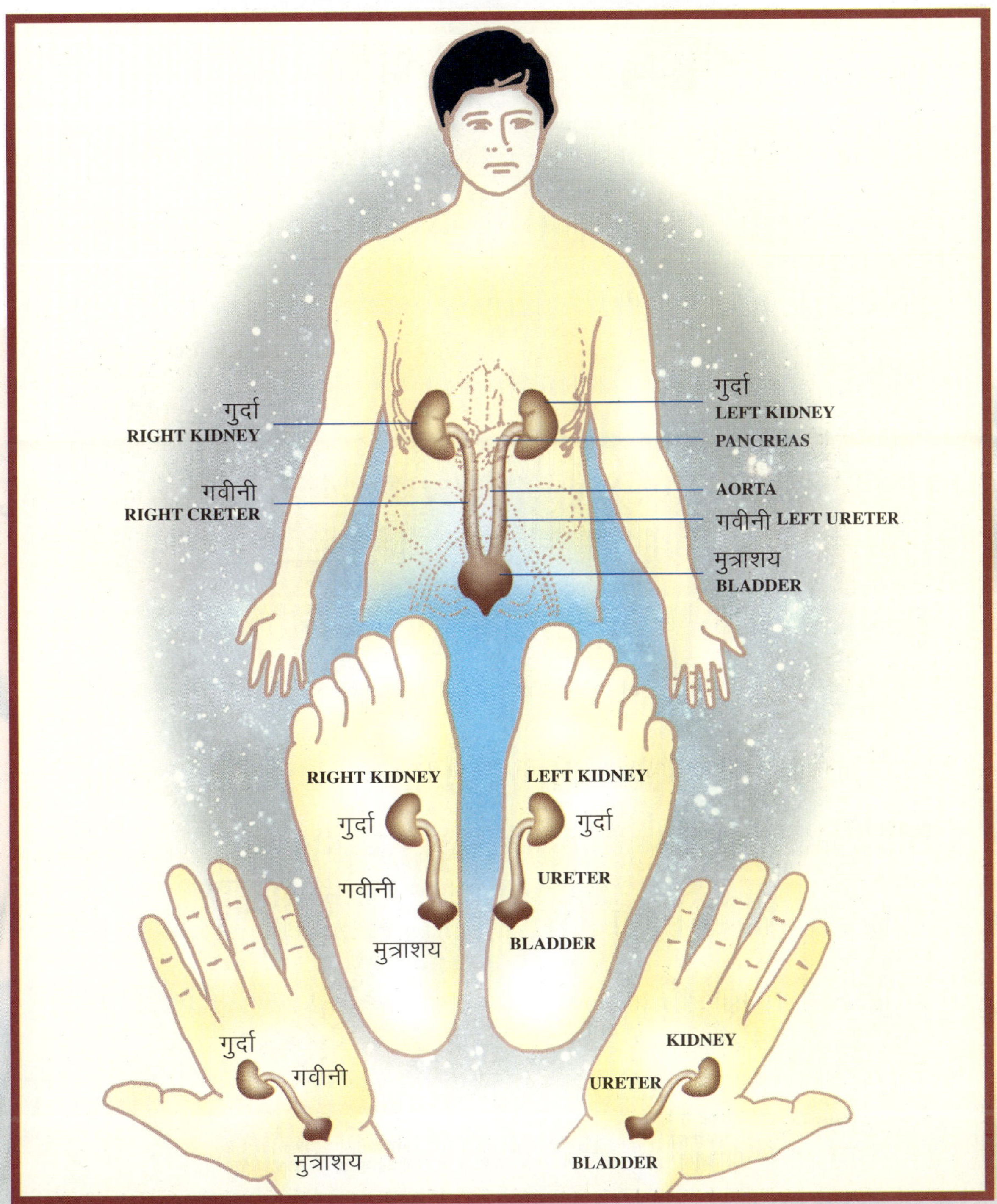

Position of organs of male and female reproductive system and related pressure points located in feet, hands and wrist

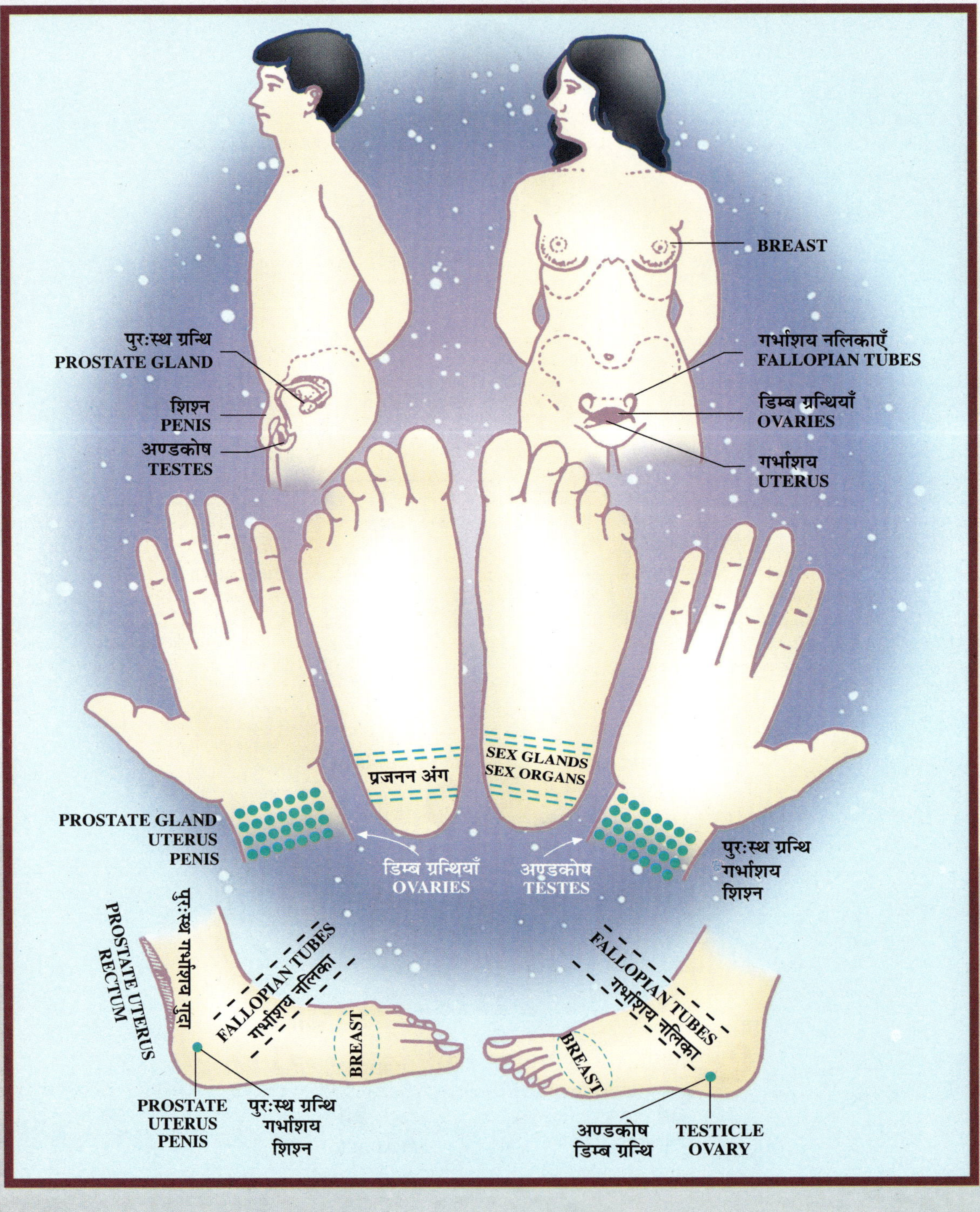

पुर:स्थ ग्रन्थि
PROSTATE GLAND
शिश्न
PENIS
अण्डकोष
TESTES

BREAST
गर्भाशय नलिकाएँ
FALLOPIAN TUBES
डिम्ब ग्रन्थियाँ
OVARIES
गर्भाशय
UTERUS

प्रजनन अंग
SEX GLANDS
SEX ORGANS

PROSTATE GLAND
UTERUS
PENIS
डिम्ब ग्रन्थियाँ
OVARIES
अण्डकोष
TESTES
पुर:स्थ ग्रन्थि
गर्भाशय
शिश्न

PROSTATE UTERUS
RECTUM
पुर:स्थ गर्भाशय गुदा
FALLOPIAN TUBES
गर्भाशय नलिका
BREAST
PROSTATE
UTERUS
PENIS
पुर:स्थ ग्रन्थि
गर्भाशय
शिश्न

FALLOPIAN TUBES
गर्भाशय नलिका
BREAST
अण्डकोष
डिम्ब ग्रन्थि
TESTICLE
OVARY

Various pressure points on the upper portion of the feet. Both the feet have same points.

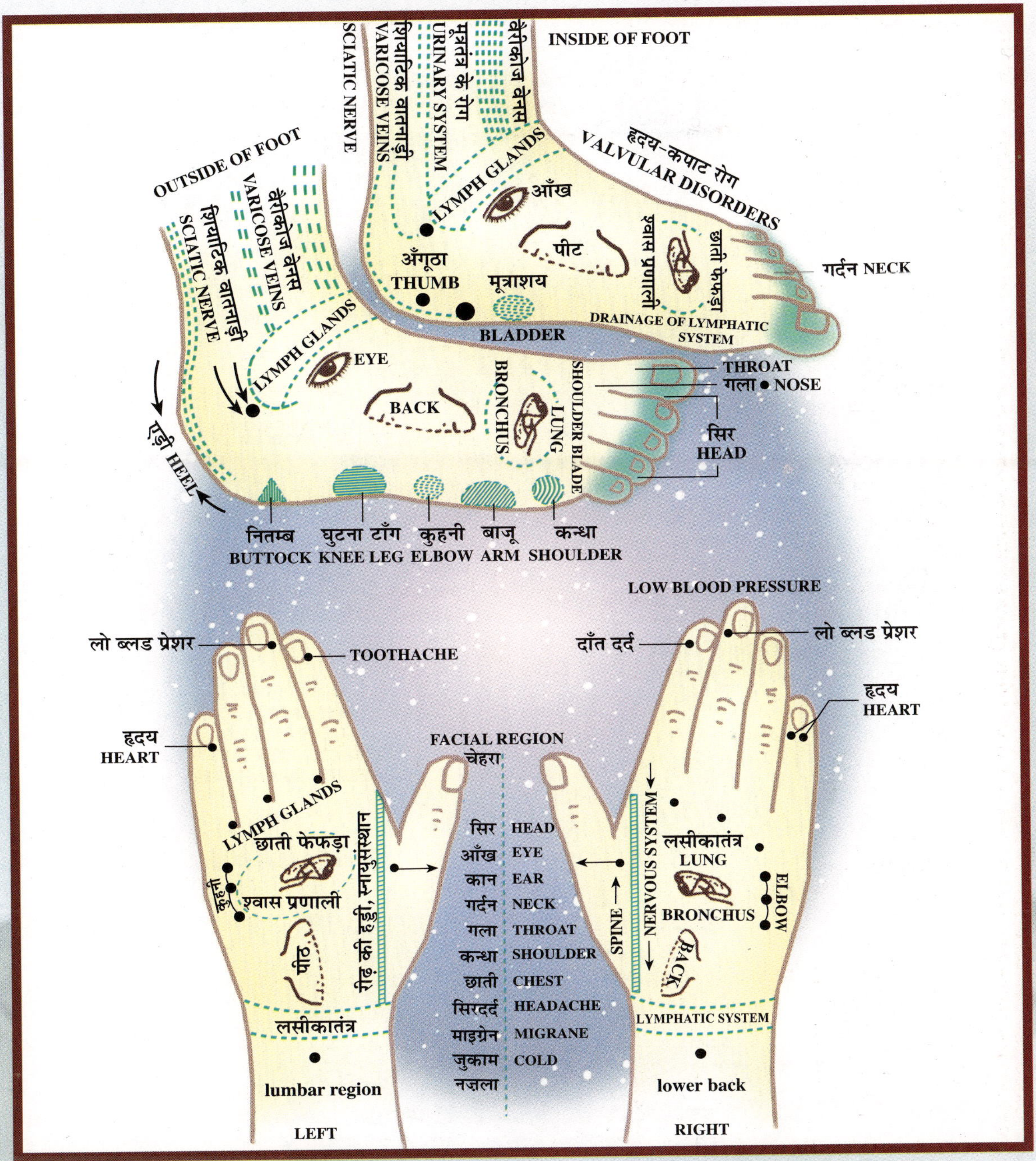

INSIDE OF FOOT

वैरिकोज वेनस

मूत्रतंत्र के रोग

URINARY SYSTEM

शियाटिक वातनाड़ी

VARICOSE VEINS

SCIATIC NERVE

LYMPH GLANDS

आँख

हृदय-कपाट रोग

VALVULAR DISORDERS

पीठ

श्वास प्रणाली

छाती फेफड़ा

गर्दन NECK

अँगूठा

THUMB

मूत्राशय

DRAINAGE OF LYMPHATIC SYSTEM

BLADDER

OUTSIDE OF FOOT

वैरिकोज वेनस

VARICOSE VEINS

शियाटिक वातनाड़ी

SCIATIC NERVE

LYMPH GLANDS

EYE

BACK

BRONCHUS

LUNG

SHOULDER BLADE

THROAT

गला • NOSE

सिर

HEAD

एड़ी HEEL

नितम्ब BUTTOCK

घुटना टाँग KNEE LEG

कुहनी ELBOW

बाजू ARM

कन्धा SHOULDER

LOW BLOOD PRESSURE

लो ब्लड प्रेशर

TOOTHACHE

दाँत दर्द

लो ब्लड प्रेशर

हृदय

HEART

हृदय

HEART

FACIAL REGION

चेहरा

LYMPH GLANDS

छाती फेफड़ा

श्वास प्रणाली

पीठ

रीढ़ की हड्डी, स्नायुसंस्थान

सिर	HEAD
आँख	EYE
कान	EAR
गर्दन	NECK
गला	THROAT
कन्धा	SHOULDER
छाती	CHEST
सिरदर्द	HEADACHE
माइग्रेन	MIGRANE
जुकाम	COLD
नज़ला	

SPINE

NERVOUS SYSTEM

लसीकातंत्र

LUNG

BRONCHUS

ELBOW

BACK

लसीकातंत्र

LYMPHATIC SYSTEM

lumbar region

lower back

LEFT

RIGHT

Various pressure points on the upper portion of hands. Both hands have same points.

Besides the pressure points of liver, heart and spleen, both the feet have same acupressure reflex centers.

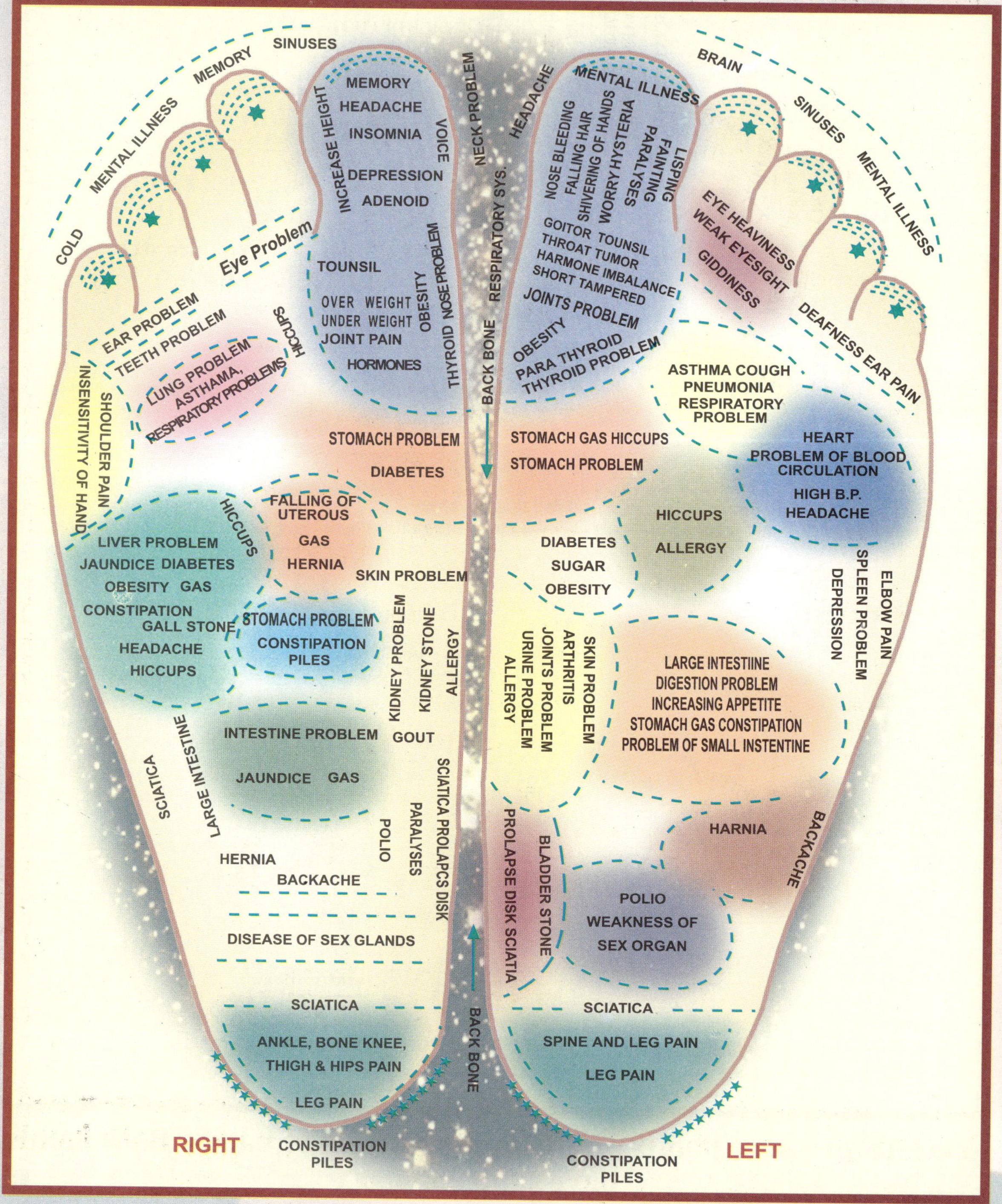

Different acupressure points located on the face

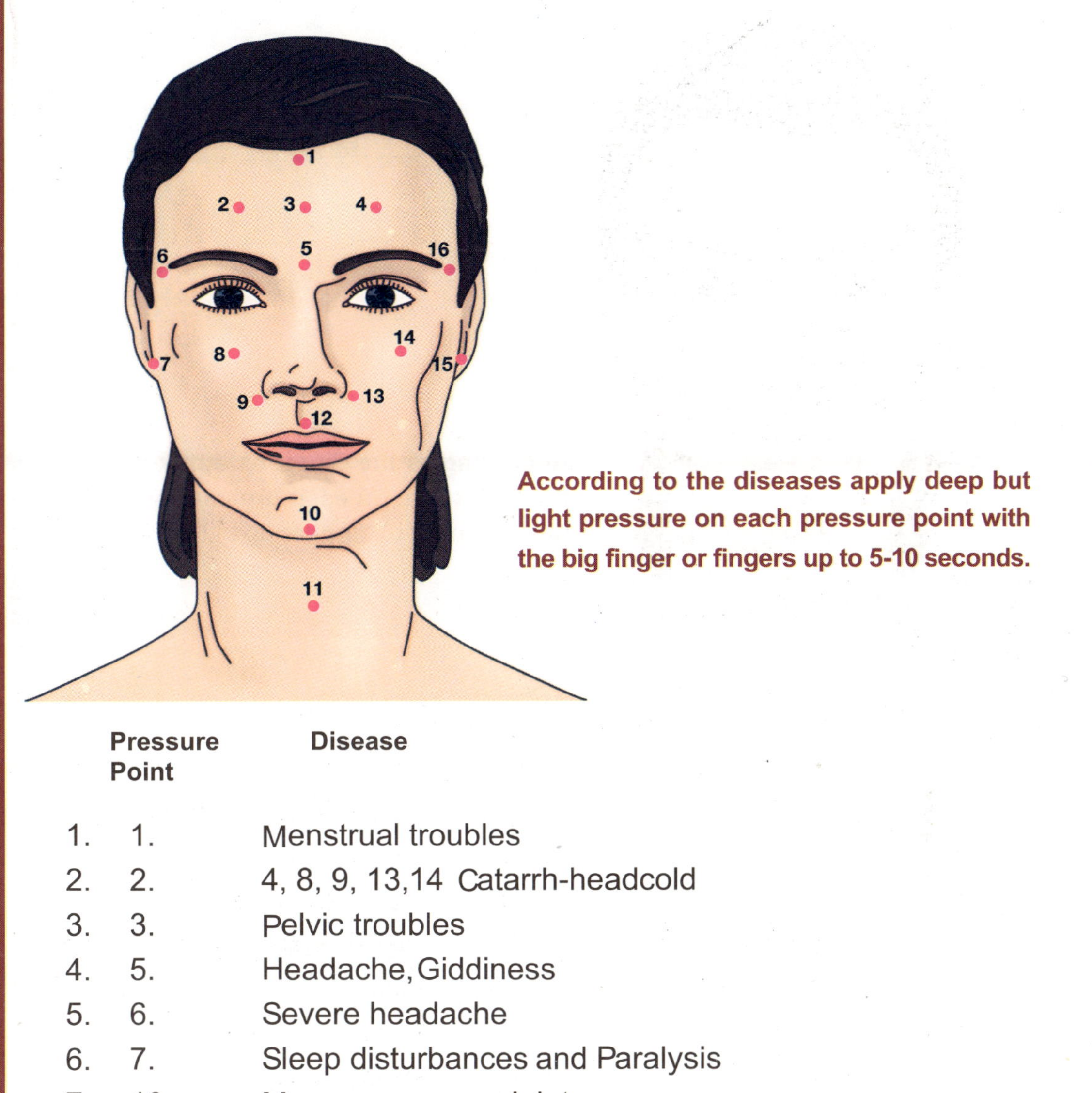

According to the diseases apply deep but light pressure on each pressure point with the big finger or fingers up to 5-10 seconds.

	Pressure Point	Disease
1.	1.	Menstrual troubles
2.	2.	4, 8, 9, 13,14 Catarrh-headcold
3.	3.	Pelvic troubles
4.	5.	Headache, Giddiness
5.	6.	Severe headache
6.	7.	Sleep disturbances and Paralysis
7.	10.	Menopause complaints
8.	11.	Throat, Cough, Dyspnea and Asthma
9.	12.	Toothache

Different acupressure points located on the face

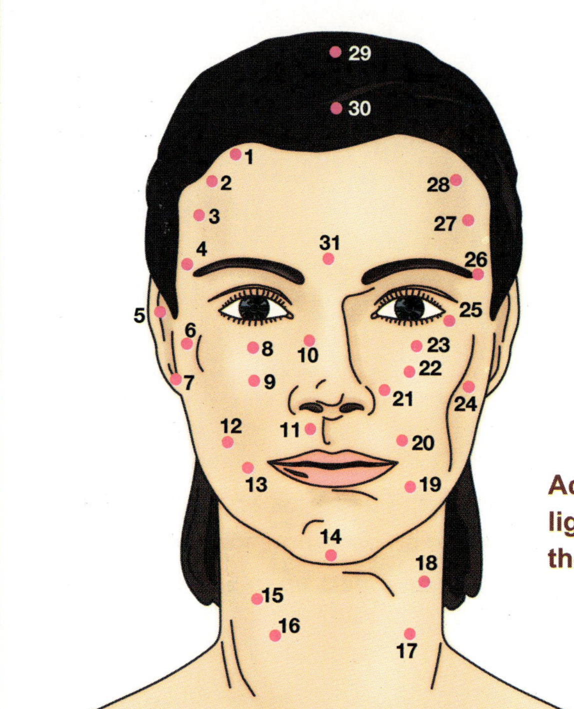

According to the diseases, apply deep but light pressure on each pressure point with the big finger or fingers up to 5-10 seconds.

Pressure Point	Disease	Pressure Point	Disease
1	Memory	12,13	Disease related to the right Lung
2	Sciatica	15,18	Erection
3,25	Gas	16,17	Abdomen problem
4	Liver problems	19,20	Diseases related to the left Lung
5	Blood pressure	23	Kidney problems
6,24	Tumour in the throat	26	Diseases of Spleen
7	Paralysis	27	Heart problem
8	Kidney problem	28	Sciatica
9,14,22	Constipation	29	Severe Headache
10, 21	Intestine problem	30	Diseases related to the Sex organs
11	Disease of pancreas	31	Headache

Different acupressure points located on the face

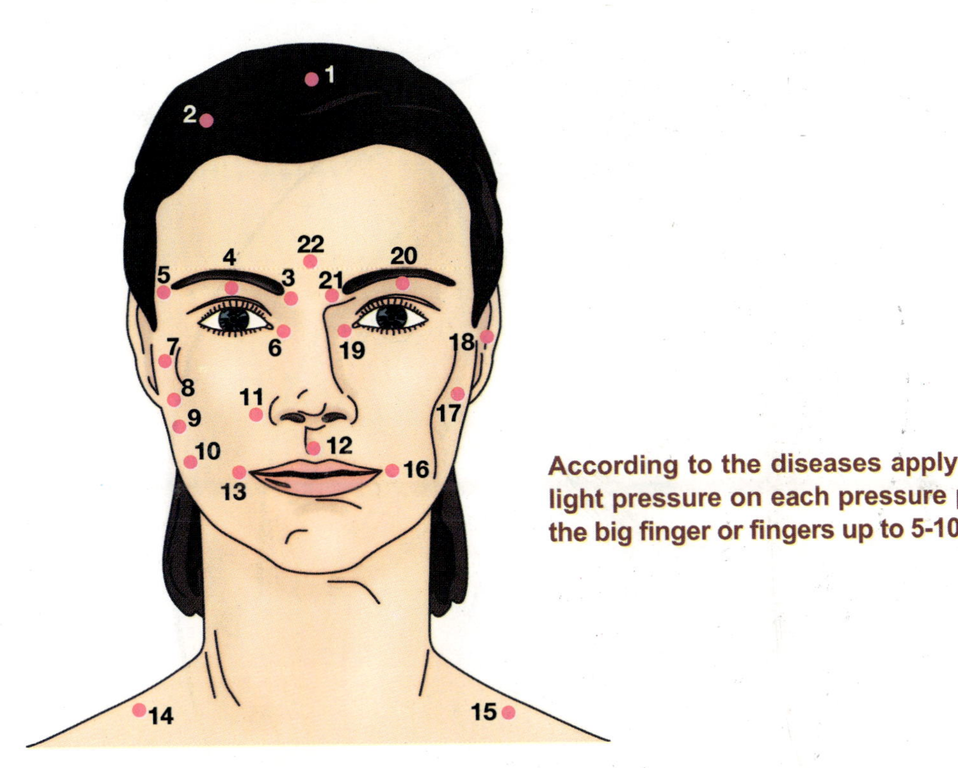

According to the diseases apply deep but light pressure on each pressure point with the big finger or fingers up to 5-10 seconds.

Pressure Point	Disease	Pressure	Disease Point
1	Piles, Bladder problems, Bed wetting	9,17	Toothache
2	Double vision diplopia	11	Nose blockage, running Nose
3,21	Brain problem, cold, insomnia	12	Paralysis, Sneezing, fainting, Unconsciousness
4,20	Sciatica, Brain, Liver and Gall Bladder Diseases	13,16	Toothache, Mental Streess
5, 6, 14, 15, 19	Eye problem	18	High Blood Pressure, Stiffness and pain in arms
7	Hearing problem	22	Diseases of Eyes, Legs and Stomach
8,10	Mental Stress & Paralysis		

Different acupressure points located on the ears

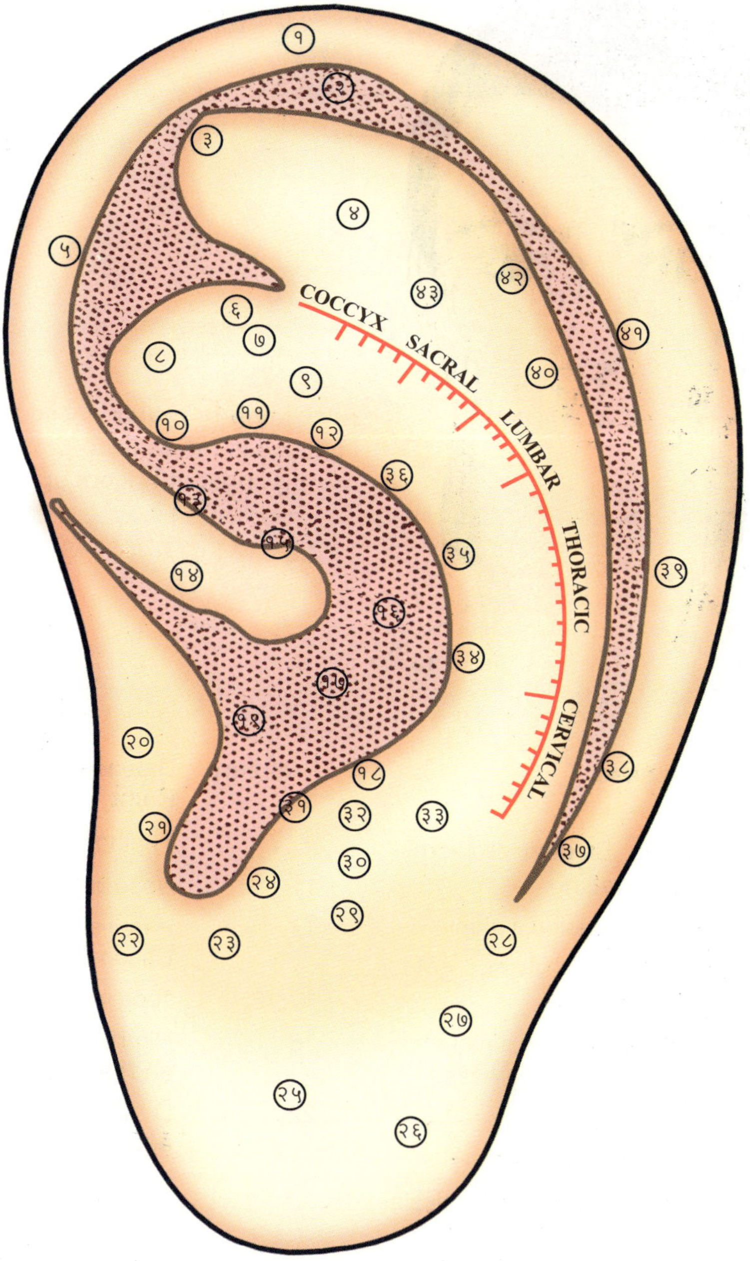

COCCYX
SACRAL
LUMBAR
THORACIC
CERVICAL

Description of the points located on ears

1. Tonsil
2. Apendix
3. Ankle
4. Knee Joint
5. High Blood Pressure
6. Asthma
7. Hips
8. Sciatica Nerve
9. Kness
10. Bladder
11. Right Vertex
12. Kidney
13. Large Intestine
14. Rectum
15. Small Instentine
16. Stomach
17. Respiratory System
18. Lungs
19. Lungs
20. High Blood Pressure
21. Internal portion of Nose
22. Eyes
23. Eyes
24. Ovary
25. Eyes
26. Internal portion of Ear
27. Upper Jaw
28. Lower Jaw
29. Lungs
30. Testes
31. Asthma
32. Brain
33. Toothache
34. Liver
35. Spleen
36. Pancreas, Gall Bladder
37. Neck
38. Shoulder Bone
39. Shoulder
40. Stomach
41. Elbow
42. Knee
43. Hip Joint

A person can treat himself in this way through acupressure

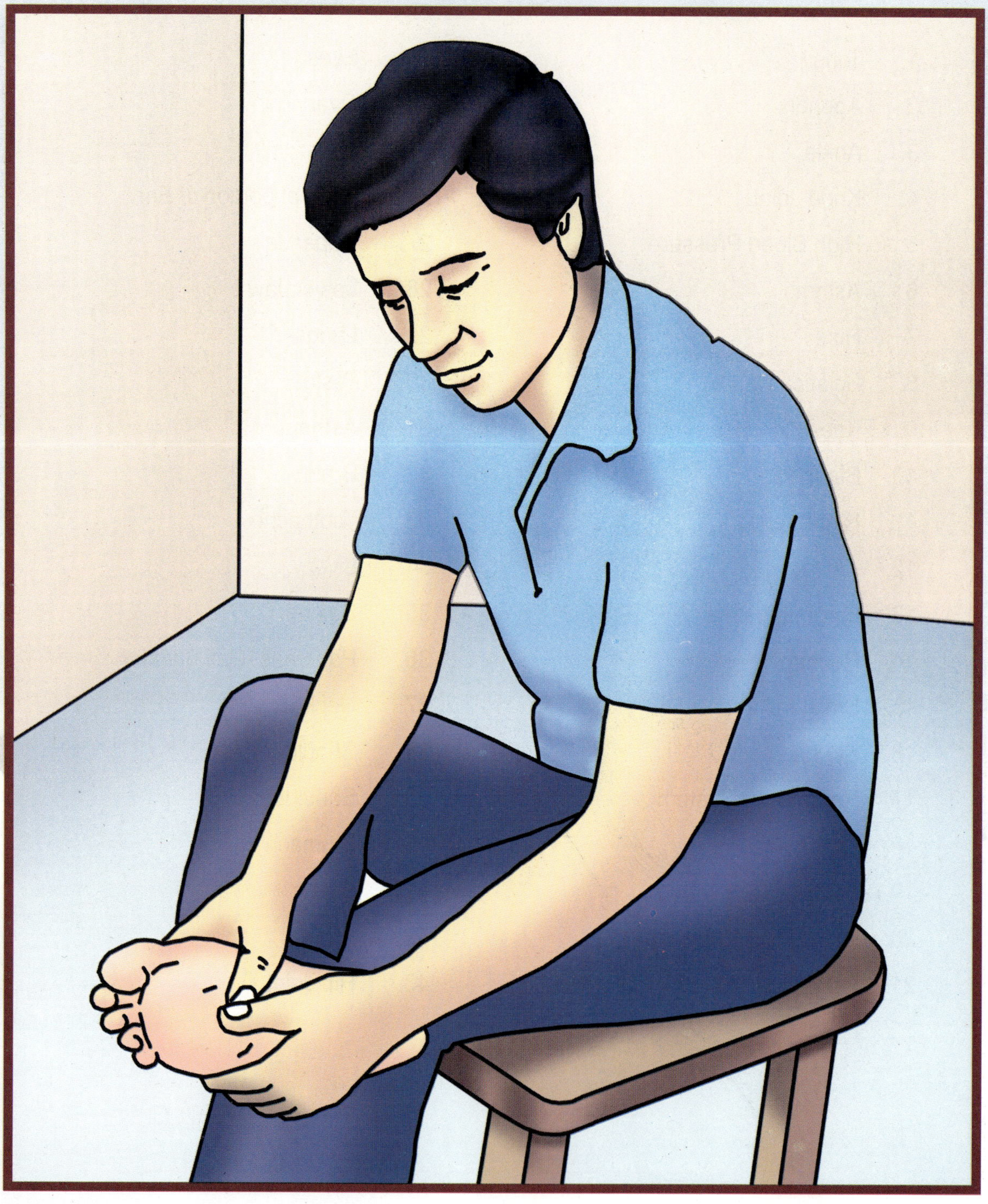

Different methods of giving acupressure

Correct method of applying pressure with big finger(thumb)

Wrong Method

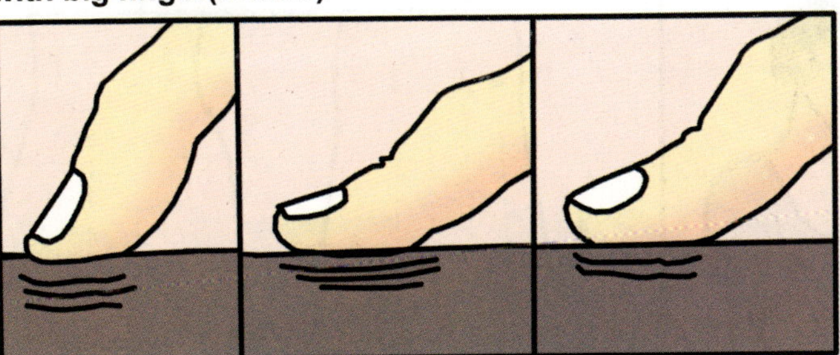

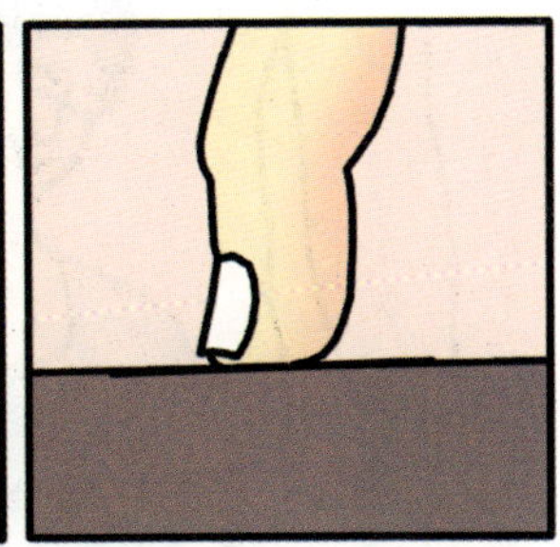

One should not lift the thumb while applying pressure

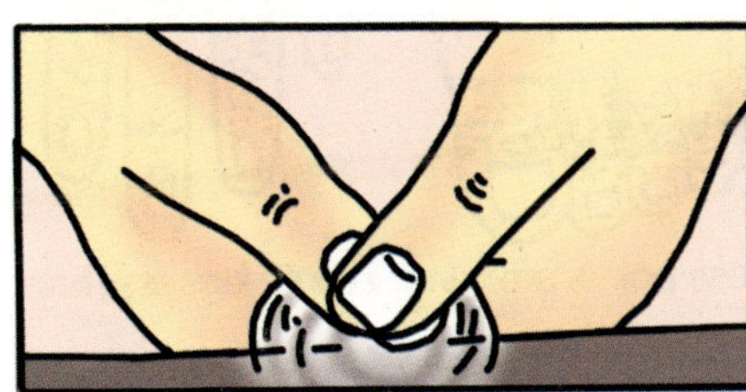

For applying more pressure one thumb should be kept on the other

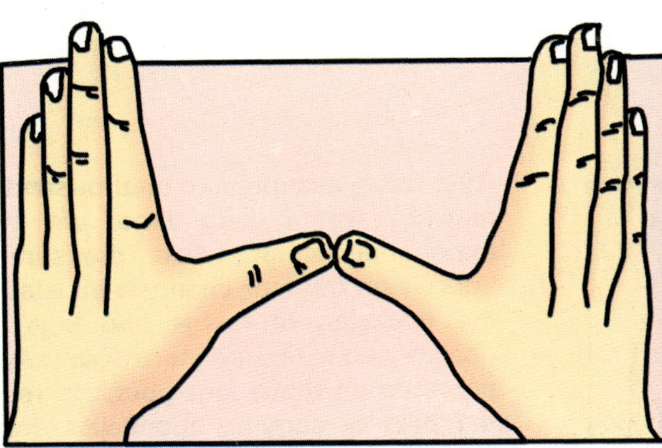

On some places, especially on the back apply pressure using both the thumbs.

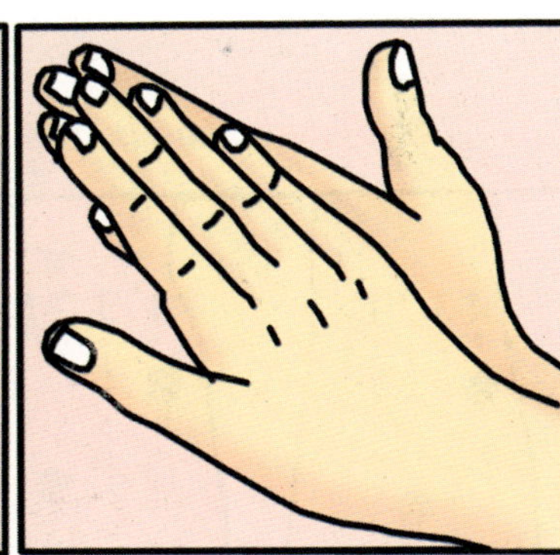

One some centres, like stomach, apply pressue with these three fingers of both hands simultaneously.

Life power centre situated on hand

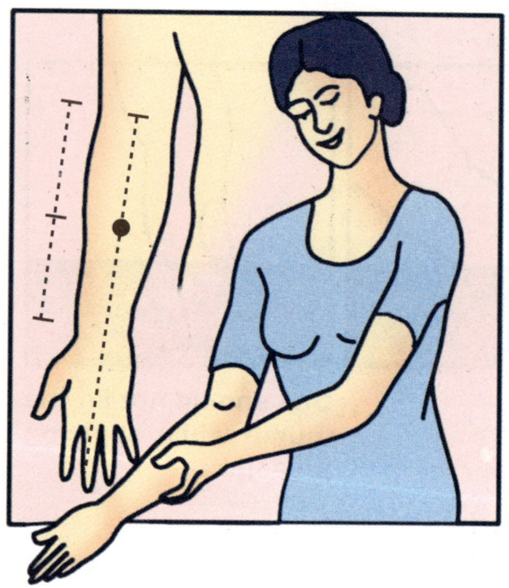

Pain relieving pressure points situated on the upper portion of hands and legs.

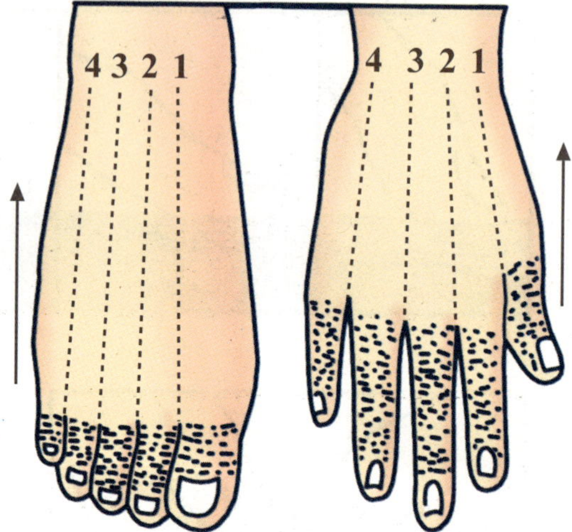

These points are same in both legs and hands.

A Illusive pains points

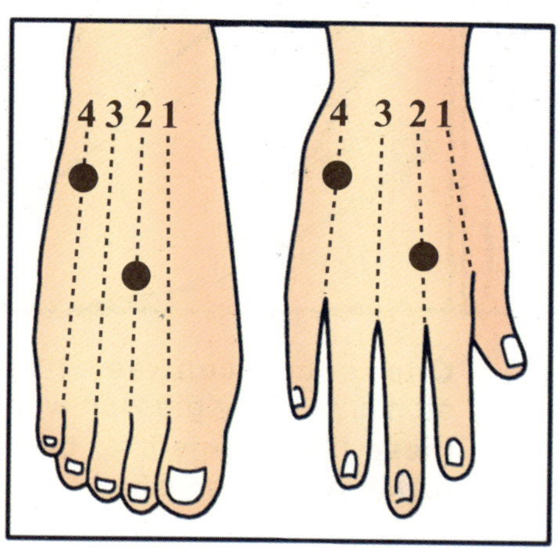

After using accupresure on thousands of patients for a long time, we have experienced that when pressure is applied on the four channels situated on the backside of hands and legs, the related pain is relaxed immediately. Apply pressure on these four points to relieve the pain of carrying spondalitis, frozen shoulder and pain at the back on the neck.

In the same way for pains related to sciatica, kness and other pains related to the legs, apply pressure on the pressure points of legs.

Divya Yog Mandir Trust - An Introduction

The headquarter of ***Divya Yog Maṇdir* Trust** is situated at *Kripālu Bagh Ashram* in *Kankhal*. This *Ashram* was established in 1932 by *Swāmī Kripālu Devji Mahārāj* who hailed from *Mewār* (*Rajasthan*) - the land of *Mhārānāpratāp*. His name before becoming a *sanyasi* was *Yati Kishore Chand*. He played an active role in the freedom movement of India. At *Hariḍwār*, he harboured many revolutionaries and helped them to carry on their mission. *Veṇī Prasād Jigyāsu,* a local freedom fighter was one of his close associates. *Kripāluji* was the man who collected around 3500 books and established the first public Library in *Hariḍwār*. He initiated dozens of schools for building the cultural base of the nation. *Swāmī Shraddhanandji*, founder of *Gurūkula Kangri* was a very good companion of *Kripāluji*. Later on, he came in contact of *Bālgaṇgādhar Tilak*, *Madan Mohan Malaviya*, *Motilal Nehru*, *Mahatma Gandhi*, *Çhiṭṭaraṇjan Das*, *Ganeśh Shankar Vidhyarthi*, *V.G. Patel*, *Hakīm Ajmal Khan* and many other nationalist leaders.

Yati Kishore Chand joined the famous *Bengali* Revolutionary Group and took the responsibility of promoting and circulating '*Yugāṇtar*' and '*Lokāṇtar*' - the mouthpiece of the revolutionaries. The British Government did not like these papers at all. The Government treated these papers like fire spitting dragon. Nobody was able to know about the place of publication of these papers. *Yati Kishore Chandji* dispatched these papers sometimes from *Çhaṇdipāhār* in *Hariḍwār* and sometimes from *Nīldhārā*. Very often he dispatched these papers from his library at *Paliwal Dharmaṣhala*. During this period, the *Bengali* Revolutionaries carried out the famous Hardings Bomb act in Delhi. *Rāsbeharī Bose* was the hero who was responsible for this act. *Yati Kishore Chand* was entrusted with the task to hide him in *Hariḍwār*. The British Government had already declared three lacs as a Prize on his head. *Yati Kishore Chandji* took him to his *Ashram* situated in a dense forest. *Rāsbeharī Bose's* friend *Harish Babu* came alongwith his three friends to see *Yati Kishore Chand* and informed him that the British Government has smelt his presence in *Hariḍwār*. He may be hunted down anytime. *Yati* acted promptly. *Rāsbeharī Bose* boarded the *Dehradun* Express going to Banaras with a band of *Patiyalvi* passengers. In the wee hours of the next day, the police raided the *ashram* but by the time Mr. *Bose* was out of reach. Later Mr. *Bose* went to Japan. Then *Yati Kishore Chand* took *Saṇyās*, and came to be known as *Swāmī Kripālu Maharaj*. He published a monthly magazine titled "*Vishwagyan*" to arouse the flame of independence among fellow Indians. Later on he switched to the *Yogic* Sciences and Spiritualism and became a great *Yogi*. He departed for his heavenly abode in the year 1968.

After *Kripālu's* death, his disciples took the mission of their *Gurū* and began to manage the *Ashram*. *Swāmī Shankardevji* is the one of his chain of disciples who is the *Gurū* of *Swāmī Ramdevji Maharaj*. *Divya Yog Maṇdir* Trust was founded in the year 1995 by Shri *Ramdevji* with active assistance of *Āchārya Balkrishanji* and *Swāmī Muktanandji* and others to carry on various selfless service project to the service of mankind. His work has deeply affected the Indian Society as a whole. They have promoted the confluence of *Veda*, *Yog* and *Āyurveda* in far and wide. Billions of people are benefited with the *Yogic* teachings by *Swāmī Ramdevji.* His every minute of life is spent only in service to humanity. Being a *sanyasi* he is relentlessly seeking the path of the benevolence of the masses. He is simply devoted to this mammoth work. He believes that all that is happening and that is going to happen in future is because of the blessings of the god.

Service Organisations run by the Trust

In such a short period of even less than ten years the trust has witnessed a phenomenal development in its various projects, from which, it seems nothing less than a divine miracle. The most ambitious project of *Patanjali Yogpēeth* has taken a multidimensional shape, looking at it people think that *Swāmī Ramdevji* is definitely blessed with some divine power. This miracle is the cumulative result of dedication towards the humble cause of serving the mankind, for which *Swāmīji* is always inspired and prepared. The brief description of the different projects run by the trust is as follows:-

Organising *Yog Sādhnā* and *Yog* Treatment Camps

The different *'Yog' Sādhnā* and *'Yog'* Treatment Camps organised in different part of the country have foiled the misbelief that *'Yog'* is merely a physical exercise. Revered *Swāmīji* has established *'Yog'* for spiritual development, physical fitness, mental, calmness, intellectual and all-round development and manifestation of human personality. In the *Yogic* Camps the eight fold path emulated by *Patanjali* is seriously dealt with. Apart from *Ashtang Yoga*, *HaṭhYoga*, Philosophy, *Upnishad, Vedas, Çharak, Suśhrut* and many other subjects also are seriously dealt with in the camps. Arrangements are being made to give practical training for *'Yog'* and *Japa-Yog*, along with all the six folds of *HaṭhYog-Yog*, *Neti, Dhōuti, Basṭi, Ṭrāṭak, Nōuli* and *Kapalbhati.*

Brahmakalpa Çhikiṭsālaya

Brahmakalpa Çhikiṭsālaya treats its patients with *Yogic Śhaṭkaṛma* and *Paṇçhkaṛmā* (Massage, Perspiration, Vomit, Purgative medicated enemas, Nasal administration of herbs) systems. Apart from that, herbal based medicines, proper and harmonious living, practicing *Brahmacharyā* and regulating the life activities are some of the tenets which are also attached with the treatment. Accupressure, *Yogasanas*, *Pranayam* and Naturopathy are taught at the centre either free or on nominal charges.

At *Brahmakalp*, High Blood Pressure, Diabetes, Heart diseases, *Asthma*, Obesity, Acidity, Allergy, Ulcer, Cervical Spondolitis, Sciatica, Arthritis, Cancer (first and second stage) and many other chronic diseases are treated without surgery.

The *Çhikiṭsālaya* is being expanded to make it a residential *Chikiṭsālaya* so that many more patients can be accommodated and benefit out of it.

Swāmīji firmly believes that we should prevent ourselves from falling ill. If unfortunately, we fall prey to illness we should prefer *'Yog'* and treat ourselves. If medicines are required, we should prefer *Āyurveda* because it is the most suitable system rooted to our environment, culture and nature and is hundred percent safe. Therefore, the medicines prepared in the pharmacy section are pure, effective and comparatively cheaper. Various preparations like *Bhāṣhyam, Pishti, Ras, Rasayan, Vati, Guggul, Churna, Awaleh, Sat, Kwath, Ghrit, Tel, Lauh Mandur, Parpati* and many more are available at *Brahmakalp*. There is a huge requirement of these medicines which we are unable to meet at present.

Very shortly this pharmacy is likely to be expanded so as to meet the requirement; the project for this is being finalized.

Research Laboratory

Divya Yog Maṇdir Trust has a very sophisticated research laboratory where continuous research on different herbs is carried out. Its main objective is to rediscover rare medicinal herbs, preparation of *Āyurvedic* medicines as per the traditional methods, to keep pace with the latest developments in the field of *Āyurvedic* research and publishing literature on *Āyurveda* in the greater interest of mankind. Our path breaking research of relocating the famous *Aṣṭavarga* Herbs is praiseworthy. It has also prepared its own formulations, which have been successful and have earned praise all over. Our researchers have located these herbs at the very high altitude of the *Himalayas*. The trust has published an exclusive book on *Aṣṭavarga* both in English and Hindi.

Herbarium

The trust is striving for plantation, preservation and promotion of rare medicines in its herbarium. Owing to space constraints the project could not be given the desired shape. In near future, the herbarium would be able to cater to the herbal desired of the pharmacy and the general masses. Medicinal Plants potted in earthen pots and seeds shall be available for sale.

Establishment of *Divya Goṣhālā*

Preservation of the Indian breed of the holy cow has been given utmost priority because various cow-related products are essential in treatment and formulation of medicines. There is a plan of preserving thousands of cows in the *Goṣhāla*. The cow dung will be used to make compost and fertilizer which will help cultivation of farm product at the *Ashram*, so that the produce free from chemical fertilizers etc. Apart from this a *Gobar* Gas Plant will also be installed to meet the energy requirement of the ashram. These Indian cows will be bred from the point of view improving the breed of the cow, as also to give respect and recognition to it.

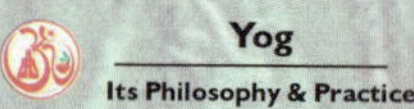

Vēdic Yagyaśhālā (Agnihoṭra)

Agnihoṭra in itself is a great science for purification of the ambience, controlling draught and over raining and treating certain diseases. *Agnihoṭra* can play a vital role in this. To perpetuate the age long *Ṛiśhi* tradition of *Agnihoṭra*, there is a proposal to build one huge *Yagyaśhālā* in the *Pataṇjali Yogapēeth* Complex. There will be scientific research on the *Yagya* and *Yagya* related benefits.

Vēdic Gurūkula

A *Vēdic Gurukūla* at *Kishangarh Ghasera*, some 8 kms away from *Rewari* Town in *Haryana*, is being run by the trust free of cost to disseminate standard teaching strictly on *Vēdic* pattern. Here both rich and poor students can obtain quality education without discrimination. The *Gurukūla* needs expansion so that greater number of students can be imparted education there.

Sādhna Ashram situated at *Gangotri*

At *Gangotri*, an *Ashram* has been established to conduct research on rare Himalayan Herbs. The *Ashram* is yet to be expanded and given a new shape.

Establishment of *Pataṇjali Yogpēeth*

This *Pēeth* is a dream project of *Diṿya Yog Maṇdir* Trust which will spread over 1,000 acres of land. This *YogPēeth* will play a vital role in spreading the message of *'Yog'* and Ā*yuṛveda* among the masses. This will be able to accommodate around 2,000 *Sādhakas* and will consists of 2500 rooms, spacious halls, Pharmacy, Hospital, *Gośhālā*, Herbarium, Publication House, Library, Printing-Press, Community Kitchen for visitors, *'Yog'* Centre and other activities centres. The visitors to this Campus will avail pure food, which will be void of L.P.G., chemical fertilizer and insecticides. It will be developed as a cosmopolitan, self-reliant complex similar to the *Shantiniketan* of Late *Rabindranath Tagore*, and will also be a place of faith in the form of a renowned institute for public at large, which will bring Health, *'Yog'*, Mental Peace and Spiritualism Development to crores of people. This ambitious project will cost around Rs. 100 crores, which will be generously offered by true *'Yog' Sādhakas* and the well wishers of *'Yog'* and Spiritualism. Swami Ramdevji has vowed by lord Shiva to complete this task with active co-operation of *'Yog'* lovers, by grace of god which is being accomplished in time on a regular basis.

The amount of contribution that has been fixed by the trust towards becoming of a member of the trust is as follows:-

1. Founder Member	Rs. 5 Lacs
2. Patron Member	Rs. 2. 51 Lacs
3. Life Member	Rs.1 Lac
4. Respected Member	Rs. 51 thousand
5. Honoured Member	Rs. 21 thousand
6. General Member	Rs. 11 thousand

Publication of *Yog - Sandesh* (Monthly Magazine in Hindi)

On demand of thousands of *Sādhaka*s related to *Divya Yog Maṇḍir* Trust, this magazine has been published (Hindi, English, Marathi, Bengali, Punjabi, Gujarati, Asamese, Nepali and Udiya editions) under the expert guidance of noted editors since September, 2003. Every month thousands of new members are adopting this magazine, which proves its popularity amongst its readers. It has been decided that in near future the views of Sages on the subjects of *'Yog'*, *Āyurveda*, Culture & Rituals and spiritualism will be distributed among lacs of readers. Apart from this, poetry, articles of interest to public at large and the activities and future projects and the experiences and feelings of the readers shall also be included in the magazine. Popularity & fame earned by any Hindi Magazine in a short span of time, clearly shows that this is due to the magnificent popularity of *Swāmī Ramdevji Maharaj*.

These references about *Prāṇāyām* have been compiled and printed along with colored illustrations in an attractive book form. We request the readers to read '*Prāṇāyām* – its philosophy and practices' written by *Swāmīji* for in-depth knowledge of the subject.

Glossary

Acupressure:

Applying pressure on the special points situated on the human body and curing of various diseases by this is called acupressure.

Agni :

It is Fire, one of the five elements. It is the biological fire that governs metabolism. It is similar in its function to *Piṭta* and can be considered an integral part of the *Piṭta* system in the body, functioning as a catalytic agent in digestion and metablism. It is known as Fire, it concerned with seeing, related to eyes by the action of movement (walking).

Ajapa-jap :

It is the recitation of the *Mantrās* without the movement of lips i.e. it is silent recitation of mantra done in mind.

Ākasha :

It is known as Ether one of the Five elements. It is concerned with sense of hearing, related to the ear, and is concerned with speech.

Āsanas :

Āsanas are the postures formed by the practitioner as per the guidance of the teacher of the *Āsanas*. These postures depend on the disease which is to be cured.

Ashtang Yog :

Translated as Eight-fold *Yoga*, it is a divine science discovered by the learned saints and seers of ancient India, brought into a disciplined manner, preserved and produced by Saint *Patanjali* in the form of eight *yogic* principles. *Yām* (Resistance to Passions), *Niyam* (Rules), *Āsana* (Postures), *Prānāyām* (Exercise of Breath), Pratyahar (Resistance to Senses), *Dhārṇa* (Concentration), *Dhyān* (Meditation), and *Samādhi* (Union with the Infinite) are the eight principles. A person practicing these principles is known to experience individual and social equality, physical health, intellectual awareness, mental peace and bliss of the soul

Aum :

It is the first cosmic soundless sound.

Āyuṛveda:

It is a holistic system of medicine that is indigenous to and widely practiced in India. The word *Āyuṛveda* is a Sanskrit term meaning "Science of life." *Āyu* means life and Veda is knowing.

BahryaKumbhak:

The stage of pranayam where the air is kept out i.e. not to inhale.

Baṇdhs :

These are the lockings which are done by holding a particular organ or movement inside the body for a prescribed time. These enhance the effect of the activity for which they are prescribed.

Braḥmā :

It means creation. Brahma is the god of creation.

Braḥmachāri :

The person who follows the path of celibacy.

Çhakṛā:

Energy centers in the body that is responsible for the different levels of consciousness; they correspond physiologically to the nerve plexus centers. They regulating the functioning of the vital organs of the physical body by providing the energy needed by them.

Çharak :

Great *Āyuṛvedic* physician who wrote one of the classic texts of *Āyuṛveda* : *Çharak Samita*.

Chiṭta :

It is the mind, the faculty of reasoning & emotions. It has the nature of always being unstable, it can be controlled by practicing certain exercises.

Dhārṇa :

It is the state of steadiness of mind.

Dhyāna:

It is concentration of mind over a thought or object. It improves mental well being of an individual who practices it.

Doshas:

These are the Humors in the body. The three *Doshas* are called *TriDosha*. They are due to three bodily organizations – *Vāta* (air) *Piṭta* (fire) and *Kapha* (water) – which govern the psychosomatic activity of daily living.

***Gāyaṭrī Mantra*:**

A *mantra* from the *Vedas*, considered one of the great, and used for the purpose of meditation or chanting

Ghēe:

Purified butter made from cow's milk.

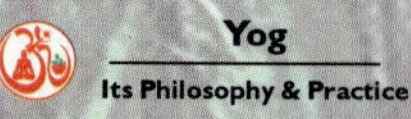

Gurū:

The teacher or the preceptor, here who initiates & guides one in the practice of *Yoga* or attainment of *Moksha* or liberation.

Jala:

It is known as Water, one of the five elements. It is concerned with taste, related to tongue by the action of procreation.

Jēevan :

It means life. It is there as long as the person is alive.

Kapha:

It is one of the *Tridoshas* translated directly as Phelgm. It is a combination of the elements Water & Earth. It is concerned with the actions of stability, energy, lubrication, greed, forgiveness, possession.

Kumbhak:

The stage in *Pranayam* where the air so inhaled is retained in the body for some time.

***Kuṇdalinī Jagaran*:**

The awakening of the divine coiled energy called *Kuṇdalinī Shakti* lying in the *Mōoladhāra Çhakra*.

Kuṇdalinī Shakti :

It is the cosmic energy situated at the base chakra in the body. It is present there in coiled form like that of a serpent.

Malas:

The body produces three waste products i.e. faeces, which are solid; and urine and sweat, which are liquid.

Mantra:

Its singular form is *Mantram*; it is a Sanskrit term denoting a word or group of words that carries certain phonetic vibrations and energy. Certain sacred Sanskrit words carry tremendous energy and chanting those words in a prescribed manner releases this energy.

Meditation:

Meditation brings awareness, harmony and natural order to human life. It awakens the intelligence to make life happy peaceful and creative. The awakening of this creative intelligence is the benediction of meditation.

Mōoladhar Çhakra:

It is the chakra located at the base of the body.

Mrityu :
When there is no inhalation and exhalation of prana in a person, the person is said to reach the state of mrityu, which is the last stage of his *jēevan*, the life as a living being.

Nādis:
These are the channels through which the energy flows in the body. They are *Pranic* currents of energy in the body.

Nādi Shodhana Pranayam:
The Prāṇāyām that purifies the channels of energy flow

Niyam:
Niyam means rules. The second principle of *Ashtang Yog* is rules. Five rules have been defined in *Ashtang Yog* they are excretion, satisfaction and devotion, regular study of Vedas and deept devotion towards God.

***Paṇchkośhas*:**
The human soul (the animating force) is surrounded by five sheaths one above the other, and the outer sheaths penetrating the inner ones. These sheaths are called *Kośha*s.

Piṭta:
It is Bile, one of the *Tridoshas*, a combination of *Agni* & *Jal*. It is concerned with the body heat, temperature, digestion, perception, understanding, intelligence, anger, hate and jealousy.

Pōorak :
It is the process of inhalation of the air.

Prāna:
It is vital energy (life-energy) which activates the body and mind. It is responsible for the higher cerebral functions, and the motor and sensory activities.

Prāṇāyām:
It is breathing exercise and is a *Yogic* healing technique that can bring extraordinary balance in the consciousness. In practicing *Prāṇāyām* one experiences Pure Being and learns the true meaning of peace and love. It has many healing benefits and also affects creativity. It can bring joy and bliss into life.

Priṭhvi: It is known as Earth, one of the five elements. It is concerned with the sense of smell, related to nose by the action of excretion.

Purusha:
It is the male energy. It is formless, colorless and beyond attributes and takes no active part in manifestation of the Universe. This energy is choiceless, passive awareness.

Rājoguna :

Derived from the word *Rajas*. It is the active vital life force in the body which moves both the organic and inorganic universes. It is the dynamic movement.

Reçhak :

The process of exhalation of air out of the body is called *Rechak.*

Sādhakā:

The seeker of knowledge, wisdom, here the person who practices *Yoga*,

Samādhi:

The merging of individual consciousness into the Cosmic Consciousness brings *samādhi*, the state of highest equilibrium. In that state peace and joy will descend as a benediction. It is a state of equilibrium giving supreme joy and bliss.

Saṃkhya:

It is the philosophy of creation.

Saṇyās :

It is abandonment of worldly ties, asceticism.

Saṇyāsi :

A person who has abandoned worldly ties or has adopted asceticism. An ascetic.

Satoguna :

Derived from the word *Satva*. It is the creative potential. It is stability.

Sātvik:

It means simple, plain, without any show off in relation to life, or spicy in relation to food.

Shiva:

A God of the Hindus, revered as the creator of this universe and an all powerful one.

Shiva Sankalpa:

A vow taken while perfoming meditation or pranayam, the objective of such practise

Tamoguna :

Derived from the word *Tamasic*. These are the inactive, potential energies which need the active, kinetic force of *Rajas*. It is static.

Tridosha:

The three bodily organizations – *Vāta* (air) *Piṭta* (fire) and *Kapha* (water) – which govern the psychosomatic activity of daily living.

Triveni:

Popularly known as the *Triveni Sangam,* it is the sacred place of confluence of the three rivers, *Ganga, Yamuna* and *Saraswati* at Prayag, India. Here it signifies the confluence of three *Nādi*'s.

Upanishads:

Vedas which contain discourses on divine knowledge.

Vanaprasthi :

It is the third grade in the life of a twice-born person.

Vāta:

It is Air, one of the *Tridoshas*. It is a combination of elements Air & Space. It is concerned with the movement, Breathing, Natural urges, secretions, fears and anxiety.

Vāyu:

It is known as Air, one of the five elements. It is concerned with the sense of touch, related to skin by the action of holding it.

Vedas:

It means world's oldest extant literature.

Yām:

Yam means resistance to passion. The first principle of *Ashtang Yog* is resistance to passions. In other words resistance to passion means to prevent deviation of senses and the mind from violence and other inauspicious feelings and concentrate the soul.

Yoga:

Yoga is the ancient life-disciplines that have been practiced in India for centuries. *Yoga* is the science of union with the Divine, with Truth. Its practice helps the individual to achieve longevity, rejuvenation and self-realization.